D0872393

The Postulates of Restorative Justice and the Continental Model of Criminal Law

Lex et Res Publica
Polish Legal and Political Studies
Edited by Anna Jaroń

Volume 3

Zur Qualitätssicherung und Peer Review
der vorliegenden Publikation

Die Qualität der in dieser Reihe
erscheinenden Arbeiten wird
vor der Publikation durch die
Herausgeberin der Reihe geprüft.

Notes on the quality assurance
and peer review of this publication

Prior to publication, the
quality of the work published
in this series is reviewed
by the editor of the series.

Teresa Dukiet-Nagórska (ed.)

The Postulates of Restorative Justice and the Continental Model of Criminal Law

As Illustrated by Polish Criminal Law

**Bibliographic Information published by
the Deutsche Nationalbibliothek**
The Deutsche Nationalbibliothek lists this publication
in the Deutsche Nationalbibliografie; detailed bibliographic
data is available in the internet at http://dnb.d-nb.de.

This publication was financially supported by the University of Silesia

Reviewed by:
Marek J. Lubelski

ISSN 2191-3250
ISBN 978-3-631-65404-0 (Print)
E-ISBN 978-3-653-04442-3 (E-Book)
DOI 10.3726/978-3-653-04442-3

www.peterlang.com

Contents

Introduction 7

Leszek Wilk and Piotr Zawiejski
The Concept of Restorative Justice 9

Piotr Zawiejski
Damage and its Redress in Criminal and Civil Law:
The Doctrinal and Case-Law Position to Date...27

Teresa Dukiet-Nagórska
An Attempt to Assess the Manner in which Damage
and its Redress can be Understood from the Point of view
of Fundamental Principles of Criminal Law..55

Dominika Bek
The Mediation Settlement as a Directive of the Level of Sanction 73

Olga Sitarz
Active Repentance at the Stage of Preparation for or Attempt
at an Offence and Restorative Justice... 115

Olga Sitarz, Leszek Wilk
Post-Perpetration Active Repentance and Restorative Justice 137

Anna Jaworska-Wieloch
Selected Aspects of Enforcement of Judicial Decisions
Awarding Redress of a Damage.. 151

Leszek Wilk
The Concept of Restorative Justice in Fiscal Penal Law.................................... 185

Jakub Hanc
The Idea of Restorative Justice: An Attempt at a Comparative Analysis 197

Final Conclusions.. 223

Introduction

The restorative model of penal law is aimed at the removal of social conflicts arising from the commission of a crime, and as such its realisation effectively depends on a framework for civil procedure that allows relations to be built up between the offender and the wronged party, essentially allowing them to achieve their desired goals. It is clearly equally important to provide specific measures which lead to that same end. Among these, a significant role should be assigned to penal measures, as is frequently emphasised. Further, it seems natural that the highest expectations are for those penal measures which involve the compensation of loss. In the Polish legal system this function is borne by the duty to redress damage. It is imposed as a penal measure, an element of probation (conditional discontinuation of proceedings, suspension of penalties and release on parole) or the penalty of the limitation of freedom.

The authors of this volume are convinced of the need to strive for the abolishment of the conflict between the offender and the wronged party (which may sometimes involve a broader social context), in particular the need to take into account, as much as is possible, the just rights and expectations of the wronged party. However, as part of the discussion devoted to these questions, there arise a number of doubts about the possibility of attaining the intended objectives through criminal law regulation (even when this is understood widely to include substantive law provisions, procedural norms and rules contained in the Penal Executive Code). This is how the idea first arose to examine whether the classical model of criminal law—which is based on assuring fundamental guarantees for the convict and offering him or her a relatively broad range of penal measures—is practically effective in achieving the ends desired. This is the subject matter of the present volume.

Katowice, December 2013   Authors

Leszek Wilk and Piotr Zawiejski

The Concept of Restorative Justice

The concept of restorative justice has evolved outside of, and at many points in contradiction to, traditional paradigms of criminal law and criminal process. Its sources may be tracked to doubts concerning the roles of many key institutions of penal law. Its founders have questioned the social benefits following the adjudication of criminal penalties and even the notion of crime itself. In addition they have put into question the way the formalised criminal process operates. Last but not least, they have spotted the negative consequences of the professional administration of justice, monopolised by "experts," i.e. lawyers, at the cost of the wronged party and the local community. Restorative justice makes manifest a profound criticism of the criminal status quo. Let us look at the arguments deployed by these critics, as well as proposals for new premises and solutions thought to produce better results. Finally, we shall analyse arguments which challenge this new trend and the potential for certain elements of this model to invade traditional criminal law.

The social utility of criminal punishment has been negated both under the retributive approach, in which a penalty is understood as just requital for a socially harmful act, and in the utilitarian conception, in which a penalty is rendered primarily as an instrument destined to protect the society from the offender and, in particular, as a means to rehabilitate the wrongdoer. While criticising both these theories, adherents of restorative justice also employ argumentation which is advanced by proponents of each of the two paradigms in their mutual disputes. Among other things, it is suggested that retributive penalties are revenge- and past-oriented, proving painful to the offender yet bringing neither relief to the victim nor benefit to the society.[1] It would be a difficult task to measure the affliction caused by this kind of punishment, especially bearing in mind the relatively simple catalogue of penalties prescribed by law, in order to adjust it to the specific circumstances of each case. As far as utilitarian punishment is concerned, critics focusing on the prevention of crime repetition point to the high

---

1   J. Consedine, *Sprawiedliwość naprawcza* (Warsaw: Przywrócenie ładu społecznego, 2004), p. 161; and "Wyrównanie szkód spowodowanych przestępstwem. Sprawiedliwość Naprawcza i Probacja," *Mediator* 4/2003, p. 6.

costs and low effectiveness of rehabilitation.[2] It is contended that such a penalty impinges excessively on human rights (e.g., with respect to unspecified punishment). With regard to general prevention, it is sometimes pointed out that the mechanism of deterrence by means of punishment might not be as efficacious as expected. In addition, it is doubtful whether the awarding of a penalty can reaffirm social norms.[3]

These arguments, traditionally resonant in disputes about the sense of punishing, are however of secondary importance to the concept of restorative justice. In fact, it questions the traditional indicator of the effects of punishment, namely the return to crime.[4] The problem is not that the criterion is artificial because of the vague number of re-offences, or the fact that crimes may even be perpetrated accidentally as a result of criminal liability by offenders who actually have changed (especially given the ample catalogue of acts considered offences). The foremost issue at stake is that the primary goal in reacting to an offender's action should be, as much as possible, the abolishment of conflicts between the offender and the wronged party and compensation to the wronged one.[5] The hierarchy of objectives is thus constructed in various ways. First of all, the solution sought is a remedy to the consequences of a crime, and not the prevention of future offences. Proponents of the concept of restorative justice put emphasis at this point on the fact that conflicts (which refers also to what are defined by law as "crimes") make up a natural social phenomenon. W. Zalewski, citing Durkheim, stresses that "crime is an inevitable social fact, permanently inscribed in social reality."[6] Crimes are committed everywhere. It is not true that there is a vast group of honest, law abiding citizens.[7] Since the conflicts at play are universal, it seems justified and socially advantageous[8] to concentrate on solving these conflicts and redressing the damage inflicted, rather than actions aimed at preventing future conflicts. A still desired (side-)effect of concrete conflict abolishment is the quantitative reduction of conflicts in the future.

---

2   M. Płatek in M. Płatek and M. Fajst (eds.), *Sprawiedliwość naprawcza. Idea. Teoria. Praktyka* (Warszawa, 2005), p. 86; W. Zalewski, *Sprawiedliwość naprawcza – początek ewolucji polskiego prawa karnego* (Gdańsk, 2006), p. 26 ff.

3   W. Zalewski, *Sprawiedliwość naprawcza*, p. 74 ff.

4   M. Płatek in M. Płatek, M. Fajst (eds.), *Sprawiedliwość naprawcza*, p. 7 ff.

5   M. Wright, 'Geneza i rozwój sprawiedliwości naprawczej', in B. Czarnecka-Dzialuk, D. Wójcik (eds.), *Mediacja. Nieletni przestępcy i ich ofiary* (Warszawa, 1999), p. 16.

6   W. Zalewski: *Sprawiedliwość naprawcza*, p. 148.

7   *Ibid.*, p. 156.

8   *Ibid.*, p. 15.

Much like the traditional understanding of penalty, crime in the traditional sense is also not always a source of social benefits. It is a formula which covers strikingly different types of behaviour, both in terms of its category and its concrete circumstances. Instead of describing a particular state of affairs, it functions as a specific stigma. Moreover, because of the fact that crime constitutes a symbol, it may be treated as one of the most significant elements of narrations within contemporary political campaigns. As a sceptre lurking over law-abiding citizens, it becomes in the political life of societies a red herring that does not solve the real problems it hides. As a result, the notion of crime not only fails to render social reality accurately, but also provides grounds for actions which are detrimental to society.

Yet, criticism of the formula of crime is deeper in character. One problem at stake is the nature of legal liability for a criminal offence. It is often argued that legal responsibility for a crime is a matter of the relationship between the offender and the state. In this conception, the wronged party is left out. This ousting can be illustrated well by the famous thesis of N. Christie on conflict appropriation. The author suggests that "the victim of a crime is wronged twice in our society – *not only by the offender but also by the state. This is the case because the victim is deprived of joint participation in his or her own conflict, which has been stolen by the state...*"[9] The problem is that the victim has been left without any possibility to settle the score with the offender. Instead, the state steps in in his or her place, and this state intervention in the prosecution of offenders is, in the views of adherents of restorative justice, detached from the victim's interest as well as irrational.

Furthermore, a crime makes up only a small part of the offender's life. The event itself does not necessarily have to be the most important factor for the wronged party and his or her relation with the offender, or to the environment in which the offender lives. Yet, the formalised criminal procedure is oriented predominantly towards that tiny fraction of life, making it difficult to account for the whole social context or even the circumstances in which the offence was perpetrated. As a result, even factors which are of vital importance to all the parties directly interested in the outcome of the process might not be taken into consideration at all. This leads to a situation in which criminal proceedings are not always an instrument for resolving conflicts in a way that would produce social benefits.

Finally, the conflict is appropriated not only by the state but also by the professionals through whose assistance justice is administered.[10] In the natural course

---

9   N. Christie, *Granice cierpienia* (Warszawa, 1991), p. 113.
10 *Ibid.*, p. 85.

of events, even when there is no abuse, legal procedures evolve in a way that is convenient to the actors involved in the administration of justice. With this in mind, any fulfillment of the functions of criminal law loses its significance. These functions are primarily declaratory in character. To go even further, a far-reaching thesis is sometimes put forward that penology and the punitive dimension of justice administered would not be able to function in their current shape but for the implementation of certain hidden goals, differing from the functions of criminal law and procedure. If "success" for the criminal justice system and the prisons were a realisation of the functions declared, these institutions would gradually disappear. Once dysfunctional, they would be replaced by other alternatives. This means that other objectives are actually pursued.[11] Distinct from the political dimension, punitive institutions have an economic sense. Penology and the punitive dimension of justice make up an important sector of public services.

Given this harsh criticism of the status quo, it does not come as a surprise that the concept of restorative justice has emerged outside penal law and has become a grassroots movement. Its origins can be traced back to initiatives by the New Zealand Movement Against Prisons. The conviction of the malfunctionality of imprisonment became an incentive for pursuing alternative solutions by the Movement's activists. It turned out that Maori traditions of dispute resolution could provide a point of reference. M. Płatek opposes this method of resolving conflicts within the traditional criminal process, depicting it in the following way:

> In the social space and charming atmosphere of Marahau, whenever a conflict took place its solution was sought—the best and most just one for the wronged party and for the society. All interested persons would gather. The meeting was presided over by the elderly men or women. In this manner neighbourhood quarrels were resolved, and conflicts ending in murder, as well as cases of rape, defilement and theft. The president of the meeting would maintain its order; however, decisions concerning solutions to the most pressing issues were worked out collectively, in the presence of all the society, as long as it was agreed upon how to redress the damage so that the entire community could be satisfied."[12]

It may be added at once that in practice the solutions achieved in the course of such meetings were focused on remedying the damage. This system, having been derogated by the colonial administration of justice, has now been partly restored in New Zealand. Naturally, there appears the question how it happened that the resolutions of such meetings actually become acceptable within the framework

---

11 M. Płatek in M. Płatek, M. Fajst, *Sprawiedliwość naprawcza*, p. 88.
12 *Ibid.*, p. 10.

of the modern legal system. It proved very helpful that this system originated in Maori culture. At first, it was accepted as a part of an experiment pertaining to juveniles of Maori origin. Its positive outcomes and popularity indicated that the experimentation could provide grounds for the restorative justice conference— this being one of the most vital methods for the new concepts.

On the one hand, there is both an ongoing practice and a general return to the roots, because the Maori procedures for resolving conflicts by the community, as can be easily guessed, are not entirely unique.[13] Similar processes, oriented primarily in the direction of compensation, and catering to the needs of the wronged party and his family, may be observed in most societies at the periphery of the contemporary state. However, this phenomenon does not only involve grassroots tendencies. Campaigners are also supported by science. Criminologist N. Christie forged a novel paradigm in horizontal justice, which differs from the traditional model of vertical justice. It essentially consists of the following:

1. Decisions are locally entrenched. […] What matters is the here and now—taking the past into account and considering the future. This may lead to inequality: "the very same act" may be qualified differently in district A and districts B and C. However, within the districts all must agree unanimously that justice was really done.
2. Questions about proper relations are approached in a manner radically different from what can be encountered within a legal system. An accurate response is considered to be a matter of primary importance, yet within the model of horizontal justice there are no predefined solutions. The proper reaction to a crime is elected in the course of the process designed to come to such a specific response. The correct answer is what participants in the procedure deem correct. Among all interested parties a minimal level of consent must subsist concerning the appropriateness of the chosen response […]
3. Compensation for both non-economic and economic loss appears as much more crucial than the urge for vengeance and the demand to punish the offender.[14]

Restorative justice is a concept in which the main goal can easily be detected as a specific synthesis of the whole movement. It is primarily about reconciliation between the wrongdoer and the wronged party, which is realised by redress to the latter. Should such a rapprochement prove impossible, an honest and frank meeting between the offender and the wronged party with a view to a mutual understanding of their positions is still meaningful. It ought to be emphasised that reconciliation, or even the meeting itself, is interpreted as a merit on its own. Still, it does allow for the implementation of other processes are traditionally

---

13 M. Wright, op. cit., p. 16 ff.
14 N. Christie, *Dogodna ilość przestępstw* (Warszawa, 2004), p. 82 ff.

associated with criminal law: that is, most importantly, the reduction of crime. In this respect, the authors stress J. Braithwaite's conception of reintegrating shame. M. Płatek, even in invoking this conception, contends that

> societies of the lowest crime indicator are not the ones which have the most severe punishments. The reverse is the case. The lowest crime level is observed where shame and a sense of shame play the most significant roles. If shame is to be effective, a specific type is needed. Braithwaite calls it "reintegrating shame." It stands in juxtaposition to stigmatisation, which is inherent to traditional justice.[15]

Stigmatisation cannot be considered an effective factor in preventing crime, because an educated person is not particularly susceptible to this type of internal stimulus. The effects of shame are also internalised. It may reaffirm the offender's morality, inclining him or her to admit that the act has been committed against the system of values which to which he or she also adheres.[16]

Already at this point it becomes apparent how important it is for restorative justice that the wronged party and the offender meet, or that their conflict becomes resolved. Confrontation by the perpetrator of the victim or relatives who are important to the perpetrator, as well as confrontation of the environment in which he or she subsists, is intended primarily to resolve the conflict permanently, and secondarily to play a purifying role. It may lead to the correction of the offender. What matters is not only the measures applied to the wrongdoer, but also in many cases the process of arriving at those measures. In fact, it may occur to the offender that the act was committed against values professed by him- or herself. It is more difficult to achieve this end by awarding a traditional criminal penalty. In particular, reconsideration is not easy in prison, where convicts tend to experience the opposite processes: denial and rationalisation of crime.

In the traditional paradigm of criminal law legal norms conceal the conflict.[17] With restorative justice, one ought to take into consideration that norms may effectively come into force and demonstrate their functionality or dysfunctionality precisely against the backdrop of conflict. Conflict resolution allows the confirmation of their social utility and significance. In other situations it may, however, point to their uselessness. In this manner, the entrenchment of norms turns out to be deeper than is the case in the traditional model of criminal law, as it is free of any idolatrous character. In addition, it is worth emphasising that adherence to the ideals of restorative justice does not usually bring abolitionism with it, or

---

15 M. Płatek in M. Płatek, M. Fajst: *Sprawiedliwość*, p. 101.

16 W. Zalewski: *Sprawiedliwość*, p. 182.

17 See also M. Płatek in M. Płatek, M. Fajst: *Sprawiedliwość*, p. 95.

even postulates to completely eliminate imprisonment as a penalty. This concept unveils only that merely servicing a penalty does not "do the trick."[18]

"Redress" refers both to economic and non-economic loss suffered as a consequence of crime. It is not so important to determine the amount of loss precisely. On the contrary, mechanisms of restorative justice seek to guarantee maximal flexibility. The parties involved are the ones to elect the most appropriate method of compensation.

There arises the question of whether there is room for restorative justice with regard to crimes without victims.[19] Attempts to apply the concept under consideration to such instances can be found in published academic work. W. Zalewski cites the example of applying restorative justice practices by the Australian National University:

> In the Canberra model, the goal is to examine the effect of "deterring by shame" potential drunken drivers or, in other words, preventing the phenomenon of driving while intoxicated. This model seems interesting, as it is applied even in situations where the directly wronged party is missing, where there is only a threat to traffic safety. The offender attends a conference in the company of at least six supporters. The role of the actual victims is assumed at the conference by inhabitants of the place where the alleged event took place— individuals potentially harmed. This points to the possibility of applying Braithwaite's theory also to crimes without victims."[20]

In consequence, the question may be raised of whether such occasions are the embodiment of restorative justice, since the offender does not restore anything. Undoubtedly, in such cases it is impossible to redress damage sustained by the wronged party. The offender may, however, assume responsibility for his or her act precisely in the process of coming to a realisation of the meaning of the act committed and may provide a remedy to the community affected by this act (usually the local community). In effect, it seems that one should not reject *a limine* the applicability of the concept of restorative justice to crimes without victims. This example clearly shows that the most crucial features of restorative justice are not compensation but the assumption of responsibility for one's conduct and reconciliation. These elements may be present even in the absence of any specific individually wronged party. On such occasions, the wrongdoer may assume responsibility for his or her act before the community affected by the

---

18 J. Consedine (*Wyrównanie szkód*, p. 9) adduces examples of offenders saying "I've served my sentence," and the positions of state authorities, "They have already been punished," "They paid their dues to the society," and emphasises that in such an approach there is no place for either victims or positive change.

19 See. N. Christie, *Dogodna*, p. 87-89.

20 W. Zalewski, *Sprawiedliwość*, p. 194.

offence (i.e., usually the local community). The notion of restorative justice (that is, de facto, responsibility) may thus extend to any action of the offender which can be viewed as a social counteraction combating all or only selected negative social ramifications of the punishable act and, most obviously, to all legal effects imputed by law to such conduct.

To sum up what has been considered thus far, it seems appropriate to say that restorative justice denotes the specifically oriented liability of the perpetrator of a punishable act to bear the consequences of his or her wrongdoing. The offender becomes a person "remedying" the evil following from his or her acts. This does not refer to the activity of the state or of any entities other than the offender who are also in a position to redress damages inflicted as an effect of a crime. Restorative justice is characterised by the following features:

- the wronged party is given a central role in the proceedings, even though benefits are also obtained by the wrongdoer, by the administration of justice, and by society (on a local or a much broader scale);
- the process of eliminating the conflict is a crucial element, not just the result of this process;[21] parties cooperate with one another—they enact the "horizontal model" of criminal process,[22] which also signifies the maximal engagement of the wronged party;[23]
- there is participation by the local community, which is in a way both responsible and harmed, because every individual functions within a group;[24]
- the liability of the perpetrator for the punishable act is specifically oriented, one crucial element being realisation (and admission) by the wrongdoer of the evil done (as well as understanding of the victim's problems);[25]

---

21 Which requires a breakthrough with regard to many cultural inhibitions. I. Wróblewska, "Rozważania na temat kulturowo-społecznych ograniczeń dla wprowadzania idei mediacji w Polsce," *Mediator* 3/2003, p. 45-47.

22 P. Szczepaniak, "Mediacja po wyroku – w stronę sprawiedliwości naprawczej," *Mediator* 1/2003, p. 57.

23 Ch. Pelikan, "Sprawiedliwość naprawcza – w poszukiwaniu pokoju i sprawiedliwości. Rola Europejskiego Forum na Rzecz mediacji między Ofiarą a Sprawcą oraz Sprawiedliwości Naprawczej," *Mediator*, 4/2004, p. 13.

24 See J. Consedine, "Wyrównanie szkód spowodowanych przestępstwem. Sprawiedliwość Naprawcza i Probacja," *Mediator*, 4/2003, p. 9.

25 This is why, for example, in the project *The Sycamore Tree*, which was carried out in Great Britain, USA and New Zealand, groups of former victims visit prisons to meet inmates and take part in therapeutic sessions which allow for therapeutic discussion of victims' problems and help the process of improving inmates' awareness.

- restorative justice covers both tangible and intangible harm rendered in statutory definitions of particular punishable acts, as well as harm that follows indirectly from such acts;
- restorative justice does not preclude punishment (or even deprivation of liberty) or contradict the functions of criminal law, although it does significantly affect how the safeguarding function is understood, since it determines, at least ostensibly, the need for its redefinition (an approach different from the one accepted thus far); restorative justice becomes an normal alternative to the punishment inscribed in the administration of criminal justice;
- restorative justice refers also to non-specified "injured parties," i.e. society (but not the state), so under this conception the notion of restorative justice refers also to so called "crimes without victims," that is offences in which the individual who could otherwise enjoy the procedural status of the "wronged party" is missing;
- in a broader context, the concept of restorative justice (i.e. de facto responsibility) encompasses each intentional punishable act performed by a perpetrator at a stage either preceding or following the offence which can be classified as a socially positive counteraction capable of removing all or some of the negative results of the punishable act;
- criminal law consequences are usually distilled into a "regress of punishment," that is the reduction of the repressive element of criminal liability (or its minimisation).

Forms of implementation of restorative justice postulates

What methods are specifically utilised by the programme of restorative justice in order to accomplish such ambitious goals? Scholars point to: negotiations, mediation, and restorative justice conferences and circles.[26] This indicates that the concept of restorative justice does not prescribe any specific means of response to the offence, but only procedures for determining such measures in concrete situations. There is no catalogue of official reactions to the offence characteristic of restorative justice which would be similar to a

---

It must be emphasized that these victims are not victims of the convicts with whom they meet as a part of the program. P. Szczepaniak, "Mediacja po wyroku – w stronę sprawiedliwości naprawczej," *Mediator*, 1/2003, p. 59.

26 M. Płatek in M. Płatek, M. Fajst: *Sprawiedliwość*, p. 19; D. Wójcik, "Rola mediacji między pokrzywdzonym a sprawcą przestępstwa," in A. Marek, ed., *System Prawa Karnego, Tom 1. Zagadnienia ogólne* (Warszawa 2010), p. 360 ff.

catalogue of penalties or punitive measures. Instead, we gain mechanisms for the pursuit of said measures. Yet these mechanisms are not formalised. They can be elaborate and require the involvement of a sizeable group of people, but they can also be very straightforward, as in the case of negotiations, which are simply carried out during an in-person meeting of the interested parties. Negotiations are not moderated, their participants can do without any external assistance.

"External" assistance is at play in the form of mediation. Does the participation of the third party lead to formalisation of the mediation procedure? At first glance, it may seem so. In Poland, for instance, mediation is an institution regulated by law. Yet, when we take a closer look at this procedure, it turns out that its regulation is incomplete and governs, not even very thoroughly, only some issues related to mediation, such as: who may mediate and on what terms, how a case is referred for mediation (especially the requirement of consent from the parties to the conflict) and rudiments of the procedure. The last of these issues has been regulated by the Regulation of the Minister of Justice of 13 June 2003 on mediation proceedings in criminal cases,[27] an enactment which merely prescribes that the mediator contact the parties, arrange separate meetings with them, instruct them about the essence and principles of mediation and their respective entitlements, hold an actual mediation meeting, and, possibly, help them formulate the settlement from the merits. It is very clear that legal provisions governing the "mode and manner" of proceedings in mediation basically give expression to what is natural. The lawmaker has clearly stepped into the shadows, leaving the task of elaborating the foundations of mediation to scholars and, most prominently, to practising mediators. As pointed out above, such a solution corresponds to postulations put forward by theorists of restorative justice. Mediation also means an informal meeting with an atmosphere of respect for the dignity of the participants and with the aim of reaching a solution that would be satisfactory for everyone. Mediation takes place outside court, and mediators must be persons not engaged in the widely conceived system of administration of justice. Nonetheless, some issues, such as the confidentiality of mediation, should be bolstered up by provisions of law and proper system of legal protection.

The foundations of mediation introduced by the doctrine of law and the practice of restorative justice are often rendered in the form of guidelines addressed to mediators, such as, for instance, the *Standards of mediation and mediator*

---

27 *Dziennik Ustaw* 2003, No. 108, item 1020.

conduct of 26 June 2006 that were prepared by the Social Council for Alternative Conflict and Dispute Resolution to the Minister of Justice. Based on these guidelines, it may be stated that a mediator should:

1) ensure voluntary participation in mediation and in forging a settlement
2) ensure safety to all parties and that their rights and dignity are not violated in the course of mediation
3) maintain neutrality in relation to the object of the dispute
4) remain unbiased towards the participants in mediation
5) assure the confidential nature of mediation
6) fairly instruct the parties about the essence and course of mediation
7) make sure that the settlement does not violate legal provisions

On the basis of the above enumeration, it is manifest how diversified a mediator's competencies should be. On one hand, he or she is to make use of all psychological and pedagogical capacities as well as personal charisma that would assist in the creation of a space for reaching an agreement. On the other hand, a mediator needs purely legal competencies which allow him or her to ensure that the settlement produced by the parties will conform to law and, what is more, be enforceable. He or she should also have a good grasp of regulations concerning law and criminal process in order to explain in a detailed way to the parties the possible consequences of agreeing on a settlement for criminal litigation.

An important characteristic of mediation is that it can be carried out without any specific entry conditions being met. The offender does not have to plead guilty or show penitence. In legal writings it is argued that the case of the restorative justice conference is different. Such a conference must not be held

> until the offender shows penitence, pleads guilty, assumes responsibility for the wrong, and displays readiness to redress the damage inflicted. When these conditions are met, in contrast to a mediation meeting in which only the wronged party and the offender participate, this kind of conference may be attended also by close relations, as well as representatives of the local community, and the person presiding over the restorative justice conference, unlike a mediator, will be able to express his or her opinion freely.[28]

Next, M. Płatek sets out the basic principles governing restorative justice conferences. These include:

- *willing parties (as in the case of negotiations and mediation);*
- *respect for all parties (similarly as in mediation and negotiations it is attainable but hard to verify);*

---

28 M. Płatek in M. Płatek, M. Fajst: *Sprawiedliwość*, p. 19-20.

- *sensitivity to the wronged party and its interest (in mediation at least);*
- *transparency of rules (in mediation at least);*
- *safety of the proceedings (as in mediation at least);*
- *confidentiality (in mediation at least);*
- *acknowledgement of responsibility by the offender;*
- *participation in the local community;*
- *acknowledgment of the right of the person presiding over the conference to express his or her opinion;*
- *the consideration of the fact that crime violates not only the interests of the wronged party, but also the sense of order of the local community, whose restoration requires that the offender take action to reinstate the order violated."*[29]

It is clear that restorative justice conferences make for the best implementation of the premises underlying the new model. It is important that it include the participation of the local community, the assumption of responsibility by the offender for his or her act and the obligation to redress the damage. On the above grounds, one might conclude that restorative justice conferences are closer to restorative orthodoxy than, say, mediation. However, it must be remembered that in the case of mediation it also seems legitimate to postulate that cases in which the accused pleads not guilty be recommended for mediation with much caution. On such occasions, there is frequently little room to discuss an amicable solution. In addition, it may be surmised that the court or prosecutor is recommending for mediation a case which is too hard from the perspective of criminal law, a case which poses too much trouble.

The restorative justice circle is a sort of middle ground between mediation and the restorative justice conference, with the additional vital involvement of collective therapy. It is not necessary that the offender should plead guilty or show remorse. This method is characterised by a specific "formalised" mode of communication. Another specification is evaluation. Once a solution is reached, how it was reached is inspected, and additional or substitute procedures can be sought.[30]

Criticism of restorative justice

That procedures of restorative justice can take various forms becomes conspicuous. At their core, however, there is always a pursuit of common understanding

---

29 *Ibid.*, p. 20.
30 http://anidur.fm.interii.pl/kregi_naprawcze.pdf

and a willingness to eliminate conflict, most frequently by way of restitution. Nevertheless, this concept is subject to criticism. The following critical arguments may be raised:

1. Restorative justice aspires to the status of a new paradigm in criminal law while in fact it refers only to a part of criminal cases (this part might not even be large), i.e. cases in which there is a wronged party and both this wronged party and the offender are willing to meet together.
2. The concept of restorative justice falsely reduces crime to conflict, while in reality we have a relation of injury, which is substantially different from a relation of conflict. As such, it generally requires the imposition of a criminal penalty. F. Ciepły indicates that

> the relation between the criminal and the victim should not be analysed in terms of "conflict." Since criminal responsibility is based on the commission of a punishable act, between the offender and the victim there subsists, in the first place, a relation of injury, the wronged party being a victim to a crime which gives him or her the right to justice being done. This justice consists in the imposition of penalty and the redress of the damage inflicted by the criminal conduct of the offender. The victim does not hold an unjustified grudge which gives rise to "conflict" with the offender, and the role of the court is not just to resolve or appease this "conflict." The victim of a crime is predominantly entitled to see the court award a just penalty to the wrongdoer. This stems from the principle of justice. This principle may be mitigated only by the ideal of clemency, which may serve as a true cornerstone of mediation.[31]

According to this, restorative justice does not serve the interests of the wronged party, as he or she is put in line with the offender by means of the concept of conflict. It may thus be ascertained that this argument essentially comes down to the fact that from the perspective of morality and justice, the offender and wronged party should not be simply aligned. The choice of a proper response as a rule necessitates the imposition of criminal punishment. This criticism is voiced from the point of view of the justice-seeking function of penal law.

3. On top of that, it is sometimes asserted that restorative justice in fact implies a resignation of the protective function, especially general prevention. Under this conception, criminal law does not deter potential offenders from crime, but, quite conversely, provokes criminal offences: "The offender risks only the possibility of being obligated to redress damage, which would already become

---

31 F. Ciepły: *Mediacja w teorii i praktyce*, ed. A. Gretkowski, D. Karbarz (Stalowa Wola 2009), p. 189-200.

his or her duty under civil law provisions."[32] This does not merely imply resignation on deterrence. The conception of restorative justice undermines the
communicative role of punishment[33] to reinforce social values.

4. Moreover, it is contended that the notion of restorative justice is characterised
by credulity, in more than just one way. Firstly, it presumes the offender's
good will for an authentic assumption of responsibility and a redress of damage. It is pointed out that this presumption is preposterous in the case of cruel
murderers[34] or corporate criminals.[35] The same goes for offenders acting
within organised criminal groups, sports fan networks, professional criminals, etc. Secondly, offenders are usually not affluent people, so how could
they repair the damage? Thirdly, it can be protested that it is naive to suppose
that a local community will be inclined to participate in conflict resolution
between the offender and the wronged party. Experiences with the social element, especially participation, in the administration of justice are, at least in
Poland, unsatisfactory. Is society ready for rational and emphatic participation in administering justice? Finally, it would gullible to assume that settlement between the offender and the wronged party will actually solve the
conflict between them, or even lead to the wrongdoer's transformation. In
practice, it is not uncommon that the contending parties become reconciled
with a sincere attitude (especially when they can hope for specific benefits),
and then the seemingly resolved dispute breaks out again with new force. In
the context of domestic violence, the term "honeymoon" was coined for the
period when a perpetrator of domestic violence changes his or her treatment
of the victim temporarily, only to return to previous habits after a time.

Let us consider whether the objections here levied against the concept of restorative justice are valid. As regards the first of them, i.e. the absence of a universal
idea of restorative justice, as has been noted above, adherents of the said theory
are already aware of this problem. At the same time, it must be emphasised that
the number of punishable deeds that can be codified as having a clear victim
is in practice quite considerable. These are not exotic offences committed only
sporadically but crimes such as the deprivation of life, health and property. It
may be thus concluded that these are the most socially significant cases. If only
restorative justice were to prove socially useful in such situations, this would

---

32 J. Wyrembak in M. Płatek, M. Fajst: *Sprawiedliwość*, p. 122.
33 K. Gradoń in M. Płatek, M. Fajst: *Sprawiedliwość*, p. 133.
34 Ibid., p. 138 ff.
35 Ibid., p. 144.

certainly constitute an effective defence for it. Regardless of this fact, a broad understanding of restorative justice as the reparation of damage not only to a specific victim but, technically, to the whole community affected by the crime, opens up the possibility to apply restorative justice in certain situations to crimes without actual victims.

The second objection made by critics of restorative justice is a philosophical declaration that differs from statements made by its proponents. Discussion on the proper paradigm of criminal law is, on its own, extremely difficult in light of the justice-seeking function, which cannot be rendered in the terms of traditional argumentation. It is evident, however, that describing a crime as conflict does not necessarily lead to questioning the injury and negating the specific, delicate, and often traumatic relation related to this injury. Theorists of restorative justice emphasise the offender's need to assume responsibility for his or her act and acknowledge the right of the wronged party to be properly redressed. Such a division of roles in the conflict clearly demonstrates who the entitled party is and who the obliged one is. We do not think it is necessary to reach for criminal penalty in order to do away with the relation of injury resulting from the crime and restore justice. It is clear that in a very large number of cases justice may be done without resorting to penalty, yet it would be difficult to dispense with redress.

The third objection raised above comes down to the question of whether this is still penal law. More specifically, the question is whether the remedy of damage can be considered the (sole) sanction for the offence committed. Is accord between the offender and the wronged party the only thing that matters, to the exclusion of the social noxiousness of the act as well as guilt? Can one avoid criminal responsibility? Does the commitment to repair damage involve an element of punishment? In our view, the generic civil law concept of redress may not include punishment.[36] It merely consists in the settling of accounts between the offender and the wronged party. Punishment is additional pain suffered for the perpetration of a punishable act, something more than mere account clearance. Moreover, the reparation of damage in civil law is measured solely by the amount of loss. It is far from flexible. In principle, it is not dependent on guilt or the social noxiousness of the act. As a consequence, as long as the typical civil law conception of obligation to redress is applied without any addition, the penalty is abandoned. This does not, however, mean that restorative justice supplants

---

36 See also B. Janiszewski: Kompensacja szkód jako zadanie prawa karnego (in:) Księga Jubileuszowa z okazji 15 – lecia Wydziału Prawa i Administracji Uniwersytetu Szczecińskiego (Szczecin 2004), p. 330.

punishment. The point is to avoid both the imposition of a penalty in place of the obligation to redress the damage and the disallowal of damage reparation as a consequence of the penalty's execution. In certain situations, penal measures may in fact secure the obligation to repair the damage (particularly probation). More importantly, however, redress of damage does not have to be conceived in the terms offered by civil law. The concept of restorative justice allows for a broader understanding. It is imaginable, for example, that private punishment is a potential response to offence that is arrived at by recourse to restorative justice procedures, recalling the traditional compensatory measures of penal law in their essence. As a result of restorative justice procedures, specific non-monetary measures of redress may be worked out. These may involve service to the benefit of the wronged party, or the performance of a specific task or type of assistance. In addition, in the context of restorative justice broadly conceived there is also room for reparation to the community affected by the offence, e.g. by community service. The offender's assumption of the obligation to carry out such services could be achieved by the utilisation of restorative justice. All of this leads to the conclusion that the measures which can be put into effect with the intention of solving conflicts that arise from the theory of restorative justice are ampler than account clearance strictly defined as referring to the detriment sustained by the wronged party.

In regard to the alleged abandonment of the general preventive function in its positive dimension that is levied against restorative justice, it ought to be stressed that, on the contrary, procedures of restorative justice emerge as dependable means of reaffirming social norms, their development and their constant practical verification. The possibility is not even ruled out that restorative justice works better in this respect than the somewhat mechanical application of legal norms that is characteristic of the traditional model. It suffices to point out the negative value of the criminal act. After all, it is the traditional model that faces far reaching criticism for its insufficient effectiveness in the general preventive function in its positive aspect.[37]

As for the fourth objection related, i.e. the gullibility inherent in the concept of restorative justice, this should be treated as a warning rather than obstacle to its operation. What is important is the will of the legislator. It is clear that the lawmaker ought to exercise caution when decreeing automatic consequences as solutions for settlement between the offender and the wronged party during criminal process, especially if these would involve the automatic

---

37 W. Zalewski, *Sprawiedliwość*, p. 308 ff.

abandonment of punishment for the wrongdoer. Legislation should, however, enable support for the wronged party at the stage of executing the settlement concluded.

Apart from the above, it must be stressed that some of the problems which cannot be effectively handled by restorative justice—by which is meant, for example, certain types of offenders and certain difficulties with strengthening the positive effects of the measures imposed—do not relate exclusively to the formula of reacting to crime. With respect to certain offenders, the same degree of credulity belongs to both the belief in the effectiveness of traditional instruments of justice and the belief in the effectiveness of restorative justice. The case of the measures imposed is similar. It is doubtless difficult to assure the permanence of restorative justice effects. It is much harder, however, to ensure durable results with the typical mechanisms of rehabilitation, meaning especially those measures utilised in the artificial conditions of incarceration.

Naturally, it must be emphasised that it would not be possible to abolish the penalty of imprisonment in reference to more serious crimes. It is also necessary to use the penalty of imprisonment as a threat in cases when the offender does not assume the required obligations, possibly as an alternative penalty. These are specific questions which call for in-depth consideration and debate.

The influence of the concept of restorative justice on modern criminal law

If one were to ascertain the way in which responses to offences in criminal law are being amended in light of the ideas of restorative justice, it emerges that the most crucial change is the return of the conflict "stolen" by the state to the wronged party (and offender) and to the local community. This may not, however, denote the complete resignation of state punishment within the traditional system. It is only possible to posit a certain pattern of regress in penalties as a consequence of the practical application of the new theory.

Mechanisms aimed at the achievement of reconciliation between the offender and the wronged party or the community affected by the crime ought most certainly to remain independent of criminal law, both substantive and procedural. The concept of restorative justice must not lose its autonomous character in this regard. Also, if these procedures are to make sense, they must have an impact on the content and severity of traditional penal law responses. The exact scope of their influence calls for further discussion.

Moreover, criminal law should account for circles of people wronged by the punishable act of the offender (intervention circles). The wronged party is the person most acutely affected by this act and, conceivably, his or her close relatives. They form the first circle of intervention. Criminal law should to the greatest possible extent seek predominantly to enable the redress of damage, to guarantee enforcement of the settlement reached with the offender (if such a settlement is reached at all). At the same time, as the occasion requires, the actual loss may be remedied with a surplus (by additional non-economic remedy or even personal penalties) or remedied in full amount.

The second circle of intervention is formed by the community in which the offence has been committed. The community is affected by the crime almost directly. Its sense of security has been violated, and its norms need to be reaffirmed. Most often, it is the local community, but this does not necessarily have to be so. Nowadays it is not distance between individuals that proves decisive in determining whether they constitute parts of the same community. Apart from territorial communities, one may speak of professional, religious or other communities. Reparation to such a community may, for instance, take form of community service. Only the last and third circle of intervention would include the state and the society at large.

Piotr Zawiejski

Damage and its Redress in Criminal and Civil Law: The Doctrinal and Case-Law Position to Date

The obligation to remedy damage in criminal law

In the restorative model of criminal law, whose central element is the liquidation of the conflict emerging between the offender and the wronged party, ascertaining damage and identifying the means of its reparation are of key importance. In light of this, findings which are intended to delimit the scope of the realisation of the goals characteristic of the restorative model in criminal proceedings must extend to an understanding of damage and its compensation in the context of penal law.

In the 1997 codifications, lawmakers reinforced the importance of the duty to redress damage inflicted by criminal conduct. Apart from criminal law institutions previously known, i.e. civil action that takes place within criminal proceedings or with the possibility to award damage *ex officio*, as well as with the obligation to repair loss as a requisite connected with the award of probative measures or community service, which were known already to the previous Criminal Code (CrimC), lawmakers introduced the obligation to repair damage as a new punitive measure.[1] In addition, a clearly compensatory function is borne by vindictive damage specified in art. 46(2) of the Criminal Code.[2] Among criminal law measures of restitution, W. Zalewski also includes apologies to the wronged party and a publication of the sentence.[3] Nevertheless, both vindictive damages and punitive measures involving an apology and a publication of the

---

1   R. A. Stefański, "Kompensacyjna rola środka karnego obowiązku naprawienia szkody," in *Kompensacyjna funkcja prawa karnego. Księga poświęcona pamięci Profesora Zbigniewa Gostyńskiego, "Czasopismo Prawa Karnego i Nauk Penalnych,"* 2002, No. 2, p. 131 ff.

2   Art. 46(2) "Instead of the obligation set out in paragraph (1) [i.e. duty to redress damage – author's annotation], the court may award vindictive damages to the wronged party."

3   W. Zalewski, *Sprawiedliwość naprawcza, początek ewolucji polskiego prawa karnego* (Gdańsk 2006), p. 265.

sentence, as clearly distinct from the strictly understood obligation to repair damage, will remain outside the scope of my further investigations.

Incorporating the obligation to redress damage in criminal law is not an easy task. It involves a private-law relationship between the offender and the wronged party, taken into account in a criminal verdict, that falls under and is in principle governed by the application of substantive penal law institutions. This is a matter that cannot be ignored in modern substantive and procedural criminal law, since fulfilment of the obligation to redress damage bears material functions in view of both legal doctrine and case law:

> The reparation of different types of damages in a pending criminal process, or even plain acts aimed at such a reparation, may result in many advantages for the wronged party, for the offender, for law enforcement authorities and for the administration of justice as such. It seems clear that the wronged party is spared time, financial means and mental stamina that would be required by subsequent civil proceedings. He or she may gain something more than financial compensation, that is a kind of moral satisfaction, or even regain the mental balance disturbed by the offence.[4]

Still, compensation is not the only thing at stake. It is additionally suggested that

> the offender himself or herself may, by realising the consequences of his or her act and acknowledging the damages and wrongs inflicted, develop a positive outlook on existing social norms, and his or her meeting with the wronged party, which seems even more apt for mediation, may in some conditions itself virtually constitute a favourable solution for both individual and social conflict.[5]

Consequently, the duty to repair damage also has an individual preventive dimension. In addition, the process of determining damage, its calculation, and its remedy allows for a better understanding of the seriousness of the committed act and its substantial value. The construction of the duty to redress damage may thus help to shape attitudes of respect towards law in society, fulfilling in other words the general preventive function.[6] Finally, it seems that reparation of damage makes a basic, natural postulation relating to the implementation of the idea of justice, prior to the imposition of penalty.

---

4   B. Janiszewski, "Kompensacja szkód jako zadanie prawa karnego" in *Księga Jubileuszowa z okazji 15-lecia Wydziału Prawa i Administracji Uniwersytetu Szczecińskiego* (Szczecin 2004), p. 317.

5   *Ibid.*, p. 318.

6   J. Lachowski, T. Oczkowski, Obowiązek naprawienia szkody jako środek karny, Prokuratura i Prawo No. 9/2007, p. 43.

The obligation imposed on the offender to repair the damage inflicted by the offence is also a notion central to the conception of restorative justice. Hence the postulation that the classical objectives of criminal law which find manifestation in the dictum *nullum crimen sine poena* be replaced with the principle nullum crimen sine obligation.[7] Naturally, as has been pointed out in the context of general remarks on restorative justice, this postulate is impossible to put into practice with respect to many types of crime. Moreover, under the theory of restorative justice, more attention is paid to the process in which the wrongdoer gradually assumes the duty to redress and discharge the conflict with the wronged party than to the compensatory obligation itself. However, this whole process of reconciliation between the offender and the wronged party takes place in combination with actual redress, which is regarded as the minimal content of this process.

The obligation to repair damage is meaningful for the fulfilment of all classical functions of criminal law.[8] It is also an important aspect of the concept of restorative justice. Contemporary substantive and procedural criminal law considers this question from a number of perspectives. First, it becomes an instrument allowing for the awarding of monetary damages to the wronged party, in consequence of which the wronged party holds an enforceable execution title against the offender with no need to initiate civil proceedings. Second, it is indispensable to assure to the wronged party and the wrongdoer an expedient forum where they can reach an agreement concerning the reparation of damage. This element is strongly accentuated by adherents of the restorative justice theory. Currently, it is traceable in Poland as mediation. Third, this obligation should translate into the sphere of the adjudication and execution of penalties.

The question arises of whether the multitude and miscellany institutions found throughout contemporary Criminal Codes which allow for the imposition on the offender of the obligation to redress damage comprise a well thought system or, quite to the contrary, a random regulation following from frictions of different traditions and conceptions. In order to answer this question, one must trace particular institutions, as suggested at the outset of this chapter, which enable the reparation of damage. The starting point should be procedural constructions: civil action within criminal proceedings and the award of damages ex officio (art. 415(4) of the Code of Criminal Procedure). To some extent, it

---

7   J. Warylewski in A. Marek (ed.), *System prawa karnego. Vol. I. Zagadnienia ogólne.*

8   See also A. Muszyńska, *Naprawienie szkody wyrządzonej przestępstwem* (Warsaw, 2010), p. 135 f.

was dissatisfaction with these institutions that led to the extension of the catalogue of measures leading to the indemnification of the damages sustained by the wronged party as a result of a crime.

Pursuant to art. 62(1) CCP, "the wronged party may, until the opening of the court proceedings at the main trial, file civil action against the accused and pursue in this way within criminal process a monetary claim arising directly from of the crime committed." The deadline to file the claim in criminal proceedings is not preclusive: "It is a term belonging to the category of terms in in the broader sense of the word (…) Subsequent action brought before entry of judgment may be considered a procedural irregularity which may have an impact on the court's verdict."[9] A substantial judicial decision allowing or dismissing the action may be delivered only in the event of entry of convicting judgment. In the case of other types of resolutions concerning the subject matter of the litigation, the court leaves the action unresolved. Importantly, the civil law claimant within criminal litigation is temporarily exempt from the judicial fee (which is still mistakenly called an entry (fee) in criminal procedural law) payable for issuing the claim. He or she will bear the costs only in the event of loss (i.e. the action's dismissal).

In civil action within a criminal lawsuit, one may only pursue economic claims arising directly from the crime. Most frequently, these are claims for redress of loss caused by a delict. At the same time, the limitation of permissible claims to material ones "does not mean (…) that within this process one could not assert claims arising out of non-material damages; this is allowable as long as pecuniary claims are concerned (compensation for non-economic loss inflicted by the punishable act)."[10]

Pursuant to art. 65 CCP, the court declines to examine the civil action or leaves it unresolved if one of the following circumstances is in effect: the action is precluded by special provision, there is no direct connection with the grounds for indictment as formulated by the prosecutor, the action has been filed by an unauthorised person, the claim pursued is examined in another pending procedure (*lis pendens*) or has already been decided finally (*res judicata*), or joint participation is necessary between the defendant and a state self-governmental and social institution or between the defendant and a person who has not been accused. The same applies to situations in which a motion has been submitted

---

9   *Ibid.*, p. 309.
10 P. Hofmański, E. Sadzik, K. Zgryzek, *Komentarz do kodeksu postępowania karnego* (Legalis, 2007).

for the imposition of the obligation to redress economic or non-economic loss (to pay the so-called atonement, as discussed below) on the offender.

A court considering a civil claim in a criminal lawsuit applies provisions of the Civil Code (CivC) in full, making it possible to provide extensive legal protection to the wronged party. The above formal conditions for filing a claim are not crucially rigorous. Yet, this institution is utilised extremely rarely in judicial practice in Poland. In scholarly writings it is suggested that one of the reasons is "the reluctance of courts to decide in civil law matters. Criminal courts usually use every opportunity to leave the action unresolved."[11] A good precedent for such an outcome may be found in art. 415(3) CCP, which allows the court to leave civil law action unsettled if the evidence heard at the trial proves insufficient to decide as to the civil claim, and supplementing the evidence gathered would considerably protract the proceedings. The low popularity of civil law actions in criminal proceedings may result from hardships surrounding the formulation of the petition.

Criminal procedural provisions make it possible for the criminal court to award damages ex officio, in light of art. 415(4) CCP.[12] The claim for compensation must be directly connected to commission of the crime and must be asserted by the party directly injured. In addition it is to be pursued directly against the accused as the offender.[13] The doctrine of law is unanimous in stipulating that the substantive law bases of the resolution indicated in art. 415(4) CCP are provisions of civil law, and the Code of Criminal Procedure sets out only the procedural framework for the delivery of such a verdict.[14] As a result, this resolution is not restrained by directives to mete out the punishment provided for in the Criminal Code. On the other hand, the court is bound by civil law provisions which determine what constitutes damage, what the prerequisites of compensatory liability are, and what remedies are available. It is also well accepted that "in lieu of statutory regulation limiting the scope of admissibility for awarding compensation from the accessory, (…) it should be concluded that the court may

---

11 K. Marszał, op. cit, p. 312. This is why the punitive measure has been introduced as well as the more or less obligatory character of judicial decisions concerning the duty to compensate (as explained below).

12 Art. 415(4): "In the event of conviction, the court may also award damages to the wronged party ex officio unless statutory provision prescribes otherwise. Imposition of compensation ex officio is not admissible in the case of circumstances set out in art. 65(1) item 2, 4 or 5."

13 A. Muszyńska, op. cit., p. 292.

14 Ibid., p. 291 and literature cited therein.

impose on the instigator compensation to the extent that they are responsible for the damages inflicted by the crime."[15]

In accordance with art. 415(4) CCP, the court awards compensation if the civil law claim arising from the offence is examined, yet it does not decide on the action. In light of the above, such a judicial resolution may surprise, or even be "unwanted" by, the wronged party. In order to protect the interests of the wronged party, it is well accepted that such a ruling has the force of *res judicata* only up to the amount of the damages awarded. As for what remains, access to civil justice is open to the wronged party.

It is easy to surmise that, since civil action within criminal proceedings constitutes an institution rarely encountered in practice, awards of damages ex officio are even more sporadic. Procedural institutions aimed at reparation of damage are practically eliminated by criminal substantive law measures.

In substantive criminal law, reparation of damage is most frequently effected by the award of the punitive measure of art. 39(5) and art 46(1) CrimC,[16] i.e. the duty to redress damage or pay compensation for non-economic loss. This regulation has evolved, and its current wording has been in force since 8 June 2010.[17] The legislator gave up on limiting the imposition of the duty to redress damage only in the case of certain exhaustively enumerated types of crimes. Currently, the obligation to redress damage is universal, and may potentially relate to all kinds of crime. Moreover, the legislator conferred on the court the possibility to adjudge the duty to redress damage ex officio, even in the absence of a respective motion from the wronged party or other entitled person. Finally, by referencing terminology from the Civil Code, the legislator indicated that the duty may refer to compensation of economic and non-economic loss. In the previous version of the provision, there was only the duty to repair (economic) damage, and since the Civil Code makes a clear distinction between the two types of compensation, i.e. economic

---

15 P. Hofmański, E. Sadzik, K. Zgryzek, *Komentarz do kodeksu postępowania karnego* (Legalis, 2011).

16 Art. 46 CrimC: "(1) In the event of conviction, the court may, at the request of the wronged party or other entitled party, adjudge the duty to repair damage inflicted by the offence in whole or in part or pay compensation for non-economic loss; civil law provisions on the statute of limitations and adjudication of annuity shall not apply. (2) Instead of the duty defined in (1), the court may award vindictive damages to the wronged party."

17 It was shaped by the Act of 5 November 2009 Amending the Criminal Code, Code of Criminal Procedure – Executive Penal Code, Fiscal Criminal Code and Certain Other Acts (Dziennik Ustaw No. 206, item. 1589).

and non-economic loss, it was not clear whether the criminal duty to compensate could also cover non-economic wrongs. Some writers were in favour of such a solution,[18] others were against.[19] At present, the legislator clearly envisages that this measure extends to compensation for both economic and non-economic loss. Unfortunately, the legislator was not consequent and forgot to adjust other provisions to the new nomenclature (by differentiating between economic and non-economic loss), in which the notion of damage is present, including reparation of loss (e.g. probation requisite of arts 67(3) and 72(2))—as discussed below.

The prerequisites for imposing the duty to redress economic or non-economic loss as a punitive measure are as follows. First, the award of such an obligation is possible only in the case of convicting judgment. Convicting judgment is not the same as judgment which conditionally discontinues the proceedings.[20] The category of convicting judgments does cover, however, verdicts in which the court refrains from imposing a penalty.[21] The Criminal Code in art. 59[22] directly provides for the possibility of refraining from adjudging a penalty in certain situations and settling for a punitive measure instead. This measure may involve the obligation to compensate for economic or non-economic loss. In the doctrine, it is indicated that this is feasible only when the measure may replace punishment *in concreto*, i.e. when it is thought also to fulfil other functions of criminal law, not merely compensation.[23]

---

18 See Z. Gostyński, *Obowiązek naprawienia szkody w ustawodawstwie karnym* (Kraków 1999), p. 65 – 76; B. Kolasiński, "Szkoda w rozumieniu art. 46 §1 Kk," *Prokuratura i Prawo* 2001/4, p. 67; A. Guzik, "Wpływ warunków materialnych sprawcy na nakładanie obowiązku naprawienia szkody," *CzPKiNP* 2002, No. 1, p. 131–132.

19 E. Hryniewicz, M. Reszka, "Odszkodowanie i zadośćuczynienie w świetle art. 46 Kodeksu karnego – uwagi krytyczne i propozycje zmian," *Monitor Prawniczy* 2007/6.

20 Resolution of Combined Criminal and Military Chambers of the SC of 29 January1971, VI KZP 26/69, OSNKW 1971/3 item. 33.

21 R. A. Stefański, "Procesowe aspekty środka karnego obowiązku naprawienia szkody" in Z. Ćwiąkalski, G. Artymiak (eds.), *Karnomaterialne i procesowe aspekty naprawienia szkody* (Warsaw, 2010), p. 223.

22 Art. 59 (1) If the offence is subject to a penalty of imprisonment up to 3 years or a less severe penalty and the social noxiousness of the act is not significant, the court may refrain from imposing the penalty if it decides to impose a punitive measure instead, and the purpose of such a penalty is thus served by the measure. (2) The provision of paragraph (1) shall not apply to the perpetrator of a misdemeanour tainted with hooliganism.

23 A. Marek, "Naprawienie szkody wyrządzonej przestępstwem. Refleksje na tle projektu nowej kodyfikacji karnej" in S. Waltoś (ed.), *Problemy kodyfikacji prawa karnego. Księga ku czci Profesora Mariana Cieślaka* (Kraków 1993), p. 212.

The Code expressly envisages in art. 46(1) CrimC the indemnification of damage inflicted by criminal offense. The second entry condition of this punitive award is that the damage (whether economic or non-economic loss) must result from the crime for which the offender is convicted. The loss must exist at the time of the judgment delivery.[24]

The award of the obligation to repair economic or non-economic loss (in whole or in part) is obligatory when the wronged party or another entitled person submits a respective motion. This application is permissible only before examination of the wronged party at the main trial (art. 49a CCP). This deadline is preclusive and it is impossible to restitute.[25] The court may, however, (optionally) impose on the accused the obligation to redress economic or non-economic loss even in the absence of said motion.

The basis for awarding the punitive measure of art. 46(1) CrimC is the presence of damage. It is consequently accepted in academic literature and case law that the concept of damage should be rendered in a manner accordant with civil law. In consequence, there arises the question of whether and to what degree the court, while awarding the punitive measure of art. 46(1) CrimC, ought to apply criminal law directives on the level of sanction, especially the guilt directive (in its limiting function). It is stressed that the measure set out in art. 46(1) CrimC is, as a rule, penal in nature; yet, with regard to its award, in the absence of an express legal provision to the contrary, the court is consequently to apply civil law regulation.[26] This follows from the strongly accentuated compensatory function of this measure. In consequence, the doctrine and case law indicate quite definitively that the rule is to obligate the offender to redress the damage in whole, and exceptions to the general principle may be justified only for very important reasons.[27] "The court may not refuse to decide in respect of the duty to redress if the motion has been filed, there are grounds for conviction and the damage has been defined and proven."[28] Directives on the level of sanction become a less important factor. It is argued that

---

24 SC judgment of 14 March 2013, III KK 27/13, Legalis 661581.
25 Judgment of the Court of Appeal in Katowice of 13 December 2007, Legalis 96231.
26 A. Muszyńska: Op. cit.
27 Z. Gostyński: op. cit, p. 180-181, SC resolution of 13 December 2000, I KZP 40/00, Legalis 48345, judgment of the Court of Appeal in Lublin of 31 July 2013, II AKa 129/13, Legalis 736142.
28 Z. Sienkiewicz in M. Filar (ed.), *Kodeks karny. Komentarz* (Warsaw, 2012), p. 199.

the directive of guilt, in the context of its restrictive function, would in principle be difficult to tie to the obligation to redress damage, all the more because it concerns factors other than the statutory description of the punishable act. The level of guilt is graded according to the seriousness of the act, and its determination requires an evaluative analysis of circumstances of the type to be taken into account when specifying the degree of the act's social noxiousness.[29]

The Supreme Court attaches such a degree of cardinal importance to the compensatory function of this punitive measure that, as the Court concluded based on art. 444(1) CrimC, its award "is admissible also in the form of joint and several obligation of all accomplices to repair the damage caused, whether in whole or in part."[30] An overwhelming majority of academics considers these views to be too far-reaching. It is contended that joint and several liability of accomplices could undermine the criminal law principle of personal and individual responsibility.[31] Instead, the doctrine is inclined in this case to impose the compensatory duty *pro rata parte*.[32] In practice, rulings are rendered which differ from the opinion of the Supreme Court in this respect. For example, the Court of Appeal in Katowice held that the duty to repair damage may not be adjudged as joint and several obligation (even though the cited decision explicitly related to the obligation of repairing damage as a precondition of probation).[33]

In the academic literature there are also doubts about the question of whether the duty to redress damage rendered as a punitive act can be reconciled with principles of criminal law, especially if one applies civil law provisions in full. B. Janiszewski draws attention to the safeguarding function of statutory definitions of crimes and their elements. The author deems it doubtful whether criminal law sanction (a notion which also extends to punitive measures) can cover circumstances beyond the statutory definition of the punishable act.[34] In particular, Janiszewski points to the problem of situations involving intentional crime, wherein the damage has nevertheless been caused unintentionally by the offender.

---

29 A. Muszyńska, *Naprawienie szkody wyrządzonej przestępstwem* (Warsaw, 2010), p. 149. See also J. Lachowski, T. Oczkowski, op. cit, p. 51.

30 SC resolution of 13 December 2000, I KZP 40/00, Legalis 48345. See, however, the S.C. judgment of 6 April 2011, III KK 399/10, Legalis 432360, in which a different kind of imposition of the duty of art. 46(1) CrimC on joint participants was allowed to the exclusion of art. 444(1) CivC.

31 Z. Gostyński: Op. cit. p. 195-196.

32 A. Muszyńska, op. cit, p. 330., J. Lachowski, T. Oczkowski, op. cit., p. 52.

33 Judgment of the Court of Appeal in Katowice of 13 December 2012, II AKa 427/12.

34 B. Janiszewski, op. cit., p. 327.

The author additionally claims that rendering the duty to redress damage as a punitive measure stands in opposition to the principle *nulla poena sine lege*:

> Once we understand what elements constitute damage, how frequently damage has to be assessed, that criteria for determining the due amount of compensation for non-economic loss are lacking in the provisions of the Civil Code, and that these criteria have been worked out in the case law of the Supreme Court, then it becomes clear that at the moment of an act's commission, the extent of damage and scope of obligation to redress it are a great unknown to the offender.[35]

Finally, according to this author, it would be strange to apply the guilt directive to the duty to redress (restrictive function of guilt).[36]

Reparation of damage can also be found in substantive criminal law as a requisite of probation. In pursuance of art. 67(3) CrimC, "when conditionally discontinuing criminal proceedings, the court shall obligate the offender to *repair damage* in whole or in part (…)," whereas, in accordance with art. 72(2) CrimC, while passing a conditionally suspended sentence, "the court may obligate the convict to redress damage in whole or in part, unless it awards the punitive measure named in art. 39 item 5," i.e. compensation for economic or non-economic loss. Similarly, in the case of release on parole of an imprisoned convict, the penitentiary court may impose on the released convict the duty to repair damage as a probation requisite (art. 159 of the Executive Penal Code (EPC)).

In the literature on reparation of damage understood as a probation requisite (as analogous to the punitive measure set forth in art. 46 CrimC), it is noted that "civil law provisions do not provide direct basis for remedying the damage but are to be applied subsidiarily where criminal law knows no separate regulation regarding the matter under consideration, in particular in determining the scope and manner of damage reparation."[37] In deed, however, this means that civil law provisions are applicable to a very wide range of cases. As ruled by the Supreme Court in one of its latest decisions,

> the norm of art. 72(2) CrimC allows the court to obligate the convict to repair damage in whole or in part, unless the punitive measure named in art. 39 item 5 CrimC has been adjudged. The duty to repair damage does not, however, comprise an element of adjudication with respect to punishment or the punitive measure. It is not a sanction imposed by the court in the name of the state that must be incurred by the offender in connection with the committed crime. The obligation to redress the damage aims only to cancel loss arising from the crime. Adjudication in this respect is thus closely connected with the

---

35 B. Janiszewski, op. cit., p. 328-329.
36 B. Janiszewski, op. cit., p. 328.
37 A. Muszyńska: op. cit, p. 174.

real damage sustained by the wronged party, as understood in the manner of civil law. In other words, obligation to repair loss may not lead, on one hand, to any additional growth of the wronged party's property or, on the other, make a *sensu stricto* element of punishment, a sanction directed against the offender to fulfill the goal determined, *inter alia*, in art. 53 CrimC.[38]

One vital way in which the duty to redress damage as a requisite to probation is dissimilar to the punitive measure is the possibility of judicial determination of the term in which the obligation is to be performed. This deadline, however, may not be longer than the period of probation.[39] This fact is related to the character of probation requisites, which are obligations imposed for the duration of probation (or a shorter period as determined by the judgment), whereby non-compliance with this obligation constitutes an optional ground for ascertaining failure of the probative measure. Nonetheless, a question may be asked if it is justifiable to differentiate in this respect between the obligation to repair damage as a probation requisite and as a punitive measure. The absence of such a deadline for the punitive measure is related to a number of negative consequences pertaining to the execution of this measure (as discussed below).

Under art. 36(2) CrimC, the obligation to repair damage may also be awarded in a situation in which the offender is sentenced to the penalty of restriction of liberty. The norm of art. 36(2) CrimC makes reference to art. 72 CrimC (in this case also to art. 72(2)), which prescribes the imposition of a duty on the same terms as the probation requisite.

Thus far, a brief overview of various institutions aimed at reparation of damage under Polish substantive and procedural criminal law has been presented, as well as a summary of doctrinal and case-law positions concerning their interpretation. The central element of these institutions, as well as the opinions expressed on them, is the civil law understanding of the notion of damage. At this point it seems appropriate to examine how the concept is conceived of in civil law, and what implications for criminal law may be drawn from that understanding.

The concept of damage in civil law

Damage (loss) is defined for the purposes of civil law as

> detriment in the assets of the wronged party amounting to the difference between the value of the assets resulting from the harmful event and the condition which would be

---

38 S.C. judgment of 9 July 2013, II k.k. 160/13, Legalis 689438.
39 S.C. judgment of the Criminal Chamber of 10 December 2008, II k.k. 106/08, Legalis 135717.

the case but for that event. The detriment takes the form of a loss, a decrease or a non-increase of the assets or an emergence of or increase in liabilities. The damage corresponds to the wronged party's interest in the co-occurrence of the event and, when it has already taken place, in restoring the state of affairs disturbed by the event. Regardless of whether non-economic loss is to be treated as an element of damage, the harmful event may touch both the tangible and personal interests of the wronged party.[40]

In order to supplement the above definition, one should pay attention to the following issues. First, damage is a legal event concerning the domain of facts (this circumstance has been underlined by the Supreme Court in its frequently cited decision of 11 July 1957[41]). It is sustained irrespective of the compensatory liability that is the legal obligation of its redress.

Approaching damage as a fact, i.e. in isolation from the rights and obligations of the parties, is also a source of certain dogmatic difficulties. As is generally accepted, the notion of damage does not extend to natural detriments emerging from it, as a result, for example, of freezing, drying up, drowning, etc.[42] It is, however, undeniable that at least some natural detriments are likewise detriments to the wronged party's assets. Where, as a result of drying up, precious liquid is lost, and the drought could have been prevented, then it is undoubtedly justified to speak of detriment to the wronged party's assets, because this process was controlled, the natural course of events could have been evaded, and the wronged party was not "condemned" to the detriment. Moreover, one may not exclude compensatory liability in the case of natural detriments. It may be the case that the detriments not only may, but also ought to be prevented (e.g. in the case of handing over a certain thing for deposit with the obligation of maintenance). In consequence, with respect to "natural detriments," distinguishing between what is covered by the obligation to redress and what is not requires in some situations a consideration of the sphere of what should be, that is a recourse to law. In light of the above, it seems that in order to keep with dogmatic consequence, all those natural detriments which could have been prevented, and to which the wronged party is not condemned, should be qualified as loss. A separate question is liability for that damage. In other words, these natural detriments may be a wrong for which nobody is held responsible. Yet if this detriment were to follow from the

---

40 M. Kaliński in *Prawo zobowiązań – część ogólna System prawa prywatnego T. VI*, (ed.) A. Olejniczak (Warsaw, 2009), p. 77.

41 II CR 304/57, OSNCK 1958/3/76, Lex No. 49753.

42 See T. Wiśniewski in G. Bieniek (ed.), *Komentarz do kodeksu cywilnego. Księga trzecia. Zobowiązania Vol. I* (Warsaw, 2009), p. 83.

event for which criminal law provides compensatory obligation, it would be loss subject to indemnification.

In addition, in literature on this subject it is suggested that damage as an event belonging to the domain of facts may also occur in a situation in which the wronged party consents to the detriment.[43] The consent of the wronged party does not exclude detriment but may only exempt its unlawfulness (SC judgment of 12 December 2006,[44] SC judgment of 30 September 2008[45]). In this case, civil law is faced with problems analogous to those relating to the construction of a person's consent to dispose of his or her interest, posing many problems for criminal lawyers. There appears the problem of what detriments in legally protected goods may be consented to. In other words, which interests are relative in character (and to what extent), meaning that their protection depends only on the disposer, and which ones are so important publicly that their disposer is not in a position to agree to the detriment (or detriment of a different type). It is worth adding that in the context of civil law and procedure this issue is a source of a peculiar paradox which is not so marked in criminal law. In the case of ineffective consent to loss in the civil law context, the person who gives such consent (or, conceivably, his or her legal successor) will be able to pursue compensation as a civil law claimant. Just as consent to the damage is his or her own free decision, also the subsequent resolution to file the lawsuit is voluntary. As a result, in certain situations, defence against actions of this type is enabled by such civil law institutions as abuse of subjective right (art. 5 CrimC), or contribution of the wronged party (art. 362 CrimC). This paradox is not perceivable with such intensity in criminal law, because of the fact that in consequence of a crime there emerges a relation between the state and the offender. For the state it is easier than for the disposer to disregard consent to the detriment where the protected interest has a public character. Nevertheless, in criminal law too, with regard to interests for which the detriment determines unlawfulness regardless of the disposer's consent, such consent is to be taken into consideration. If this cannot be done by reference to unlawfulness, there remains the standard of social noxiousness, guilt, and directives on the level of sanction.

It should be emphasized that there are serious difficulties with ascertaining which interests may and which may not be disposed of. Legislation in this respect is only rudimentary, and the issue at hand is deeply entangled in axiology

---

43 See M. Kaliński; op. cit., p. 79-80.
44 II CSK 280/06,. Lex No. 232817.
45 II CSK 144/08, publ. Lex No. 465951.

and disputable as a result. The pursuit of such a catalogue should undoubtedly start with the Constitution; however, bearing in mind the general character of this regulation, this source provides only very general guidelines. Primacy belongs to the principle of proportionality. Another source of law that may be of certain help is statutory provisions relating to different types of interests, as well as criminal law regulations pointing directly to, for example, the invalidity of consent to deprivation of life of a human being (regulation of euthanasic murder or human trafficking).

One can most certainly consent validly to merely financial or proprietary detriment. However, a problem arises when particular assets pose some significance, e.g. when for reasons of culture or natural environment they are generally protected by provisions of public law. In the judgment of 29 November 1999, the Supreme Court pointed out that

> awareness of the owners of neighbouring properties concerning the possibility of unfavourable influence of the landfill on their garden output may be qualified as consent of the injured parties to the emergence of loss. This consent may allow the offender's conduct to be exempted from unlawfulness. It would not, however, be possible to approve of illegal activity that causes devastation to the natural environment. The environment itself constitutes a universal asset, protected by art. 5 of the Constitution of the Republic of Poland, hence the consent of the wronged party to its pollution may not exempt the unlawfulness of the offender's activity.[46]

Despite the economic character of the damages and the civil law character of the case, the SC took the stance that consent to the detriment is not effective (it did not exclude unlawfulness of conduct) if the conduct leads to devastation of the natural environment, and so mandatory rules have been violated (in this particular case public law norms). This resolution seems disputable, as one could argue that damage to environment is one thing and private law loss is yet another.

In view of such argumentation, consent would only exclude the compensatory claims of the owners, without any impact on public law liability for damage to environment. However, SN decided to elect a different solution oriented around the construction of compensatory liability, and indicated that where consent fails to exclude unlawfulness, premises of compensatory liability are fulfilled. The conclusive factor, therefore, was unlawfulness. Applying this statement to the criminal law obligation to repair damage calls for a consideration of the following paradox. In criminal law, because of the principle of specificity, the protection of interests is assured by way of diversified typologies, which in principle

---

46 III CKN 473/98, Legalis.

are organised according to types of legally protected interest. In reference to devastation of natural environment, one should bear in mind that there are crimes against natural environment (Chapter XXII CrimC) and crimes against property (Chapter XXXV CrimC). The devastation of natural environment may fall under one of the crimes against environment and at the same time under the crime of a thing's destruction defined in art. 288 CrimC, or of the felling of trees defined in art. 299 PC. In the absence of consent from the owner of the thing or tree to its destruction or felling, cumulative qualification of the act is in effect as a rule. The so called consent of the entitled party (e.g. the owner of the thing) most certainly excludes criminal liability for the crime against property, but cannot exempt liability for devastation of environment. In consequence, the matter to be dealt with is an offence against natural environment. However, it would not be unfeasible to award the criminal law obligation to repair the damage to the benefit of the affected property's owner. Naturally, this is the case only if we accept the position that consent which does not exempt unlawfulness (of any type) still may not bar claims for redress, and only insofar as the remaining preconditions of the obligation to repair the damages are met. Still, there arises the question of whether such state of affairs would conform to the aims and principles of criminal law regulation.

Types of loss in civil law

It is emphasized in legal literature that

> in the language of law and legal practice, there is a distinction between economic and non-economic loss (also known as "harm," "non-material loss," or "non economic harm"). This distinction is made on the highest level of classifications of the notion of damage according to the objective criterion of the harmful event's impact on the interests of the wronged party. Economic loss comprises detriments to assets and interests of calculable financial value, capable of being expressed in monetary terms,[47]

while non-economic loss affects other interests of the wronged party (the resolution of the full Civil Chamber of the SC of 8 December 1973[48]).

It is not entirely clear if the concept of "non-economic loss" corresponds precisely to the term "harm" set out in the Civil Code, i.e. encroachment of the personal interests of the wronged party. There are authors who do not accept the synonymy of these terms. It is pointed out that

---

47   M. Kaliński; op. cit., p. 91.
48   III CZP 37/73, Lex Polonica 301116.

non-economic loss includes the realm of negative human experiences involving physical and emotional suffering. Within this category, one can isolate "harm," that is, non-economic detriment arising out of a violation of the personal interests of the entitled person which does not translate into a financial issue for the wronged party. In consequence, there is a difference between non-economic loss *sensu largo*, covering harm and those cases of non-economic detriment which are not the effects of a transgression of personal interests. Under this typology, harm may be conventionally defined as non economic loss *sensu stricto*.[49]

Other authors confine the scope of non-economic loss to instances of violations against personal interests. They argue that non-economic loss corresponds to "that type of infringement of the personal interests of the wronged party which causes no detriment to his or her property."[50] According to this latter stance, non-economic loss is identified with harm.

In fact this disagreement concerning the relationship between the concepts of non-economic loss and harm has little practical importance. There is no doubt that beside economic detriments, civil law indemnification may extend only to detriments affecting non-economic interests: harm, in other words. For the purpose of the present analysis, the terms "harm" and "non-economic loss" are used interchangeably.

The difference between economic and non-economic loss is reflected by terminology referring to types of indemnification. Whereas economic loss collocates in Polish with repair or compensation, with regard to non-economic loss "the provision aimed at its indemnification is generally referred to as atonement, which, as opposed to redress of economic loss, always involves the payment of a specific amount of money. Although such detriment cannot be assessed in terms of monetary funds, a particularity that does not merely arise from difficulties of proof but also from its nature, the legislator considered it necessary to confer on the wronged party a claim intended to compensate for non-economic loss."[51]

In doctrinal writings, it is argued that claims for atonement are not a logical consequence of the general protection afforded to personal interests but need a special express statutory ground. As a result, unlike the duty to repair economic damage, atonement for harm sustained is payable only in situations set out in statutory provisions. Under the current legislative framework, atonement for harm may be awarded only within the regime of delictual liability. Still, it should be noted that its scope is quite considerable. Regardless of the

---

49 M. Kaliński; op. cit. p., 91.
50 A. Szpunar, *Zadośćuczynienie za szkodę niemajątkową* (Bydgoszcz 1999), p. 68.
51 M. Kaliński; op. cit., p. 91.

protection following from other provisions, pursuant to art. 448 CivC, "in the event of violation of personal interest, the court may award to the one whose interest has been transgressed a respective sum as pecuniary atonement for the harm suffered…" The character of the personal interest has not been specified in art. 448 of the Civil Code. This means that this provision applies in the event of any violation concerning personal interest, whether or not it is explicitly named in art. 23 of the Civil Code, but only as long as legal protection has been afforded.[52] Nonetheless, in the body of case law, it is emphasised that under this provision the court is not under the duty to award damages ("the court may award"). Whether atonement is granted depends on the fulfilment of the remaining conditions of compensatory liability (SC judgment of 19 April 2006[53]), as explained below.

It should be emphasized that non-economic loss may affect both natural and juridical persons. This thesis is accepted both in legal literature[54] and, with some uncertainties, in case-law (SC judgment of 24 September 2008[55]). When the judgment concerning the non-economic loss of juridical persons was entered, the facts of the case were highly interesting. The claimant was a juridical person who was the publisher of a daily newspaper whose title was included in its business name, but had a trademark legally reserved to the claimant. In the area where the daily was issued, a respondent pasted posters which mocked the newspaper (targeting its title among other things). The Supreme Court held that the publisher deserved atonement. The Court ruled that

> the meaning of a trademark frequently reaches beyond (…) the function derived from provisions of industrial property law. The sensory perception of the trademark is related specifically to the positive, negative and neutral opinions of third parties (especially consumers) pertaining to goods bearing the trademark, and consequently to expectations concerning the quality of goods made by a particular enterprise, and finally to the reception of the entity holding the enterprise for which the trademark was registered. In this view, the trademark, just as other marks which represent juridical persons, may be seen as a personal interest of the juridical person without which it cannot function within the scope of its activity.

Then, when justifying the award of the atonement, the Supreme Court concluded that

---

52 See T. Wiśniewski, op. cit., p. 456.
53 II PK 245/05, OSNP 2007/7-8/101, Lex No. 243923.
54 See T. Wiśniewski, op. cit., p. 456; M. Safjan, "Komentarz do art. 448 k.c.," *Legalis*.
55 Sygn. II CSK 126/08, publ. OSNC-ZD 2009/2/58, Palestra 2008/11-12/309, Lex No. 464461.

for obvious reasons, juridical persons do not experience physical or mental suffering. Yet, juridical persons do incur the damage of non-economic loss as a result of the infringement of their personal interests, which cannot be measured in money, and which justifies the appropriate application of art. 448 of the Civil Code in conjunction with art. 24(1) CivC and art. 43 CivC in order to achieve compensation for the sustainment of non-economic loss.

The facts of the case cited aptly render the need to protect juridical persons against detriments of a non-economic character. One effect of encroachment on the pseudonym of a juridical person may be the considerable limitation of its commercial capacities. In the case of a newspaper, it means not only a decrease in sales but also, for example, lesser public confidence, and lesser opinion-making impact.

As regards economic loss, one should pay attention to one distinction inscribed in the Civil Code, namely damage relating to property and damage relating to persons: "Damage to property involves negative repercussions of infringements concerning property and other tangible interests of the wronged party. This concept is qualified by the legal definition of property in art. 44 CivC."[56] Damage to a person, on the other hand, involves negative consequences of the infringement of personal interests. Naturally, when dealing with economic loss, indemnification of damage, both when relating to property and persons, takes the form of compensation.

It appears, however, that the most significant classification pertaining to economic loss is the distinction, backed by the Civil Code, between direct loss (*damnum emergens*) and lost profits (lucrum cessans). Pursuant to art. 361(2) CivC, in principle (in the absence of contrary contractual or statutory provision), redress of damage covers direct loss sustained by the wronged party and benefits he or she could have reaped if the damage had not been inflicted. In literature, it is accepted that *damnum emergens* consists of

> a decrease in assets or an increase in liabilities. As a result of damage, the wronged party becomes poorer than before—his or her property is diminished. Assets are decreased as a result of their destruction, damage (decline), loss or decrease of value. Liabilities, on the other hand, grow by way of the emergence of new, previously (before the harmful event) non-existent debts or an increase in the value of already existing debts."[57]

As opposed to *damnum emergens*, loss within the scope of *lucrum cessans* is purely hypothetical. Such loss is made up of

---

56 M. Kaliński; op. cit., p. 97.
57 *Ibid.*, p. 89.

a reflection of the economic value of an event which has not happened, yet which, by occurring, would cause the assets of the wronged party to grow, which simply means a a positive modification of his or her financial position. The frustration of this enrichment follows from a harmful event attributable to the debtor on statutory or contractual grounds.[58]

It is pointed out that this notion extends to:

1) lost earnings (*lucrum cessans sensu stricto*), either from one's own business activity (e.g. the carriage of persons by a taxi driver becomes impossible as a result of the harmful event) or employment;
2) loss of expected income from future transactions (*lucrum speratum*). As an example, one can point to profits from the sale of transported goods that would have been reaped if they had reached the destination point;
3) loss of fruits and incomes from a thing;
4) loss of the possibility to avail of a thing.[59]

Ascertaining and determining the size of damage amounting to *lucrum cessans* usually poses more serious problems than ascertaining and determining *damnum emergens*, since it is necessary to take into consideration a purely hypothetical course of events. In consequence, it is stressed in judicial decisions that "with regard to pursuing redress of a loss amounting to lost profits, they must be proven by the party claiming compensation to such a degree of plausibility that, in the light of life experience, one may actually determine that loss of profits really took place." (SC judgment of 21 June 2001[60]).

Lost profits should be differentiated from possible damage (loss of chance or hope). One element accounting for the difference between these two concepts is the degree of hypothetical probability of profit had the damage not occurred:

When it comes to lost profits, the reception of income must be highly probable. On the other hand, potential damage deriving from a loss of opportunity is at play if the probability of using the opportunity was more than high. In such situations, one cannot require proof of absolute certainty, because hypothetical deliberations are always marked by a margin of error. In order to minimise error, it is necessary for the court to consider all knowledge of the individual situation of the wronged party.[61]

Possible damage, as opposed to lost profits, is in principle not subject to indemnification. There are only two exceptional enactments envisaging repair of possible

---

58 *Ibid.*, p. 115.
59 *Ibid.*
60 IV CKN 382/00, publ. M.P. 2003/1/33, Lex No. 52543.
61 M. Kaliński; op. cit., p. 103-104.

damage. These involve art. 444(2) CivC to the extent in which compensation refers to the worsening of professional prospects in the future and art. 446(3) CivC relating to loss of opportunity to obtain means of subsistence from the deceased. Generally speaking, however, setting aside the above exceptional situations, the borderline between lost profits and possible loss is a border between those detriments which are subject to indemnification and all other detriments. It is clearly apparent that this distinction is not clear (it is based on the level of probability of the hypothetical course of events).

Rulings in which it was decided whether a particular detriment constitutes lost profits or only a possible loss indicate that the problem itself is very difficult. A matter of primary importance in deciding the quandary are issues related to evidence, and it is often difficult for the parties to predict the outcome of the case in advance. For example, one claimant, a constructor, contended that but for the defect of his construction machine he would have reaped profits related to works normally performed with the aid of the defective equipment. In the end, it was decided that the claimant failed to prove that he would have really earned the profit in connection with the operation of the machine.[62] In another case, respondents undertook to find and buy for the claimant for a specific price an attic in a house within a specific location, with a view of adopting it as housing premises. They failed to perform the contract, in consequence of which the claimant sued for lost profits related to rise of the market value of residential units. The claim was awarded. The Supreme Court indicated that if the respondents had complied with the contract and the claimant had obtained the lodging, it was very probable that the market value of the unit could have been higher than expenses incurred by the claimant in obtaining the premises. The respondents' thwarting of the claimant's potential increase in assets should, in principle, be treated as loss of an expected, real benefit (SC judgment of 28 April 2004).[63] In another relevant decision, the question of benefits lost in stock exchange operations was taken up. This rather complicated account may be reduced to the failure of the brokerage office, despite its obligation, to carry out its client's dispositions concerning the purchase of shares whose price then went up. The court faced a difficult quandary when determining the moment in which the wronged party would have sold the shares if he had received them, and, thus, the amount of ceased profits. Courts of fact hold that the relevant moment is the stock exchange trading session immediately following the session at which the shares

---

62 S.C. judgment of 21 June 2002, IV CKN 382/00, Legalis.
63 V CKN 111/00, Lex No. 52740.

should have been bought to the benefit of the wronged party. In other words, one has to compare the value of shares at two subsequent trading sessions. This view was rejected as excessively schematic by the SC (in a judgment of 18 October 2000).[64] The Supreme Court admitted that because of the unpredictability of the actions of participants in the stock market game, it is hard to pinpoint a specific moment at which the hypothetical loss of the wronged party ought to be calculated. The court put forward the notion, which can also be found in other SC decisions, of searching for the most probable conduct of the wronged party. This concept seems dogmatically justified, yet it multiplies the hardships having to do with evidence. It is clear that in many cases specifying lost profits is extremely difficult.

It is interesting that the creditor's deprivation of his or her claim is treated in the literature as *damnum emergens*, rather than *lucrum cessans*. It is pointed out that "a claim is an asset in the creditor's patrimony, and so its forfeiture or curtailment must be qualified as loss. This should be the qualification in situations of limitation expiry or preclusion periods relating to a claim that results from an attorney's negligent conduct."[65]

In academic writings, and frequently also in contractual practice, one comes across the distinction between direct and indirect damage. Judicial decisions in criminal cases sometimes mention "loss directly caused by criminal offence." The SC stresses that "the loss whose repair may by imposed on the offender is determined only by the amount of actual loss inflicted directly by the crime, not its further ramifications (indirectly related to its commission), e.g. interests" (SC judgment of 9 July 2008,[66][66] SC judgment of 16 May 2002[67]). This position, however, refers merely to the obligation to redress damage awarded as punitive measure, and as probative requisite. Yet, it would be hard to establish precisely, based on the case law of the Supreme Court, the borderline between damage directly and indirectly caused by a crime. As regards interests, which were referred to in the judgment cited above, in civil law they make up an institution separate from compensation. Their exclusion from the scope of the obligation to repair the damage does not trigger the need to coin new procedures.

In other decisions, the Supreme Court refers to loss directly inflicted by criminal offence, asserting, for example, that it is not possible either to adjudge the obligation to repair damage beyond the actually ascertained amount of loss, to

---

64 III CK 495/02, publ. Lex No. 164003.
65 M. Kaliński; op. cit., p. 111.
66 II KK 137/08, Lex No. 436369.
67 III KK 189/02, Lex No. 53327.

impose the duty to repair damage to the extent it has been already redressed, or to award the obligation to repair damage to the benefit of parties other than the wronged one. It seems worthwhile only in this last case to invoke the difference between the losses directly and indirectly caused by the crime. The other ones simply do not refer to loss. In light of this, there arises the question of whether the distinction made in civil law doctrine between direct and indirect damage may be of any use to criminal law.

At the outset of the investigation to answer this question, it ought to be underlined that it would be difficult to adduce a single, generally applicable and accurate definition of "direct loss" and "indirect loss." It is suggested that

> the notions of direct and indirect loss may be understood in three different ways. According to the subjective criterion, loss is direct where effects of the harmful event are assessed in the sphere of the interests of the person directly aggrieved, while indirect loss affects other parties. Secondly, one may resort to the criterion of causal link, reducing direct loss to detriment covered by direct causal link (*causa proxima*) with the harmful event. Third, direct loss may be defined as a result of the violation of either an interest directly affected by the harmful event or the integrity of the whole property of the wronged party regardless of the violation of any particular interest, whereas indirect losses follow from the transgression of other interests of the wronged party.[68]

The first of these meanings of the term indirect damage was often found in earlier judicial rulings, but it seems that this usage is not sufficiently justified. As far as the second and third proposals are concerned, they are equally viable. The criterion of indirectness of damage based on causal link was invoked by T. Dybowski.[69] On the other hand, B. Lackoroński contends that loss is indirect if the actions of the actor who caused it are not directed against the diminished interest.[70] At the current stage of the debate, it would be difficult to predict which of the meanings of the concept "indirect damage" will permanently prevail in the Polish legal system. Despite the relative popularity of the exemption of liability for indirect loss in contractual practice, the meaning of this concept still has not been fixed in Supreme Court case law. Nevertheless, in one of the latest rulings, the judgment of the Supreme Court of 22 June 2012,[71] it was indicated that "compensation covers not just direct damage but also so-called indirect damage as long as it is normally causally linked with unlawful conduct on the part of the

---

68 M. Kaliński, op. cit., p. 105.
69 See T. Dybowski, in Z. Radwański (ed.), *System prawa cywilnego, vol. III, part. 1,* p. 217.
70 B. Lackoroński, in J. Jastrzębski, *Odpowiedzialność odszkodowawcza* (Warsaw, 2007).
71 V CSK 282/11, publ. OSP 2013/5/48, Lex No. 1313749.

offender (art. 361(1) CivC)." This rule applies obviously only in the absence of any contractual stipulation to the contrary.

It thus seems that the notion if indirect loss, which escapes precise definitions in civil law, would not be of much use in determining limits to the criminal law duty to repair damage.

Grounds for compensatory delictual (tortious) liability in civil law

Traditionally, it is accepted that civil law liability for damage may be based on delictual grounds, on one hand, or the non-performance or default of a contract (liability *ex contractu*), on the other. Yet, it turns out that there are still other sources of compensatory liability. Beside the two grounds just distinguished, one may point, for example, to liability for damages caused in the course of the performance of public functions, to liability for damages inflicted while performing one's subjective right, to a guarantor's liability for damage (e.g. in commercial insurance), and, finally, to liability for damage sustained in another party's interest or common interest.[72]

In the context of the criminal law duty to repair damage, irrespective of how it is defined, the regime of delictual responsibility is of most relevance. We may speak here of the reparation of damage inflicted by criminal offence. It seems that in light of criminal law subsidiarity, the class of criminal offences is subordinate to the class of delicts, as understood by civil law provisions. Deliberations pertaining to the grounds of civil law responsibility may thus be limited to delictual liability.

As regards the premises of delictual liability, they may be said to comprise:

1) the event which gives rise to delictual liability in light of civil law provisions;
2) damage;
3) a causal link between the event which gives rise to delictual liability in light of civil law provisions and the damage.[73]

Ad. 1) The catalogue of events which make up the foundation of delictual responsibility under civil law provisions is extremely broad. They are differently classified and it would not be possible to refer here to all the classifications one encounters. Traditionally, the premises are grouped under "principles of liability."

---

72 M. Kaliński; op. cit., p. 23.
73 *Ibid.*, p. 348; see also W. Czachórski, Zobowiązania. *Zarys wykładu* (Warsaw, 1994), p. 186.

It is thus legitimate to talk about liability based on guilt, risk, and, finally, equity. The present considerations may be limited to liability based on guilt, since this principle is closest to the mechanism of criminal accountability. Evidently, liability attaches to the perpetrator of an act, which may take form of either an action or an omission, but must be unlawful and culpable. Most clearly, there are also differences between criminal and civil law. First, the catalogue of persons that may be held responsible under civil law is broader. In civil law, one may speak of the liability of juridical persons, or other entities with legal capacity conferred under respective legal provisions, whereas criminal liability relates only to natural persons. However, what is even more important than the catalogue of persons capable of incurring liability is the fact that civil law defines the act differently. Under criminal law, the act always relates to human behaviour. Under civil law, on the other hand, with regard to the responsibility of legal persons, one may adduce the concept of "guilt in organisation." Under this conception, responsibility for the conduct of anonymous persons associated with the organisation comes into question.[74] Liability attaches to juridical persons for acts which cannot be and do not even need to be attributed to individuals.

As regards the other premises of liability, i.e. unlawfulness and guilt, there are certain doubts in the doctrine of civil law about whether unlawfulness constitutes guilt or is a separate requisite of responsibility. This question, however, is of little meaning to the scope of compensatory liability based on guilt. Hence, it seems that it is not necessary to resolve that query, since unlawfulness and guilt may be approached as separate conditions of liability. It should, however, be noted that under the current criminal law regulation which reflects the normative theory of guilt, intention and its absence are handled at the level of the definition of the punishable act. Quite to the contrary, intention in civil law and various types of non-intentionality are generally rendered as guilt. In addition, civil law doctrine classifies unintentional forms of guilt in a more detailed manner. Authors differentiate, for instance, between recklessness, negligence (including gross negligence), *culpa levis*, and *culpa levissima*.[75]

Regardless of constructional dissimilarities concerning the classification of intentionality and various types of non-intentionality, it must be stressed that under the framework of compensatory liability based on guilt, the intensity of guilt is reflected in the amount of compensation.[76] This remark is entirely valid with

---

74 See Z. Banaszczyk, "Komentarz do art. 416 k.c.," *Legalis*.
75 See W. Czachórski, op. cit., p. 192-194.
76 M. Kaliński, op. cit., p. 64.

respect to economic loss. On the other hand, when it comes to non-economic loss, this issue becomes complicated. It is pointed out in case law that the court awarding compensation for non-economic loss (atonement) should consider in particular the type and degree of guilt of the person infringing a personal good, the purpose and motivation of his or her conduct, his or her financial standing, the behaviour of the offender after the violation of personal interests, the type and scale of the infringement encroached on, the results of the encroachment to the wronged party, and the extent to which removal of the results of infringement to personal interests requires allowance of the claim pursued under art. 448 CivC apart from non-economic remedies envisaged in art. 24(1) CivC (SC judgment of 16 April 2002).[77] At first glance, criminal lawyers might see a similarity between these elements, which have an impact on the possibility to adjudge atonement and its amount, on one hand, and criteria for evaluating the level of social noxiousness of the punishable act and factors determining the level of sanction, on the other. In assessing the circumstances which determine the possibility of awarding atonement and determining its amount, attention ought to be paid to the compensatory character of this institution. It is emphasised by the Supreme Court that "the basic function of monetary compensation for infringement of personal interests (art. 448 CivC) is compensatory. Atonement is meant to indemnify the harm sustained, and should cover all the aspects of this harm. As a result, it may not be of a solely symbolic character. Although differing from compensation for economic loss, it must still have a palpable material value. The deciding court must account for the type of interest infringed, the character, intensity and duration of the suffering of the wronged party, and negative emotional experiences induced by the violation (harm). In the process of this assessment, the court also takes into consideration the level of guilt of the wrongdoer, the purpose he or she had in mind while acting in a manner harmful to the relevant interest and the financial gain attained or expected to be attained by the wrongdoer" (SC judgment of 11 April 2006).[78]

Ad. 2) Two basic methods of calculating economic damage have been suggested: the differential model and the objective model. The differential model consists in the comparison between the condition in which the property of the wronged party would hypothetically be, in the absence of the delict, and the condition that has emerged as a result of the civil wrong.[79] In the literature, it is

77 V CKN 1010/00, Lex No. 55467.
78 I CSK 159/05, publ. Lex No. 371773.
79 See T. Dybowski, op. cit, p. 218.

indicated that "the object of comparison is the difference between the true state of affairs at the time of the determination of damage and the hypothetical condition, i.e. an arrangement of facts which would be observable had the wrongful event not taken place, even though the overall situation of a given wronged party is related to both of these states. In the absence of a legal regulation to the contrary, it is not admissible to restrict the analysis to interests directly affected by the harmful event."[80]

The objective method, in contrast, consists in "determining the amount of damage in reference to a particular interest."[81] This method is "detached from the effects of the harmful event on the total property of the wronged party."[82] Undoubtedly, the objective method is easier to apply in practice. It aims at assessing the value of specific lost or damaged wronged party interests, and not the hypothetical condition of the whole patrimony. Nonetheless, the differential method makes for a better implement intended to fulfil the principle of full compensation, which has been defined in art. 361(2) CivC. Bearing this in mind, it is the differential model that has been accepted in Polish legal literature and case law as the right one for determining the scope of damage. For example, by reference to recent judicature, one may calculate that according to the resolution of the Seven Judges of the Supreme Court of 17 November 2011,[83] in a case of automobile damage, loss not only covers the costs of the replacement or repair of its parts but also reasonable costs for the lease of a replacement vehicle for the period of repair.

Naturally, the acceptance of the differential method does not mean that the objective method is not applied at all. In fact, calculating loss by reference to the objective method is easier. It is more difficult to grasp, and, more importantly, prove within a pending process what the hypothetical condition of the wronged party's assets would be if it had not been for the harmful event than to actually render the value of specific interests. For this very reason, it can be concluded that determining full damage in accordance with the differential method is impossible in many individual cases. The differential method is more like a postulation and eventuality that the wronged party may avail of as claimant in the proceeding. The wronged party usually manages to prove some of the aspects of loss by recourse to the differential method, and with regard to other elements he or she is likely to rely on the objective method by pointing to the value of particular the interests injured.

---

80 See M. Kaliński, op. cit., p. 82-83.
81 K. Pietrzykowski, "Komentarz do art. 361 k.c.," *Legalis*.
82 *Ibid.*
83 III CZP 5/11, publ. OSNC 2012/3/28, Lex No. 1011468.

Generally speaking, reparation encompasses loss existent at the time of a case's decision. This conclusion follows from art. 361(2) CivC. This principle may be superseded by a special provision, such as art. 444(2) CivC, which provides for annuity as a mechanism of redressing future damage.

Ad. 3) Under art. 361(1) CivC, the person obligated to compensate is liable only for the normal consequences of his or her actions or omissions which caused the damage.

The causal link is the prism through which the question of the wronged party's or third person's or third factor's contribution to the emergence or enhancement of the damage are evaluated. In accordance with art. 362 CivC, "where the wronged party has contributed to the emergence or enhancement of damage, the obligation to repair it shall be proportionally decreased, as circumstances require, with a view in particular to the level of guilt of both parties." When it comes to contribution of third parties to the damage, as long as their conduct may be qualified in the category of delictual behaviour, the liability of all contributors is joint and several. This conclusion follows from art. 441 CivC, which provides that "where a number of persons is accountable for damage inflicted by a delict, their liability shall be joint and several."

An interesting problem is the susceptibility of the wronged party to the wrong. It is pointed out that susceptibility does not contradict "the normality of a causal link between the event attributable to another person and its consequences. As an example, some authors point to a case of death resulting from a slap to the victim's face because the victim's skull bones were so thin that even a light blow could turn out to be fatal. This issue comes down to a determination of the admissible degree of generalisation when ascertaining whether the requisites of normality have been met. This position is justified as long as the generalisation is not too far reaching and as long as, when asking the question about increased probability, we consider the factor whose occurrence with regard to the wronged party enabled emergence of this particular detriment."[84]

Means of redressing damage in civil law

Under art. 363(1) CivC, "Repair of damage should be done, in accordance with the preference of the wronged party, either by restitution of previous condition or payment of a specific amount of money. Nevertheless, if restitution of the previous state of affairs proves impossible, or if it is connected with excessive

---

84 M. Kaliński, op. cit., p. 135-136.

hardships or costs incurred by the obliged party, the claim raised by the wronged party may only be awarded in money." Legislation leaves it to the choice of the wronged party whether repair of loss takes form of restitution in kind or the rendering of pecuniary compensation. Nowadays, the most frequent choice on the part of the wronged party will be the latter. Restitution in kind could be of more significance in the times of constant deficiency of goods and services on the market. Now that money may be invested in practically any goods, pecuniary compensation has become more universal and usually more advantageous to the wronged party.

Then also the Civil Code provides that "where redress of damage is to assume monetary form, the amount of compensation ought to be determined according to prices on the date of its calculation unless special circumstances require that another moment be relevant for this determination" (art. 362(2)) CivC.

When it comes to the possible means of natural restitution, legal literature points out that it may take the form of:

1) repair of the damaged thing or achievement of its compliance with the contract;
2) delivery of the thing whose control was forfeited by the wronged party as a result of the harmful event;
3) delivery of non-pecuniary profits that would fall to the wronged party in the absence of the harmful event;
4) provision of services in kind;
5) press announcement (a provision made use of especially in instances of encroachments on personal interests and acts of unfair competition).[85]

---

85 *Ibid.*, p. 177.

Teresa Dukiet-Nagórska

An Attempt to Assess the Manner in which Damage and its Redress can be Understood from the Point of view of Fundamental Principles of Criminal Law

Introductory remarks

As has been stated above, the doctrine is dominated by the view that damage, as a concept associated with civil law, is to be defined according to findings made on the level of the language of law and legal practice, as they are appropriate. *Mutatis mutandis*, the same applies to redress of damage. Accepting this view requires a consideration of arguments for and against the thesis that it is necessary to understand damage within criminal law autonomously. What follows is devoted to balancing the arguments against each other and choosing one of these alternatives.

Polish lawmakers, with respect to the solutions adopted in the Criminal Code of 1997, decided to take restitution and compensation into broader consideration than had been done before, an event that was connected to the changing status of the wronged party in criminal process and to attempts to solve the conflict which arises between the offender and the victim in consequence of the offence. The justification of the Criminal Code reads that this purpose is served by the institution of active repentance (its task is, among other things, to prevent damage from happening or to redress it) which involves a duty to redress the damage. Along with this, it is stressed that the institution of the redress of damage "(...) is embedded in civil law, thus the court awarding redress of damage should use relevant provisions of civil law, with the exception of the provisions on the limitation of claims (limitation periods in civil law are shorter than in provisions of penal law concerning the statute of limitations) and the possibility of awarding annuity."[1] This decision in the legislature reflects views expressed in legal doctrine, according to which the route of criminal proceedings is necessary

---

1 *Kodeks karny. Kodeks postępowania karnego. Kodeks karny wykonawczy*, Warsaw, 1997, p. 147. The justification of the Criminal Code did not mention non-economic loss because both types of damage were distinguished in further amendments to the Code.

in this matter, since civil law cannot focus on the negative meaning of the act committed by the offender and the harm suffered by the victim. The view held by M. Cieślak and A. Murzynowski serves as an example: "(…) in the area of civil law, the suffering of the victim of a crime by itself does not present a satisfactorily autonomous and coherent legal issue. It is embedded in a system of various financial clearances and considered in various contexts which dilute its appropriate and sharp social meaning (…) In the area of property insurance, theft is treated equally to a flooded house, and arson is equal to a stroke of lightning."[2]

This focus on the wronged party was met with approval in the doctrine. Many scholars highlighted the necessity of providing the wronged party with a real possibility to obtain quick compensation with no extra procedures or costs: "It seems that the concept of turning to the victim of the crime, particularly by redress of damage, could not be more appropriate. Other functions, although important and in some cases of very high priority, emerge as of lesser importance."[3] It was also widely stressed that redress of damage fulfils the social sense of justice and serves general and individual prevention purposes well.[4] Yet, upon further consideration, the matter turned out to be more complicated.

It was underlined in the early stage of more detailed studies on the problem of the criminal-law duty to redress damage that the penal nature of this measure necessitates an examination of it in reference to the purpose of the penalty,[5] which leads to the conclusion that in some cases the compensatory purpose has to be pushed into the background, and allowed to give way to preventive purposes.[6] Moreover, resignation on fine as penalty is recommended for better fulfilment of the compensation purpose.[7] This line of thought on the obligation to redress damage was continued and developed in the later period. What fits well into this view is the statement by B. Janiszewski that "The content of art. 53

---

2   M. Cieślak, A. Murzynowski, "Wynagrodzenie szkody osobie pokrzywdzonej przestępstwem – jego znaczenie w sferze prawa karnego," *Studia Prawnicze*, 1974, No. 2, p. 46 ff.

3   B. Janiszewski, "Naprawienie szkody a cele wymiaru kary," *CzPKiNP*, 2002, No. 2, p. 53.

4   See W. Zalewski, "Naprawienie szkody w polskim prawie karnym a postulaty restorative justice," in S. Waltoś, B. Nita, P. Trzaska, M. Żurek (eds.), *Kompensacyjna funkcja prawa karnego*, Zakamycze, 2002, p. 67, and the source cited therein, W. Zalewski, *Sprawiedliwość naprawcza, początek ewolucji polskiego prawa karnego*, Gdańsk, 2006.

5   Z. Gostyński, *Karnoprawny obowiązek naprawienia szkody*, Katowice 1984, p. 73.

6   *Ibid.*, p. 66.

7   Z. Gostyński, *Obowiązek naprawienia szkody w nowym ustawodawstwie karnym*, Zakamycze, 1999, p. 38.

CrimC raises the problem of the relationship of redressing damage to the elements included in that provision, which are mostly the social noxiousness of an act and guilt, but also factors of individual prognosis." Moreover, this author very accurately signals that a broad understanding of damage—including both *damnum emergens* and *lucrum cessans*—indeed well serves the goal of safeguarding the interests of the victim and is morally right; still, it raises questions about the compatibility of its definition with the principle of certainty.[8] He also asks the question of the acceptability of widening the extent of damage beyond the legal definition of a prohibited act, paying attention to the possible incongruence of criminally relevant damage with definitions of crime, assessments of the social noxiousness of an act, and circumstances affecting the level of penalty.[9] Another essential point is the author's remark on complications in terms of *mens rea* with regard to the broad understanding of damage.[10]

B. Janiszewski limited his thesis to presenting certain doubts and outlining various perspectives of their dispersal. Sadly, his premature death, preceded by serious illness, prevented him from developing his thoughts. This thread of research can and should be continued. This is the nature of the present study, for which the questions asked by Janiszewski were an inspiration.

The Criminal Code does not define either the essence of damage or the way it should be redressed. In this situation, as indicated above, criminal court judges usually quote conclusions reached in the study of civil law, a tendency that is necessary for coherence within the legal system. I have substantial doubts about whether this attitude conforms to fundamental principles of criminal liability, that is principles included in the Constitution. The following remarks refer to the principles of certainty, culpability and proportionality.[11]

---

8   B. Janiszewski, op.cit., p. 54.

9   *Ibid.*, p. 56-57.

10 *Ibid.*, p. 59.

11 "Art. 42(1) Only a person who has committed an act prohibited by a statute in force at the moment of the commission thereof, and which is subject to a penalty, shall be held criminally responsible. This principle shall not prevent punishment of any act which, at the moment of its commission, constituted an offence within the meaning of international law. [...] (3) Everyone shall be presumed innocent of a charge until his or her guilt is determined by the final judgment of a court."

"Art. 31 [...] (3) Any limitation upon the exercise of constitutional freedoms and rights may be imposed only by statute, and only when necessary in a democratic state for the protection of its security or public order, or to protect the natural environment, public health or public morals, or the freedoms and rights of other persons. Such limitations shall not violate the essence of freedoms and rights."

The principles of nullum crimen and nulla poena sine lege

The constitutional principle of certainty (Art. 42(1) of the Constitution) states that penal responsibility can only be based on acts defined by statute; therefore, only such acts may be considered the determinants of criminal law reaction. The essence of a formal crime is that the results of the offender's acts do not have any significance for criminal liability, which is instead determined only by his or her conduct. Since, in crimes without effects, the form of criminal liability does not depend on the result of the act, the economic (or non-economic) loss caused by such offences cannot give rise to an imposition of the duty to compensate. This is possible only in the case of result crimes. If, for example, as a result of false testimony, someone were to suffer damage or grievance, there would be no grounds to impose the obligation of compensation in any manner. The same must be said of the negative consequences of defamation; therefore, for eample, a surgeon cosmetologist whose number of patients has decreased as a result of false information being uploaded to the internet about his medical errors cannot recover his or her losses by imposing the obligation of compensation on the offender by means of criminal action.

In reference to result crimes, the principle of certainty causes the scope of the duty to redress to be determined only by reference to the result as expressed in the legal description; therefore, if the offender commits a theft of an item of little value, which, however, is of great value to the victim because it is a family heirloom, then only the objective market value shall be taken into consideration when determining the obligation to redress the damage, because the definition of theft only protects property and ownership. Therefore, non-economic loss cannot be compensated for here.

Following these conclusions, a further question must be asked: can all result crimes justify the obligation to pay compensation, or only those whose constituent elements mention damage? I am for allowing such a possibility with reference to every crime which causes certain effects, including the crime of exposure to danger (which I classify as a result crime). Therefore, if there occurs, for example, a risk of death which results in the long-term mental destabilization of the victim, there is no contradiction in awarding compensation for non-economic loss as well as for economic loss if it is necessary to pay the costs of therapy. Of course, this refers to those result crimes for which a victim can be distinguished (I leave out any doubts about whether there really are crimes without victims).

Assault on legal interests can lead both to economic loss (e.g. theft—in the most typical situation, loss of possession leads to a reduction of one's property) and non-economic loss (e.g. as a cause of injury connected with pain), both directly and indirectly (for example, the theft of a work of art not only leads to the reduction of one's property, but also reduces the ability to earn income as remuneration for lending the work of art for exhibition).

The most difficult question concerning the principle of certainty pertains to the scope of the duty to compensate in situations where the act of the offender is against one legal interest but the loss (economic or non-economic) involves more than this specific legal interest; for example, a person deprived of liberty does not fulfil his or her obligations because he or she does not have freedom of movement and, as a result of the crime, is obliged to pay a contractual penalty. In my opinion, only a detriment that is an assault on a legal interest described in the specific definition of a given crime can determine the extent of the obligation to redress. Of course, in this matter we should consider both the main object of protection and the secondary one, as well as any legal interest included by an application of the cumulative legal qualification. As a consequence, I posit that the extent of the obligation to redress should be determined on the basis of detriments which are inherently connected with assaults on a given legal interest (this corresponds to the essence of the sufficiency condition, which is expressed by the phrase "always if p, then q"). Therefore, in the example just mentioned, the reduction of property caused by the payment of a contractual penalty cannot be compensated by imposing on the imprisoning party an obligation to remedy the damage, as this sort of detriment to property is not an inevitable consequence of imprisonment.

A similar problem arises as a consequence of the postulate to transpose the civil law conception of damage into criminal law. The civil law conception of damage includes both *damnum emergens* and *lucrum cessans*—which is usually fully accepted in legal literature and jurisdiction.[12] I cannot share this view without reservation. In the light of the above considerations, the imposition of the duty to compensate, when it involves lost benefits, can take place only insofar as the benefits would have been clearly reaped if the criminal assault on legal interests had not occurred (the absence of any assault on legal rights would in each case lead to the attainment of the benefit). It should be noted here that further restrictions in this regard might involve issues of (un)intentionality (*mens rea*), which will be further described below.

---

12 As in A. Marek, T. Oczkowski in M. Melezini (eds.), *System prawa karnego. Kary i środki karne. Poddanie sprawcy próbie*, Warsaw, 2010, p. 710; W. Zalewski in M. Królikowski, R. Zawłocki (eds), *Kodeks karny. Część ogólna, Komentarz do artykułów 32-116, vol. II*, Warsaw, 2010, p. 204.

The principle of certainty imposes the necessity to apply a literal interpretation; therefore, in disputes pertaining to the duty to compensate, an interpretation of the term *damage*, which appears in numerous provisions of the Criminal Code, must be undertaken.

Damage is referred to in the general part of the Criminal Code mainly in provisions which concern the duty to redress it (art. 39 item 5), art. 46(1), art. 67(3), art. 72(2)). In addition, the term appears in art. 51 (providing for the notification of the family court *inter alia* in the event of an offence to the detriment of a minor), 66(3) (modifying the circumstances of conditional discontinuance of criminal proceedings), art. 115(2) (indicating the criteria for assessing levels of social noxiousness), art. 155(7) (defining "considerable damage" and "damage of great size"). However, in the special part of the Criminal Code, *damage* is used to describe the effects of the basic and qualified offence types, wherein it describes the effects related to miscellaneous legal interests such as property, natural environment, the proper functioning of state and self-government institutions, and business trading. It is also included in many cases describing active repentance (e.g. art. 295 CrimC).

Interpretations attempting to define the meaning and scope of this concept are hindered by the lack of uniformity in the terminology used in the Criminal Code: art 39 item 5 and 46(1) CrimC differentiate between economic and non-economic loss, but this distinction does not appear in other provisions of the Criminal Code, and furthermore there is heterogeneity in doctrinal opinions and judicial decisions. Therefore we must consider whether this situation is justified, which raises a further question: If a given statutory provision fails to mention non-economic loss, does it narrow damage to economic loss?

It seems that for the question of how significant the principle of certainty is for understanding *damage*, any further consideration of Article 51 of the Criminal Code needs to be eliminated, as it has no linkage with the safeguarding function. It serves the interest of a child in situations when danger to children comes into question. The notification specified in this rule should not be limited by issues pertaining to the offender, thus it should be understood as broadly as possible. This leads to the conclusion that *damage* within the meaning of this rule includes both economic and non-economic loss; direct and indirect damage.[13] When a child has been sexually abused, leading to extensive disruption of psychological and physical development and making it necessary for guardians to

---

13 This view is presented by N. Kłączyńska in J. Giezek (eds.), *Kodeks Karny, Część ogólna, Komentarz, Lex 125556*. Also P. Kozłowska-Kalisz in M. Mozgawa (eds.), *Kodeks Karny, Komentarz, Lex 140835*.

incur treatment and psychotherapy costs, compensation shall include economic as well as non-economic loss.

This rule is significant in this analysis, because it illustrates the necessity of a broad understanding of *damage* (otherwise the notification would not fulfil its function), which contradicts the thesis that whenever the Criminal Code refers to damage, a distinction following from the wording of art. 39 item 5 CrimC and art. 46(1) CrimC should be observed.

The distinction between economic and non-economic loss (unknown to the original draft of the Criminal Code from 1997, which used only the name "damage," the distinction was applied as a result of the amendment to the Criminal Code, the Code of Criminal Procedure, the Executive Penal Code, the Fiscal Criminal Code and some other statutes by the Act of 5th November 2009[14]) refers exclusively to a specification of the essence of the punitive measure. It is not a legal definition according to which each reference to the term would necessitate an interpretation conforming with the definition. Therefore the meaning of *damage* must be ascertained in another way.

The distinction between *economic* and *non-economic loss* made in art. 39 item 5 and art. 46(1) CrimC is a consequence of the belief that compensation is an institution of civil law; therefore, according to this view (as described in Chapter 2), the meanings of these terms are to be found in this branch of law. Yet I am not convinced of the validity of this thesis.

In the first place, it is difficult to speak of a legal definition of economic and non-economic loss in civil law, because the basis for defining them in civil law lies solely in the distinction between the compensation accordant to each type of detriment. The language of law also does not define damage in any uniform way: the doctrine tends to use the terms delictual (tortious) damage and contractual damage (emphasizing that contractual damage does not include non-economic loss, because the obligation to compensate for non-economic loss requires an explicit statutory basis, which is provided only with respect to delictual liability). This was mentioned in Chapter 2.

Therefore, in neither criminal nor civil law is there a legal definition for *damage*, and the legal language even lacks semantic uniformity. Thus the meanings of the general language have to be taken into consideration. This would be justified even if a legal definition existed in civil law, because the functions of these two legal disciplines are so different that one could not rule out the possibility of the malfunctioning in criminal law of definitions formed in civil law.

---

14 *Dziennik Ustaw* No. 206, item 1589.

The Polish language generally allows *economic loss (szkoda)* and *non-economic loss (krzywda)* to be treated as nearly synonymous, since the latter Polish expression is understood as "moral, physical, or economic harm, inflicted to somebody undeservedly, unlawfully,"[15] while *damage* means "economic or moral loss; detriment."[16] In substance (and this was the only aspect emphasized in Art. 39 item 5 and Art. 46(1) CrimC), they reveal no difference, thus despite the absence of any statutory reference in this matter, there would be grounds to cover economic as well as non-economic loss with the duty to redress damage. In this case, although the legislator is articulate only with reference to the punitive measure that both types of loss are to be considered, in all other usages of the term "damage" in a statutory provision, in pursuance of literal interpretation, both economic and non-economic loss are to be borne in mind since such are the connotations of the plain and ordinary language. It is therefore impossible to meet the requirement according to which a single term should be given the same meaning in all parts of a single legislative act. Tightly clinging to this rule would lead to situations in which restricting liberty, conditionally discontinuing criminal proceedings, and suspending penalties, combined with the duty to redress damage, would never lead to compensation for non-economic loss, because the relevant provisions refer only to economic loss (*szkoda*). Therefore, a perpetrator of, for example, light or medium health impairment could not be awarded the obligation to compensate for the non-economic loss suffered.

The view expressed thus far in relation to the understanding of *damage* in the Criminal Code does not violate the safeguarding function because it is based on general, plain and ordinary language. The fact that it is only under this approach that the compensatory function can be completely fulfilled might be an argument in its favour. Therefore, the opinions based on the assumption that distinguishing between *economic* and *noneconomic loss* under art. 39 item 5 and art. 46(1) CrimC implies that any reference to damage in the Criminal Code indicates material damage only are not correct,[17] as this point of view leads to significant dysfunctions.

In light of this, the thesis is justified that each time the Criminal Code mentions the duty to compensate, it means a potential redress of an economic and

---

15 M. Szymczak (ed.), *Słownik Języka Polskiego, vol. I*, Warsaw 1978, p. 1069, own translation.

16 M. Szymczak (ed.), *Słownik Języka Polskiego, vol. III*, Warsaw 1981, p. 413, own translation.

17 This view on Art. 67 § 3 CrimC. is shared by: A. Zoll, "Komentarz do art. 67 kodeksu karnego," *Lex*; G. Łabuda, "Komentarz do art. 67 kodeksu karnego," *Lex*.

non-economic loss. This regards specifically those provisions which connect the obligation to compensate with probative measures (art. 66(3), art. 67(3), art. 72(2) CrimC) and the penalty of restriction of liberty (art. 36(2) CrimC).

This observation does not mean that in every case of imposing an obligation to redress, assessing the effectiveness of active repentance, or instantiating an element of crime definition which uses the term *damage*, both forms of damage should be taken into consideration. A need for correction might occur based on a specific definition type, or, to be more specific, based on the description of the criminal offence, since what counts as the essence of redressing damage is determined as a result of the given set of elements that define a criminal offence. This attitude is a consequence of the aforementioned view, according to which priority is given, in this case, to the legal interests protected by the given command or prohibition.

In concluding this topic, it has to be asserted that the form of the imposed duty to compensate is a result of a consideration of its conception in the general part of the Criminal Code and the set of elements which define a given crime. *Mutatis mutandis*, this refers to an element of crime definition formulated with the use of the term *damage*.

The principle of certainty requires that the criminal law reaction be properly specified. The Criminal Code uses the quite general notion of *duty to redress economic and non-economic loss* (Art. 39 (5)). The compensation mechanism is not clearly specified, and there is only the stipulation that civil law provisions on the limitation of claims and annuity are not to be applied (art. 46(1) CrimC). Furthermore, no comment on this notion can be found in other provisions of the general part of the Criminal Code which refer to the duty to compensate, or in the Executive Penal Code.

The argument that a full blanket clause has been introduced here is fully justified, because the essence of the punitive measure, as well as the penal measure accompanying restriction of liberty and probation, have not been defined in the Criminal Code. In such a situation, the doctrine of the criminal law allows for the (direct rather than appropriate) application of civil law provisions (which has been indicated in Chapter II). This gives rise to doubt about the compatibility of this approach with the principle of certainty.

The Civil Code contains provisions related to redress of economic and non-economic loss. These provisions indicate their essence, their applicability and the mechanism of their calculation (as presented above). Although the requirement is met to lay down criminal sanctions in a legislative act of statutory rank, doubts arise concerning the fact that criminalization is envisaged in a different legislative act than the one providing criminal sanctions, wherein these legal acts have different functions to perform (which means dissimilar terminology, as has been suggested). One example of this is Article 415 of the Civil Code, which contains elementary regulation on tort liability for damages, and in which the lawmaker refers to the concept of guilt as understood differently than in criminal law.[18]

The mechanism of referring to civil law also entails certain doubts. Objections might derive from specifying civil law provisions which are not applicable (as set out in art. 46(1) CrimC). This technique is understood as the recommendation to apply all other provisions of civil law relating to redress of damage. However, it is not only the Criminal Code which fail to indicate such provisions in a positive manner. Supporters of this concept too make no efforts to prepare such a list. Indeed, the form of criminal sanction is determined by blanket reference. A clear illustration of the imperfection of this approach to the problem is the view expressed in the Supreme Court decision of 6 March 2008, III KK 345/07.[19] The question examined was the issue of awarding compensation for non-economic loss to the parents of a fatally beaten victim. The courts adjudicating on this matter admitted that the mental shock which the parents had suffered justified the award of compensation. The Supreme Court gave the following justification:

> Although the obligation to redress damage is rooted in civil law, and applied as a criminal measure, it is in its essence a penal sanction. The criminal law nature of this obligation means that it should be applied in accordance with provisions of criminal law. In the opinion of the Court, it is not contrary to these provisions to use an interpretation of the provisions of Art. 445(1) of the Civil Code, which make it possible to award compensation in order to remedy an instance of suffering resulting from a health disorder in a close relative of a victim to intentional crime against life, where the disorder is suffered as a result of emotional upset following the crime. Since this interpretation appeared in civil judicature and was accepted as the basis for awarding compensation to a close relative of the deceased victim of a delict (crime) for a health disorder resulting from this act (causally linked) in accordance with art. 445(1) of the Civil Code, and since such an interpretation is in accordance with provisions of criminal law, its application constitutes grounds for concluding that the penal measure specified in Article 39 item 5 CrimC does not violate substantive law.

---

18 In civil law there is a complex theory of guilt. The wrongdoer is accused of taking inappropriate action, or not taking appropriate action. He or she is therefore judged by behaviour. The basis of this judgment, leading to possible claims, is both his or her mental state and existing norms (W. Czachórski, *System prawa cywilnego. Tom III. Część 1. Prawo zobowiązań - część ogólna*, Ossolineum, 1981, p. 540). Therefore, as far as guilt is concerned, intentionality and many levels of unintentionality are distinguished.

19 Lex No. 361539.

The Supreme Court here presents a view, which is by all accounts correct, of the necessity to consider provisions of criminal law when applying the punitive measure specified in Art. 39 item 5 CrimC, but then the Court acts in a way which seems incompatible with this view, since instead of justifying compatibility with provisions of criminal law as an argument, it refers to an interpretation found in decisions of civil courts which allows the awarding of compensation for non-economic loss in such situations. The final result of this line of argumentation is that the requisites for imposing a punitive measure follow from interpretations adopted by civil courts. This state of affairs is far from satisfactory.

Another consequence of applying provisions of civil law in criminal cases is the "borrowing" of the manners of redress of damage from this area of law (as indicated above). For the purpose of the present analysis, it is essential that civil law itself does not indicate the means of restitution; only the doctrine provides examples in this respect. Thus, no further increase takes place in the level of encroachment on the principle of the specificity of penal sanction; however, referrals to the civil law legacy do not serve the end of diluting the conflict between the offender and the victim, or even the compensatory function itself. For this, actions of a completely different character carried out by the offender might prove more functional. As an example, a car accident caused by a moment of driver inattention leads to death of a person who was building a house for his large family. The offender turns out to be an experienced construction worker who is struggling to make ends meet. In this situation, a fair solution would be to hire the offender to finish the construction initiated by the victim.

Doubt arises about the factors which determine the due amount of compensation. On this issue, the Supreme Court held, "The damage which the court imposes on the offender the duty to redress shall correspond to the actual damage resulting directly from the crime, and it is not permissible to include elements which followed from subsequent consequences of the act; that is, interests are not considered" (Judgment of 4 February 2002, II KKN 385/01).[20] Unfortunately, this judgment does not contribute much to a solution, as it is not obvious how "damage resulting directly from the crime" is to be understood. It is particularly difficult to find a justification for the point that a consequence of a wrongful act does not determine the amount of due compensation. On the contrary, if the concept of *damage* is to refer to the result which constitutes an element of a crime's definition, including the qualified type of the offence, then, participants of battery, for example, defined under art. 158(2) CrimC, should of course cover

---

20 Lex No. 53028.

the expenses of treatment caused by heavy health impairment and non-economic loss caused as a result of the act. When it comes to interests, it is beyond doubt that the duty to redress arises at the moment of the validation of the criminal court judgment; therefore, in such judgments there is no place for imposing interests accrued after that date (these issues will be further discussed below).

It has to be noted that, by and large, civil law allows the victim to choose the means of redressing the damage, which is reflected in the content of the claim. However, in a criminal actions, this end cannot be met, as it would allow the victim to shape the form of criminal law response to the offence. Of course, decisions of this nature may be made by means of mediation, but their situation differs significantly from instances of direct dictation by a wronged party and is by all means acceptable under the rules of restorative criminal law. The result of a mediation process, *de lege lata*, is not binding for the criminal court, and there is no contradiction in applying a penal sanction other than the one agreed on in the settlement, whereas the civil court may not adjudge beyond the wronged party's claim, and examples of objections to the settlement are rare—they can only be justified by defiance of the principles of social coexistence.

Another point is the difficulty resulting from concurrent application of provisions of the Civil Code and the Criminal Code. For example, in the case of conditional discontinuance of criminal proceedings and suspension of penalty, an obligation to apologize to the victim may be imposed (art. 67(3) and art. 72(1) item 2 CrimC), while, according to the Civil Code, the infringement of personal rights may result in an order by the court to make a statement of appropriate content. The question arises of whether commission of a crime of personal interest violation (e.g. liberty), which is addressed by imposing the duty to redress damage in the form of a probative measure, may involve the obligation to make a declaration other than an apology which would itself be treated as compensation for non-economic loss?

To sum up this part of discussion, it ought to be noted that the catalogue of rules determining the form of the penal measure imposing the obligation to redress the damage is not definite; therefore, its essence is vague, which does not contribute to fulfilling the objectives of restorative criminal law.

The principle of guilt

Guilt legitimises punishing: there is no crime without guilt, and without crime penal measures cannot be applied—this refers to penalties, punitive measures, and probation measures. Only preventive measures are not determined by the underlying principle of guilt (this is why in the case of insane offenders, according to art. 99 CrimC, preventive measures are used rather than punitive measures, although their content is identical to the punitive measures specified in this rule).

An offender can be charged only if the features of the criminal act (the elements of its definition) have been realised, including, of course, the elements related to *mens rea*. As a consequence, economic and non-economic loss may be compensated only if the elements of intentionality referring to the result have been actualised—wherein, as mentioned before, the basis for the duty to compensate may only be a detriment to interests protected by a given command or prohibition. This can be illustrated with the example of an offender who has locked the victim of deprivation of liberty in a room, causing the latter's particular anguish. Yet, it was not intentional (the offender was negligent and did not check the conditions of the place of the victim's isolation). It is beyond doubt that the suffering of the victim has been intensified by the conditions where he has been kept, but this could not influence the amount of damage, because the type of crime qualified by circumstances described in Art. 189(3) *in fine* CrimC requires intention, and mixed *mens rea* does not qualify at this point. A similar case would concern the amount of indemnity awarded to an offender who, while maliciously interfering with the public performance of a religious ceremony (crime under art. 195(1) CrimC), at the same time negligently destroys décor articles of the temple, meaning that the crime under art. 288(1) CrimC must be intentional. Therefore, the non-economic loss of the persons participating in the religious ceremony may be compensated, but the damage resulting from the destruction of décor may not, even though the offender acted against two legal interests. Analogical assessment should be made in cases in which the offender is deemed unaware of the great monetary value or particular importance to Polish culture of the stolen object, as a result of the absence of elements of an intentional qualified type defined for the crime in art. 294 CrimC. The scope of the duty to redress damage is thus determined by the basic type of the offence (art. 278(1) CrimC).

Particular emphasis should be put on the significance of *mens rea* for imposing the duty to compensate in respect of lost profits: in the case of intentional offence, the offender must at least be aware of the possibility of lost profits and of accepting this eventuality. This requirement, in connection with the aforementioned significance of detriment to the object of assault, means that instances of imposing the duty to repair damage in the form of lost profits will be very rare – it would require a case in which, for example, a famous figure-skater deliberately hurts her rival in a training session, causing an injury that prevents the rival from participating in a show which is a source of income, and knows in advance about this likelihood.

When considering negligence, the prerequisite for awarding the obligation to compensate is in this case the actual prediction of the possibility of lost profits in the event of conscious recklessness and (abstract) predictability of lost profits in the event of unconscious unintentionality.

The relevance of directives on the level of sanction

According to the Criminal Code, the level of sanction is ascertained by the penal sanction assigned to a specific crime, the provisions of the general part of the Criminal Code which refer to specific penal measures, the provisions of the general part of the Code which set forth principles concerning the level of sanction (that is provisions of elementary importance to degree of penalty), and directives on the level of sanction (specified mainly in art. 53 CrimC).[21] It is clear that it is not possible to cover all issues raised by the level of sanction, therefore only those that seem fundamental to this topic will be discussed below.

Provisions concerning the level of penalty, under art. 56 CrimC, are applicable as appropriate to the remaining penal measures (excluding preventive measures). Therefore the obligation to compensation is also subject to this rule.

The general directives on the level of sanction have been regulated in art. 53 CrimC, which indicated the criterion of the degree of guilt, the directive of proportionality to the degree of social noxiousness of the act and the directive of prevention (specific and general).

---

21 (1) The court shall impose the penalty according to its own discretion, within the limits prescribed by law, bearing in mind that its harshness should not exceed the degree of guilt, considering the level of social noxiousness of the act committed, and taking into account the preventive and educational objectives which the penalty has to attain with regard to the convict, as well as the need to develop a legal conscience among the public. (2) In imposing the penalty, the court shall above all take into account the motivation and the manner of conduct of the perpetrator, the commission of an offence together with a minor, the type and degree of transgression against obligations imposed on the perpetrator, the type and dimension of any adverse consequences of the offence, the characteristics and personal conditions of perpetrator, his way of life prior to the commission of the offence and his conduct thereafter, and particularly his efforts to redress the damage or to compensate the public perception of justice in another form. The court shall also consider the behaviour of the injured person. (3) In imposing the penalty, the court shall also take into consideration the positive results of the mediation between the injured person and the perpetrator, or the settlement reached by them in the proceedings before the state prosecutor or the court.

Particular emphasis should be put on the principle of the proportionality of a sanction to the degree of social noxiousness, due to its correlation with the constitutional principle of proportionality. Polish lawmakers provided a normative, exhaustive list of determinants of the degree of social noxiousness in art. 155(2) CrimC.[22] This assessment is determined solely by the circumstances of a given act and a particular offender. The prevalent role has been attributed to elements of an objective nature, as only the form of intent and the motivation of the offender were mentioned in the provision cited as criteria of a subjective nature. Among circumstances of an objective nature, damage is only one, therefore it cannot be given particular significance.

Art. 53 CrimC also identifies specific directives concerning the level of sanction, among which the type and size of detrimental consequences of an offence are enumerated. From the point of view of this analysis, it must be stressed that the meanings of specific directives are equal, precluding any recognition of any one of them as dominant. Therefore, it would not be possible to state that priority has been assigned to detrimental effects.

Guilt is the determinant of penalty (here excluded is the dispute over whether a law shares only a limiting function with guilt or in fact results in an injunction to impose penalties commensurate to the degree of guilt), whereas its attribution follows from a realisation of elements of a definition of crime which pertain to *mens rea*. Therefore, in a case in which monetary damage is considerable, and even of great size, but the offence happens to be negligent, there arises a justification to mitigate the amount of the duty to redress damages on the part of the criminal court. Otherwise, one could speak of infringement of the limiting function of guilt.

In criminal law, legislators bear in mind that economic distress (which is not intended to be caused by the duty to repair damage, but in fact is) should not be excessive; therefore a fine is not imposed if it cannot be executed (art. 58(2) CrimC), and the daily rates system takes into consideration the offender's income, his or her personal situation, family situation, property relations and earning capacities (art. 33(3) CrimC). Taking into consideration, among other

---

22 "Art. 155. (...) (2) In assessing the level of the social consequences of an act, the court shall take into account the type and nature of the infringed interest, the dimension of the damage caused or anticipated, the method and circumstances of the act's perpetration, the importance of the duties breached by the perpetrator, the form of intent and motivation of the perpetrator, the type of precautionary rules breached, and the degree of the transgression."

things,[23] the above aspects, the Criminal Code provides for the possibility of redressing damage in part or in whole (art. 36(2) in conjunction with art. 72 CrimC, art. 46(1), art. 67(3), art. 72(2) CrimC). Civil law, on the other hand, follows a rule that damage must be completely redressed and mitigation of the amount of compensation is possible only in special circumstances.

Civil law distinguishes between two means of redressing damage: restitution (of the previous condition) and monetary provision. Non-economic loss may be compensated only by provision of money. In the case of criminally unlawful acts, *status quo ante* can rarely be achieved (e.g. death or severe bodily harm cannot be undone, but returning a stolen good without deterioration is possible). Therefore, in most cases (if not in every case) the duty to repair damage means an obligation to pay a specified amount. Non-economic loss is compensated only by monetary payment (whether it is a periodic payment or not is irrelevant here). As a result of that and due to the mandatory nature of the provision which envisages the duty to compensate (art. 46(1) CrimC), and when the judgment of a criminal court is based on the provisions of civil law, there could easily result an award of a compensation which exceeds the financial capacities of the sentenced. This aspect has been taken into consideration in the Supreme Court judgment of 23 July 2009, V KK 124/09,[24] in which the Court held, by reference to the judgment of the Supreme Court of 2 February 2002, II KKN 3585/01,[25] that

> It ought to be stated that the very essence of the punitive measure prescribed in art. 39 item 5 CrimC and art. 46(1) CrimC points to its criminal, repressive nature, and only subsequently to its compensatory nature. Therefore, in the judgment cited, the Court emphasises elements concerning "the actual damage" and its "direct" connection to the committed crime. These are elements of the "degree of guilt" mentioned in art. 53(1) CrimC and art. 56 CrimC, which refer solely to the act itself and not the further consequences which are not always connected to the "degree of guilt." This case is a good illustration of a situation in which the affluence of the offender (or, actually, absence thereof) could be a circumstance having considerable influence on the level of sanction envisaged in the sentence, where the lack of the possibility to pay interests on one hand would lead to augmentation of the obligation in light of continually accruing interests. On the other hand, this could be the basis for ordering execution of penalty in pursuance of art. 75(2) CrimC.

---

23 Imposing only partly the duty to compensate may follow from other reasons – e.g. earlier, partial redress of damage, contribution of the victim.

24 Lex No. 519632.

25 Lex No. 53028.

This view is fully acceptable, except for its reference to actual damage and its direct connection with the committed crime as the elements of the degree of guilt.

In summing up all the deliberations outlined, it has to be emphasized that both the principle of certainty and the principle of culpability, as well as directives of the level of penalty, preclude any imposition of the duty to repair damage by mechanical transposition of terms and principles from civil law to criminal law; and this concerns both damage and redress of the damage. Moreover, the aforementioned fundamental rules of liability for offences greatly hinder actual compensation for economic and non-economic loss sustained by the victim. In other words: both safeguards provided for the accused and the accurate expectations of the victim oppose the notion that criminal law creates the right base for amends satisfying the victim. Without this realization, one cannot speak of the due fulfilment of aims characteristic of the model of restorative criminal law.

Dominika Bek

The Mediation Settlement as a Directive of the Level of Sanction

When Polish legislators codified criminal law anew in 1997, they built mediation into criminal process and accounted for the impact of its results on the type
of conclusion reached in the proceedings. The aim of this chapter is an analysis
of the significance of this incorporation, both for the imposition of penalties of
different level or other penal measures and for a realisation of the idea of restorative justice. First it must be emphasised that, at present, Polish criminal law
provides only for optional influence of the agreement between the offender and
the wronged party on the outcome of criminal proceedings. However, as of 1 July
2015, the situation will change because of the amendment of art. 59a CrimC,[1] to
be discussed further in the text.

Positive effects of mediation carried out between the wronged party and the offender or
the settlement reached between the two during the stage of proceedings before the court
or prosecutor as general directive on the level of sanction.

The starting point for investigations on the present subject must be art. 53(3) of the
Criminal Code of 6 June 1997 (Dziennik Ustaw of 1997, No. 88, item 553), according to
which "the court, while meting out punishment, shall take into account positive effects
of mediation between the wronged party and the offender or the settlement reached
between the two in the proceeding before the court or prosecutor." This provision is particularly clear for the functioning and development of restorative justice within Polish
criminal law, at least for the reason that as the only one in the Criminal Code it mentions
mediation, an institution inseparably associated with restorative justice. The role of the
cited provision is to establish substantive law grounds for considering concord between
the offender and the wronged party in resolution of criminal process (owing to art. 56
CrimC,[2] it is the case also when the court considers for measures other than penalty).
The introduction of the discussed directive in the Criminal Code does not mean a resignation of other general directives of the level of sanction imposed by court (especially
the limiting function of guilt),[3] and this poses to the court the challenge of reconciling

---

1   Act of 27 September 2013 on the amendment of the statute – The Code of Criminal
    Procedure and Some Other statutes (Dziennik Ustaw 2013, item 1247).
2   Art. 56. The provisions of art. 53, art. 54(1) and art. 55 shall be applied accordingly to
    the imposition of other measures provided for in this Code.
3   *Art. 53(1) The court shall impose the penalty according to its own discretion, within
    the limits prescribed by law, bearing in mind that its distress should not exceed the*

certain assumptions of restorative justice with the retributive model of criminal law. This task is most definitely not easy. The interpretation of art. 53(3) CrimC itself raises much doubt.

The rule quoted above points to two separate situations to be considered by court. The basic thing is to clarify the notion of "positive effects of mediation" and determine the character of "the settlement reached in proceedings before the court or prosecutor." The positive effects of mediation may signify merely that a settlement has been concluded or that its clauses have been put into practice. In the literature of the field, it is generally accepted, although not without restrictions, that in order to ascertain that mediation has concluded with success, settlement itself is sufficient.[4] The same phrase refers, in the opinion of E. Bieńkowska, even to "any result of mediation which would be acceptable to the parties to the conflict, especially the victim."[5] This last stance ought to be analysed in more detail. One can imagine a situation in which both parties are satisfied with the effects of mediation despite the absence of a settlement, or in which the meeting with the wronged party influences the offender's attitude very positively, while the lack of settlement follows from factors impossible to control. It is not accidental that the legislator differentiates in art. 53(3)

---

degree of guilt, considering the level of social noxiousness of the act committed, and taking into account the preventive and educational objectives which the penalty has to attain with regard to the convict, as well as the need to develop a legal awareness among the public.

(2) While imposing the penalty, the court shall above all take into account the motivation and the manner of conduct of the perpetrator, the commission of the offence together with a minor, the type and degree of transgression against obligation imposed on the perpetrator, the type and dimension of any adverse consequences of the offence, the characteristics and personal conditions of the perpetrator, his way of life prior to commission of the offence and his conduct thereafter, and particularly his efforts to redress the damage or to compensate the public perception of justice in another form. The court shall also consider the behavior of the wronged party.

(3) While imposing the penalty, the court shall also take into account positive effects of mediation between the wronged party and the perpetrator, or the settlement reached by them in proceedings before the state prosecutor or the court.

4   See D. Wójcik in A. Marek (eds.), *System prawa karnego. Zagadnienia ogólne* (Warszawa 2010), p. 386.

5   E. Bieńkowska, *Mediacja w sprawach karnych. Stan prawny na 1 września 2011 r.* (Warszawa 2011); see also P. Rączkowski, "Postępowanie mediacyjne według Kodeksu postępowania karnego" in L. Bogunia (eds.), *Nowa kodyfikacja prawa karnego*, t. IV (Wrocław 1999), p. 228.

CrimC between "positive effects of mediation" and "the settlement reached in proceedings before a court or prosecutor" even though the same effect could be achieved in a shorter way, e.g. by use of the formulation "settlement reached in mediation or proceedings before court or prosecutor." The specific basis of the justification of judgment may stem not only from settlement but also positive effects of mediation, e.g. termination of conflict. This would mean, inter alia, that at the parties' request, the mediator should include these other positive consequences of mediation in the report sent to court. Otherwise, the court would have no chance to verify "positive effects" that were not reflected in the content of settlement. Because of the function of art. 53 CrimC, it would not be easy to accept the thesis that the positive outcome of mediation is no less than implementation of all elements of the settlement. Oftentimes, the very content of the settlement gives rise to an obligation whose performance is stretched over time, and to wait for its implementation would protract criminal proceedings. Evaluating the offender's attitude before the latter complies with the obligations undertaken involves a certain risk which may, however, be reduced by properly selecting the criminal law response and correctly incorporating the provisions of settlement in the content of the judgment, as will be elaborated below. One should also emphasise that the expression "the court shall take positive effects of mediation into account" denotes *a contrario* that the court ought not to take into consideration any negative results.[6] Unsuccessful mediation may not encumber the defendant at least for the very reason that diffusion of conflict requires the shared intention of both parties, and not just the good will of the offender.

These deliberations lead to the conclusion that the factor to be taken into account by the court in accordance with art. 53(3) CrimC while meting out punishment is either the settlement concluded between the offender and the wronged party or, conceivably, some other positive effect of mediation. At this point the question arises of what is to be understood as settlement. After the entry into force of the current Criminal Code, W. Daszkiewicz defined settlement in criminal proceedings as a civil law agreement regarding civil law claims, both for economic and non-economic provisions, which also covers claims that only

---

6   See K. Buchała in K. Buchała, A. Zoll, *Komentarz do k.k., t.1, Kodeks karny. Część ogólna. Komentarz do art. 1-116 Kodeksu karnego* (Zakamycze 1998), p. 400.; A. Murzynowski, "Rola mediacji w osiąganiu sprawiedliwości w procesie karnym" in M. Płatek and M. Fajst (eds.) *Sprawiedliwość naprawcza. Idea. Teoria. Praktyka* (Warszawa 2005), p. 63.

indirectly derive from the offence.[7] If one were to accept such an understanding of settlement, declarations merely concerning apologies and forgiveness could not be called settlement. Furthermore, recognizing this type of written statement by the parties as a "positive effect of mediation" other than settlement would produce serious practical complications. Accepted apologies are treated by mediators as settlement and they are included as such in the report. Dividing various types of party declarations would blur the general picture of the effects of mediation. It must be thus concluded that for the purposes of mediation the concept of settlement is broader than in the civilian *sensu stricto*. It may also cover written apology and its acceptance, and expressions of understanding or even forgiveness by the wronged party that are unconnected to any commitments to pay compensation for economic or non-economic loss. It may happen as well that a wronged party who does not feel entirely innocent in his or her relations with the offender also undertakes certain commitments in the settlement. Moreover, declarations contained in a mediation settlement quite often directly concern claims asserted by both parties which do not follow even indirectly from crime, but which remain relevant to the conflict which comprised the background of the crime. It seems that also these elements are admissible in a mediation settlement and may be translated in the resolution of the criminal court.

Thus, an acceptance of apologies (sometimes mutual) which puts an end to conflict may be called reconciliation when it is accompanied by forgiveness. In academic writings, the distinction between "settlement" and "reconciliation" is not clear. W. Daszkiewicz clearly differentiates between the two, and adds at the same time that "foundations of settlement are always set by some kind of reconciliation."[8] More emphasis is put on the distinction by D. Gil, who writes that "reconciliation does not have to come in a pair with a settlement, yet prior reconciliation between the parties is a necessary condition of a settlement's conclusion."[9] Both authors, while analysing the concept of "reconciliation," adduce enactments related to private prosecution, placed among other provisions of the Code of Criminal Procedure.[10] They also cite an earlier statement (made before the introduction of mediation to criminal procedure) by S. Waltoś that

---

7   W. Daszkiewicz, *Pojednanie, ugoda i mediacja w procesie karnym, Nowa kodyfikacja karna. Krótkie komentarze*, No. 8 (Warszawa 1998), p. 60-61.

8   W. Daszkiewicz, *Pojednanie, ugoda i mediacja w procesie karnym, Nowa kodyfikacja karna. Krótkie komentarze*, p. 61-62.

9   D. Gil, *Postępowanie w sprawach z oskarżenia prywatnego w polskim procesie karnym* (Wolters Kluwer Polska 2011), p. 227.

10 Arts 485-499 PCCP.

"reconciliation makes up an agreement of the private prosecutor and the accused in which both parties pledge not to lodge any complaints against one another in relation to the crime, and agree for that reason to discontinue the criminal process initiated by a private accusation."[11] For another thing, D. Wójcik, in discussing the current model of mediation, contends that reconciliation "involves a deeper emotional engagement by the parties in the mediation process, including even expiation and forgiveness," and that agreeing on the means of redress does not always come in combination with this understanding of rapprochement, which means that a settlement is conceivable which would not be based on reconciliation.[12] The conception presented by D. Wójcik is constant with the idea of mediation, but is it, at the same time, in congruence with nomenclature of the Criminal Code? In the CrimC, the term "reconciliation" appears only twice,[13] in similar contexts: as a requisite of optional mitigation of punishment and a requisite of extended application of conditional discontinuance of the proceeding.[14] A more thorough analysis of the premises of both these institutions will be provided below. At this point, it must be indicated that in these provisions the term "reconciliation" is used beside the requirement of damage reparation and the agreement of the means of redress. This implies that the legislator has distinguished between reconciliation and civil law obligations. Z. Ćwiąkalski, in the context of art. 60 CrimC, writes: "Reconciliation with the offender should be understood as sui generis forgiveness by the wronged party towards the one who committed a crime against him or her, his or her close relations or entity represented by the wronged party (e.g. economic operator). This refers to rapprochement with the offender and renouncement of any grudge against the latter."[15] Such an approach comes in line with an implementation of the theory of restorative justice, and reconciliation based on forgiveness may be also coupled with an expression of common intent to end the proceedings in a specific way (e.g. by discontinuance or conditional discontinuance), or obligations of the civil law

---

11 P. Waltoś, *Postępowania szczególne w procesie karnym* (Warszawa 1973), p. 206.

12 D. Wójcik, "Rola mediacji między pokrzywdzonym a sprawcą przestępstwa" in A. Marek (eds.) *System prawa karnego. Tom I. Zagadnienia ogólne*, p. 379.

13 The Act of 27 September 2013, which has already been cited in the first footnote of this chapter, will remove the notion of reconciliation out of the regulation on conditional discontinuance; the notion will not appear in the new art. 59a but it will still function as requisite for extraordinary mitigation of punishment.

14 Art. 60(2) item 1 and art. 66(3) CrimC.; both institutions will be discussed below.

15 Z. Ćwiąkalski in A. Zoll (eds.), *Kodeks karny. Część ogólna. Komentarz, t.1, Komentarz do art. 1-116 Kodeksu karnego* (Zakamycze 2007), p. 753.

type. However, reconciliation understood in this manner, i.e. based on genuine forgiveness and the abandonment of regrets, seems an over-idealistic goal in the context of the application of criminal law instruments.[16] Controversies pertaining to the nature of settlement and reconciliation, although they unveil far reaching terminological discrepancies, do not bar the way to the pursuit of a common denominator for restorative justice and traditional criminal law.

Another open question refers to the circumstances in which reconciliation or settlement may be achieved. E. Bieńkowska rightly asks whether one should also take into account settlements made as a consequence of mediation proceedings carried out under the agreement specified in art. 183[1] of the Civil Procedure Code (CPC).[17] The same question may refer to agreements concluded between the same parties in other procedures, especially civil and criminal ones. Since the legislator has not pinpointed in art. 53(3) CrimC the type of mediation, and, at the same time, has aligned it with results of settlements reached before a court or prosecutor, I think there are no contradictions in accounting for all mediation settlements adduced by the parties in the decision concluding criminal proceedings, as long as they relate to the subject matter of criminal court deliberations. In case of doubt, mere and common adduction by the accused and the wronged party of the content of a mediation settlement which binds the parties outside

---

16 This discord between "reconciliation," understood as the most ambitious objective of mediation, and "reconciliation," as understood in the light of substantive and procedural criminal law, might be one of the reasons to abandon the term "reconciliation" in the regulation of the Criminal Code amended by the Act of 27 September 2013. There is a lack of consistency, however, as the term "reconciliation" still appears in art. 66 of the Criminal Code.

17 E. Bieńkowska, "Mediacje w sprawach karnych: analiza obowiązującej regulacji prawnej," *Jurysta*, No. 3/2008, p. 6.

Civil Procedure Code of 17 November1964 r. (Dziennik Ustaw 1964, No. 43, item 296).

Art. 183[1] (1) Mediation is voluntary.

(2) Mediation shall be carried out on the basis of an agreement referring a dispute to mediation, or a decision made by the court referring the parties to mediation. An agreement shall be deemed to be concluded also by consent to mediation of a party once the other party has submitted the application referred to in Art. 183[6](1).

(3) In a mediation agreement the parties shall agree, in particular, on the subject of mediation and shall identify the mediator or establish the manner of his or her choice.

(4) Mediation shall be conducted prior to initiating the proceedings, and also during the proceedings if the parties agree.

the pending proceeding may be treated as a new settlement made before a court or prosecutor, as long as the conditions set out below are met. Such a solution is undoubtedly favourable to the idea of restorative justice and takes into account the will of the parties to the fullest possible extent, and, at the same time, benefits the economic dimension of the process by shortening criminal proceedings and reducing their costs. In practice, it is not uncommon that the disputing parties are involved simultaneously not in one but several processes in which they act in different roles, and the source of all these litigations is the same dispute. It would be insensitive and bothersome to the parties to make them come back again and again to the same topic during subsequent meetings with a mediator, despite the existence already of a settlement covering the whole subject matter.

Another interpretive doubt suggested above concerns the issue of the settlement concluded in a proceeding before a court or prosecutor. E. Bieńkowska argues that the final fragment of art. 53(3) CrimC "is completely unclear, as there is no single provision which would envisage conclusion of settlement by any party at whatever stage of criminal proceedings, either before court or prosecutor."[18] This finding is, however, at least in my opinion, no reason for anxiety. What is more, it seems that no separate legal basis is necessary. A. Murzynowski seems right in asserting that "the conclusion of a direct settlement between the offender and the victim to a crime in the course of proceedings before prosecutor (or court – D.B.) may often result from an intention which is shared between these parties and which deserves to be taken into account, to the exclusion of mediation."[19] It seems there are no convincing arguments that the settlement prepared by the parties should be of less value to the authority carrying out the proceedings than settlement entered into during a meeting with a mediator. Most obviously, parties often need a qualified third person to open the way to agreement in a situation where a conclusion in settlement would not be feasible in the absence of mediator. Still, the remark made over ten years ago by A. Murzynowski still retains validity, in which the author points to the absence of a sufficiently developed structure of qualified mediators in the whole country and the resulting need to "mediate" in other form.[20]

---

18 E. Bieńkowska, "Mediacje w sprawach karnych: analiza obowiązującej regulacji prawnej," *Jurysta* No. 3/2008, p. 6.

19 A. Murzynowski, "Mediacja w toku postępowania przygotowawczego" in P. Stachowiak (eds.), *Współczesny polski proces karny. Księga ofiarowana Profesorowi Tadeuszowi Nowakowi* (Poznań 2002), p. 247.

20 *Ibid.*

The expression "settlement reached in a proceeding before a court or prosecutor" suggests that the process of arriving at the agreement should advance in the presence of the person conducting mediation. It seems, however, that this does not entirely exclude the submission to the authorities of a settlement independently worked out by the parties. However, this requires intensified caution on the part of the public officials about the conformity of the settlement reached with law and the non-vitiated consent of the parties. The prosecutor or judge ought to discuss provisions of the settlement with both parties and make sure that they are understandable and acceptable in their entirety by both parties. It ought to be explained that even the involvement of the mediator does not relieve the court from the obligation to independently evaluate the value of the agreement, and it would be illegitimate to state that additional duties are imposed on the authorities. Also art. 53(3) CrimC *in fine*, to my mind, opens up a broad though non-utilised path for the development of various forms of restorative justice. It enables not only a consideration of mediation settlements made in different proceedings and agreements reached independently by the parties, but also accords reached within a larger group, with the participation of the local community. One can imagine a situation in which the wronged party and the offender coming from the same local environment, i.e. family, neighbourhood, colleagues, professional group, national or ethnic minority, etc., work out a compromise for a solution of the criminal conflict with the involvement of representatives of the environment forming a kind of circle or conference of restorative justice.[21] If the requirements of art. 53(3) CrimC are to be met, such a conference would have to proceed in the prosecutor's presence, though not necessarily at his or her initiative. Because of the low popularity of such methods of conflict resolution among Poles, a sound example may be the customs of cultural minorities, e.g. the Roma population.[22] The independent resolution of insider conflicts by representatives of local communities makes up one of the foundations of civil society and is in accord with the constitutional principle of subsidiarity.

Another question which is no less important than the above ones is the issue of the "consideration" of a settlement and other positive outcomes of mediation by the court. Once again, it must be emphasised that art. 53(3) CrimC might refer to a situation of meting out the penalty, yet in light of the wording of art. 56 CrimC, this directive is to be extended to the imposition of penal measures

---

21 See P. McCold, *Restorative Justice Practice – The State of The Field*, 1999, http://www.iirp.org/article_detail.php?article_id=NTA0

22 See D. Lorek, "Romski model sprawiedliwości naprawczej," *Ruch prawniczy, ekonomiczny i socjologiczny*, No. 2/2012, p. 239-249.

other than punishment itself, which also refers to instances in which the court reprieves from awarding the sentence or conditionally discontinues proceedings.[23] In light of the above, how should consideration of a settlement look? In the literature, it is rightly indicated that this expression does not denote that the court is bound by the resolution found in the settlement, but only ought to frame its verdict so as to baffle the parties' accord as little as possible.[24] This is all the more important because at present settlements made as a result of mediation in public prosecution proceedings do not enjoy the status of court settlement, and, consequently, execution of their provisions is possible only after their incorporation in a judicial judgment concluding the process or a civil court judgment rendered in separate proceeding.[25] The situation will change as of 1 July 2015, the date of entry into force of the amendment to art. 107 CCP, pursuant to which an enforcement clause may be affixed as well to settlements reached in mediation.[26] This does not change the fact that settlement ought to be taken into account by the court deciding a particular case. At the same time, however, the court, by electing the criminal law response to the criminal offence, must bear in mind the

---

23 In the initial period of mediation in the Polish system of penal law, the institution was erroneously linked to the possibility of conditional discontinuance, which was criticized by P. Waltoś (P. Waltoś, "Główne nurty nowelizacji procedury karnej," *Państwo i Prawo* 2004, no 4, p. 141.).

24 See e.g. E. Bieńkowska, B. Kunicka-Michalska, G. Rejman, J. Wojciechowska, *Kodeks karny. Część ogólna. Komentarz* (Warszawa 1999), p. 926.; D. Kużelewski, 'Wpływ prawa karnego materialnego na mediacje między pokrzywdzonym i oskarżonym – wybrane aspekty' in Z. Ćwiąkalski, G. Artymiuk (eds.), *Współzależność prawa karnego materialnego i procesowego w świetle kodyfikacji karnych z 1997 r. i propozycji ich zmian* (Warszawa 2009), p. 350.; D. Wójcik in A. Marek (eds.), *System prawa karnego. Zagadnienia ogólne* (Warszawa 2010), p. 384.

25 W. Daszkiewicz, "Pojednanie, ugoda, mediacja w procesie karnym," *Nowa kodyfikacja karna. Krótkie komentarze* 1998, No. 8, p. 57-92.; A. Rękas, *Mediacja w polskim prawie karnym* (Warszawa 2004), p. 14-15.

26 Act of 27 September 2013 Amending the Code of Criminal Procedure and Certain Other Acts (Dziennik Ustaw 2013, item 1247)
    Art. 1(35) in art. 107:
    a) paragraph (1) shall be worded as follows:
    (1) The court or the court referendary shall attach an execution clause to a ruling subject for execution upon the request of an authorized person.
    b) paragraph (3) shall be amended to read:
    (3) provisions of paragraphs (1) and (2) shall respectively be applied to the obligation arising from a settlement reached in court or in the presence of a court referendary, and the settlement concluded in mediation.

aggregate of directives to be found in art. 53 CrimC, and not only paragraph (3) of this provision pertaining to mediation.[27] The court thus faces the uneasy task of accommodating the multiple objectives of criminal proceedings.

The notions of reconciliation and settlement already functioned before the introduction of mediation into Polish criminal procedure as viable options in litigation initiated by private prosecution. There remains the query of whether art. 53(3) CrimC is applicable at all to private prosecution cases. Art. 489 and subsequent CCP cover this mode of proceeding, suggesting that reconciliation of the parties always results in a discontinuance of the process, and that such reconciliation may be, but does not have to be, accompanied by settlement.[28] It is thus true that in private prosecution cases settlement must always be based on reconciliation (understood as mutual commitment of the parties not to lodge

---

27 Art. 53(1) The court shall impose penalty according to its own discretion, within the limits prescribed by law, bearing in mind that its distress should not exceed the degree of guilt, considering the level of social noxiousness of the act committed, and taking into account the preventive and educational objectives which the penalty has to attain with regard to the convict, as well as the need to develop legal awareness among the public.

(2) While imposing the penalty, the court shall above all take into account the motivation and the manner of conduct of the perpetrator, the commission of the offence together with a minor, the type and degree of transgression against the obligation imposed on the perpetrator, the type and dimension of any adverse consequences of the offence, the characteristics and personal conditions of the perpetrator, his way of life prior to commission of the offence and his subsequent conduct, and, particularly, his efforts to redress the damage or to compensate to the public perception of justice in another form. The court shall also consider the behavior of the wronged party.

(3) While imposing the penalty, the court shall also take into account the positive results of mediation between the wronged party and the perpetrator, or the settlement reached by them in proceedings before a prosecutor or a court.

28 Code of Criminal Procedure of 6 June 1997 (Dziennik Ustaw 1997, No. 89, item 555, as amended).

Art. 489 (1) The main trial shall be preceded by a conciliatory session led by a judge. (2) Upon a motion by the parties or at their consent, the court may, instead of designating a conciliatory session, designate a suitable date for conducting mediation proceedings. Art. 23a shall be applied accordingly.

Art. 490(1) A conciliatory session shall begin by calling upon the parties to reach reconciliation. (2) The minutes of a conciliatory session should in particular include the position taken by the parties with regard to the call for reconciliation, as well as the results of the session; if a reconciliation is reached, the report shall also be signed by the parties.

Art. 492(1) In case of reconciliation, the proceedings shall be discontinued. (2) If reconciliation has been reached as a result of mediation, article 490(2) shall apply accordingly.

complaints against one another following from the criminal offence and to discontinue the private prosecution proceeding on such grounds[29], rather than actual forgiveness), whereas such reconciliation always implies discontinuance, that is termination of the pending case, without application of penal measures. This does not, however, entirely preclude the application of the aforesaid directive of the level of sanction to litigation initiated by private prosecution. The assumption that reconciliation and settlement are not the only positive results of mediation means that if in the course of the proceedings mediation is referred to, and this mediation is concluded not with a settlement but with, for example, profound understanding on the part of the perpetrator of the harm inflicted to the victim, this fact as well should be reflected in the judgment's justification.

Remaining general directives of the level of sanction and restorative justice

Apart from manifest reference to mediation in art. 53(3), the legislator also introduced to the Criminal Code other factors destined to shape the merits of the judgment, among which one can find a number of aspects which are favourable, at least indirectly, to a realisation of the assumptions behind restorative justice. This category of circumstances definitely includes the type and scope of crime's negative consequences, the offender's demeanour after the commission of crime, attempts to redress damage, and other amends in the social sense of justice.

Immediately after committing an offence, and later, during the pending criminal proceeding, the offender may express his or her attitude toward the criminal offence and the wronged party in various ways. As a part of the right to defence, the accused may plead not guilty and accordingly may refuse to strive for reconciliation with the wronged party and for redress of the damage, which may not be interpreted as an aggravating circumstance should his or her guilt be proven.[30] On the other hand, it is generally known that actions such as repenting, pleading guilty, revealing the crime's details, and repairing the damage speak in favour of the offender.[31] Art. 53(2) CrimC provides general grounds for considering these circumstances, irrespective of other solutions offered by the general and special part of the Criminal Code, which will be discussed further

---

29 P. Waltoś, *Postępowania szczególne w procesie karnym* (Warszawa 1973), p. 206.

30 As in the S. C. judgment of 6 December 1971, RW 1260/71, OSNPG 1972, No. 4, item 77; SC judgment of 6 March 1973, V KRN 591/72, OSNKW 1973, No. 9, item 108.

31 J. Wojciechowska in *Kodeks karny. Część ogólna. Komentarz*, ed. G. Rejman, C.H.BECK 1999, p. 924.

below. As a consequence, elements of restorative justice may find manifestation in the court verdict even in situations when officially there was no mediation. For example, negative consequences, that is primarily economic losses, but also non-economic effects of crime, e.g. moral crime, sense of humiliation, loss of confidence or authority of the wronged party, breach of family and social relations, depravity,[32] may be mitigated depending on the offender's attitude. In the course of mediation, but also outside it (owing to an informal agreement between the offender and the wronged party or actions taken by representatives of the local community) the accused may take restorative steps, which are not only helpful to the wronged party but also give the offender a chance for a less severe sentence. From the point of view of restorative justice, one negative aspect of the solution adopted is the obligation imposed on the court to consider even ineffective attempts to remedy the damage. Inefficacy may obviously follow from reasons which have an objective nature and which are difficult to surmount, yet this assumption, although it fulfils the rehabilitative and preventive function of sanctioning, pushes the needs of the wronged party to the margin. Moreover, the reparation of damage as such, when not preceded by agreement with the wronged party, is not in accord with basic assumptions behind criminal justice, even though it should naturally reflect an evaluation of the offender's attitude and even though it bears the compensatory function of criminal law. In consequence, the court should also take into consideration, along with circumstances concordant with the spirit of restorative justice, those facts which are disadvantageous to the concept.

For an application of the idea of restorative justice, it is also important that "other amends in the social sense of justice" be made, also when the offence at hand is a so-called crime without a victim or where the party wronged by the offender's act has not been determined. A community which holds especially strongly to its local forms frequently feels a sense of injustice and insecurity in connection with a violation of the legal order, and the offender's manifestations of repentance, willingness to change, and reparation of damage or community service may be of much assistance in restoring social order and mitigating the expectations of the public as to the severity of punishment. One may only agree with M. Płatek that specific means of "amends in the social sense of justice" may be worked out, e.g. within negotiations, mediations or

---

32 Z. Sienkiewicz in O. Górniok, P. Hoc, M. Kalitowski, P. Przyjemski, Z. Sienkiewicz, J. Szumski, L. Tyszkiewicz, A. Wąsek, *Kodeks karny. Komentarz, t.1* (Gdańsk 2005), p. 527; W. Wróbel in A. Zoll (ed.), *Kodeks karny. Część ogólna. Komentarz, t.1, Komentarz do art. 1-116 Kodeksu karnego* (Zakamycze 2007), p. 695.

restorative justice conferences, even when statutory provisions fail to provide for their form.[33]

Probation measures in light of the theory of restorative justice

Among special measures provided by legislation, the institution of substantive criminal law which has been most closely associated with mediation since its very beginning was a set of measures related to the submission of an offender for probation. It found expression, for instance, in the Resolution of the Senate of the Republic of Poland of 3 June 2004 concerning criminal policy in Poland,[34] which sets forth in item 2 that

> The best means of implementing the idea of restorative justice are non-custodial penalties correlated with submitting the offender to a temporary probation in which the offender ought to comply with the obligations imposed on him or her. Among these obligations, the reparation of damage and moral harm inflicted on the wronged party ought to be considered the most important. When courts are awarding probative measures, in particular the conditional discontinuance of criminal proceedings or the suspension of imprisonment, it is recommended that they impose on the offender the duties which are extensively catalogued in the Criminal Code, and that they ensure these duties are enforced.

The Criminal Code differentiates between three measures involving probation which are imposed on the offender, but from the point of view of the level of sanction only two of them are crucial: conditional discontinuance of criminal proceedings and conditional suspension of penalty.[35]

Currently,[36] the most far reaching consequence of a settlement concluded in a process initiated by public prosecution is the conditional discontinuance of criminal proceedings. One should remember that conditional discontinuance of criminal proceedings is not tantamount to conviction of the offender, although it is undoubtedly a form of criminal law response to a criminal offence which has been ascertained.[37] The requisites of conditional discontinuance of proceedings

---

33 M. Płatek, "Wstęp I" in M. Płatek i M. Fajsta (eds.), *Sprawiedliwość naprawcza. Idea. Teoria. Praktyka* (Warszawa 2005), p. 17-18.

34 Monitor Prawniczy 2004, No. 26, item 431.

35 Release on parole from service of the rest of the penalty of imprisonment is listed as a third measure of this nature.

36 Before 1 July 2015, i.e. the date of entry into force of the reform of the Act of 27 September 2013.

37 A. Marek, *Warunkowe umorzenie postępowania karnego w polskim ustawodawstwie karnym* (Toruń 1971), p. 37-38.; B. Kunicka-Michalska in G. Rejman (eds.), *Kodeks*

include low statutory penalty range. This benevolence may only be applied to perpetrators of crimes punishable by no more than 3 years of imprisonment or, as long as all specific conditions are met, no more than 5 years of imprisonment.[38] Conditional discontinuance is admissible when the process pertains to an offence punishable even by 5 years of imprisonment as long as:

a) the wronged party has reconciled himself with the offender;
b) the offender has redressed the damage;
c) the wronged party and the offender have agreed on the manner of remedying the damage.

These conditions comprise three independent premises of conditional discontinuance in the case of more severe crimes[39] which, however, must be fulfilled jointly with the requisites set out in art. 66(1) CrimC. Nonetheless, attention should be paid to the stance of K. Buchała, who argues that the condition for recognizing reconciliation between the offender and the wronged person by judicial decision is either repair of damage or specification of the manner of its

---

karny. Część ogólna. Komentarz (C.H.BECK 1999), p. 1027-1031; E. A. Wdzięczna, *Warunkowe umorzenie postępowania karnego w świetle koncepcji sprawiedliwości naprawczej* (Toruń 2010), p. 121-122.

38 *Art. 66 (1) The court might conditionally discontinue the criminal proceedings if the guilt and social noxiousness of the act are not significant, the circumstances of its commission do not raise doubts, and the attitude of the perpetrator not previously penalized for an intentional offence, his personal characteristics and his way of life to date provide reasonable grounds for the assumption that even in the event of discontinuance of the proceedings he will observe the legal order and particularly that he will not commit any offence.*

(2) Conditional discontinuance shall not be applied to the perpetrator of an offence for which the statutory penalty range exceeds 3 years of imprisonment.

(3) In the event that the wronged party has been reconciled with the perpetrator, the perpetrator has redressed the damage or the wronged party and the perpetrator have agreed on the method of redressing the damage, conditional discontinuance may be applied to a perpetrator of an offence for which the statutory penalty does not exceed 5 years of imprisonment.

39 This position is presented e.g. by M. Kalitowski in O. Górniok, P. Hoc, M. Kalitowski, P. Przyjemski, Z. Sienkiewicz, J. Szumski, L. Tyszkiewicz, A. Wąsek, *Kodeks karny. Komentarz, t.1* (Gdańsk 2005), p. 605; B. Kunicka-Michalska in G. Rejman (eds.), *Kodeks karny. Część ogólna. Komentarz* (C.H.BECK 1999), p. 1044; E.A. Wdzięczna, *Warunkowe umorzenie postępowania karnego w świetle koncepcji sprawiedliwości naprawczej* (Toruń 2010), p. 254-255.

reparation.[40] This would mean that reconciliation does not constitute independent grounds for conditional discontinuance of proceedings, and yet, on the other hand, neither of the other two remaining requisites should be effective without reconciliation. It seems that this interpretation ought to be rejected because of its contradiction with the linguistic interpretation of art. 66(3) CrimC, but, at the same time, the requirement of reconciliation, or at least of agreement between the parties, would render the spirit of restorative justice more fully. A redress of damage which does not follow from any arrangements between the parties and which is unrelated to dissolution of the conflict constitutes, as has already been mentioned, an obvious manifestation of the compensatory function of penal law, even though it does not follow the assumptions of restorative justice. Simultaneously, the premise of reconciliation, which, as I have pointed out above, necessitates forgiveness, seems an overly idealistic ambition. One should bear in mind as well that the legal regulation of conditional discontinuance does not explicitly mention mediation, and that the application of art. 66(3) CrimC does not require any type of settlement. Moreover, E. Bieńkowska observes, not without a certain anxiety, that the Polish Code of Criminal Procedure does not correlate the institution of conditional discontinuance with the outcome of mediation in articles 341 and 414,[41] but only with the results of "concord between the offender and the wronged party with regard to repair of damage or compensation for

---

40 K. Buchała in K. Buchała, A. Zoll, *Komentarz do k.k., t.1, Kodeks karny. Część ogólna. Komentarz do art. 1-116 Kodeksu karnego* (Zakamycze 1998), p. 441.; as in J. Wojciechowska in Kodeks G. Rejman (eds.), *Kodeks karny. Część ogólna. Komentarz* (C.H.BECK 1999), p. 941 (comments on analogous formulation referring to the extraordinary mitigation of penalty).

41 *Art. 341 (3) If the court finds it purposeful because of the possibility of reaching an agreement between the accused and the wronged party on the matter of redressing damage or compensation, the court may adjourn the session and designate a suitable date for the parties. At the request of the accused and the wronged party justified by the need to settle, the court shall announce a suitable break or adjourn the session.*

(4) Upon deciding on conditional discontinuance, the court shall take into account the results of the agreement between the accused and the wronged party on the matters specified in paragraph (3).

Art. 414 (4) While discontinuing the proceedings conditionally, the court shall accordingly apply Article 341.

(5) When expecting the possibility of conditional discontinuance of the proceedings or the possibility of imposing a conditionally suspended penalty, the court may re-open the proceedings in order to apply Article 341(3) accordingly; then the court may adjourn the case.

non-economic loss."[42] It seems that this formulation does not prevent mediation, and at the same time opens the way for the utilisation of other forms of arriving at an agreement. For the sake of clarity of legal regulation, it would be useful to provide for the possibility to refer the case to mediation. Other methods of reaching consensus with the participation of representatives of the local community are neither popular nor developed in Poland, and arrangements worked out independently by the parties may involve too many threats, threats which could be lifted by mediation (this refers primarily to coercion of the wronged party's consent and faked apologies).[43] Guarantees for the wronged party are all the more important as the voluntary and genuine character of art. 66(3) CrimC does not secure benevolent consequences of reconciliation, and only a wary judge, or possibly mediator (in cases when agreement has been reached by means of mediation) safeguard the rights of the wronged party.[44]

A certain threat to the position of the wronged party may also be posed by the wording of the requisites framed by lawmakers. B. Kunicka-Michalska argues that the requisite, "the wronged party has reconciled with the offender," and the requisite, "the wronged party and the offender have agreed on the manner of repair of the damage," are contrary to "the spirit of contemporary Polish criminal law, which demands that each individual be held liable for his or her own acts, but not for what another person does or omits to do."[45] In addition, the author emphasises that this provision imposes "voluntary obligations" on the wronged party, which may lead to his or her extra victimization.[46] Although it could not be denied that in the situation under analysis, the conduct of the wronged party exerts influence on the criminal law response to the offender's act, one should remember that reconciliation may bring about much benefit to both parties, and participation in mediation, as the preferred route for arriving at an agreement, is entirely voluntary. Conditional discontinuance does not constitute the sole institution alleviating the responsibility of the offender, whose application is partly

---

42 E. Bieńkowska, "Mediacje w sprawach karnych: analiza obowiązującej regulacji prawnej," *Jurysta* No. 3/2008, p. 6.

43 *Ibid.*

44 See A. Zoll in *Kodeks karny. Część ogólna. Komentarz*, t.1, Komentarz do art. 1-116 Kodeksu karnego, pod eds. A. Zoll, Zakamycze 2007, p. 832.; E.A. Wdzięczna, *Warunkowe umorzenie postępowania karnego w świetle koncepcji sprawiedliwości naprawczej*, Toruń 2010, p. 255.

45 B. Kunicka-Michalska in G. Rejman (eds.), *Kodeks karny. Część ogólna. Komentarz* (C.H.BECK 1999), p. 1036-1037.

46 *Ibid.*, p. 1043.

dependent on the wronged party's position. Moreover, the author criticises the wording of the conditions envisaged in art. 66(3) CrimC, arguing that placing the wronged party first may suggest that the lawmaker supports the concept of the wronged party's contribution to the offence and acknowledges, in the same way, that it is the wronged party that should take the initiative in the process of reconciliation.[47] This provision, however, may also be understood in the manner proposed by M. Kalitowski, who contends that the position of the wronged party is a key factor for reconciliation.[48]

Commentary also seems necessary on the two remaining requisites, repair of loss and determination of the manner of its redress. Repair of loss by the offender signifies that the damage inflicted as a result of the commission of the crime is no longer observable, owing to efforts made by the offender. In my opinion, if this requisite is to be deemed fulfilled, the damage must be redressed in whole.[49] This does not mean that partial reparation of loss is meaningless for the possibility of conditional discontinuance of the proceedings. Such efforts on the part of the offender may constitute an element of reconciliation with the wronged party or initiate negotiations as to repair of the damage. Agreement about the manner of redress as such does not yet guarantee that these arrangements will be put into practice. On the contrary, it may appear that the benevolence of conditional discontinuance of criminal proceedings has been awarded too early to the offender. This result may be mitigated by the proper exercise of the possibilities provided for in the CrimC as to duties that may be imposed by court in the probation period.

The connections between the institution of conditional discontinuance of criminal proceedings and the idea of restorative justice are not exhausted by the mere requisites of its application. Aspirations for conditional discontinuance on the part of the offender may mobilise him or her to take steps leading in the direction of reconciliation with the wronged party. In addition, proper utilisation of this institution may further subsequent compensatory measures. Provisions of the conceivable settlement ought to be reflected, as far as possible, in the content of the judgment. From this perspective, art. 67 CrimC seems of much

---

47 *Ibid.*, p. 1046-1047.
48 M. Kalitowski in O. Górniok, P. Hoc, M. Kalitowski, P. Przyjemski, Z. Sienkiewicz, J. Szumski, L. Tyszkiewicz, A. Wąsek, *Kodeks karny. Komentarz, t.1* (Gdańsk 2005), p. 604.
49 In light of the above considerations of the understanding of loss in criminal law, assessing the size of damage to be repaired by the offender seems highly problematic.

importance.[50] This provision specifies the period of probation, which may span between one and two years, and which should be precisely defined in the content of the judgment or the order of conditional discontinuance of the process. In paragraph (2) of the provision discussed, the Code authorised the court to put the offender under the supervision of a probation officer or trustworthy person, association, institution or social organisation, whose activities cover care for the upbringing, prevention of demoralisation or assistance of criminal convicts. Supervision of non-professional character should in particular bolster grass-roots initiatives close to restorative justice, however, as follows from scholarly studies, it is not applied in practice.[51] Art. 67(3) CrimC also provides for duties connected with submitting the offender to probation that may be imposed on him or her in the event of conditional discontinuance of the proceedings. These comprise the following:

    a) redress of damage in whole or in part,
    b) informing the court or probation officer about the course of the duration period,
    c) apologies to the wronged party,
    d) performance of the duty encumbering the offender to provide means of subsistence
       to another person (alimony),

---

50 *Art. 67(1) Conditional discontinuance shall be adjudged for the term of probation which is between one and two years running from the date when the judgment becomes final and binding.*

    (2) In conditionally discontinuing the criminal proceedings, the court may, within the probation period, put the perpetrator under the surveillance of a probation officer or a person of public trust, association, or community organization whose activities include educational care, preventing demoralization or providing assistance to convicts.

    (3) In conditionally discontinuing the criminal proceedings, the court shall require the perpetrator to redress the damage in whole or in part, and may impose on him the obligation specified in Art. 72 (1) items 1-3, 5-6a or 7a-7b, and also adjudge a pecuniary provision as specified in Art. 39(7), and an interdiction on driving a vehicle as specified in Art. 39(3), for a period of up to 2 years. By imposing the obligation specified in Art. 72(1) item 7b on a perpetrator of the crime committed with the use of violence or with the threat to the next of kin, the court shall specify the manner of contact between the perpetrator and the wronged party. (4) The provision of Article 74 shall be applied accordingly.

51 Although offenders might be supervised by various entities, they are actually supervised exclusively by probation officers; for example, as of 31 December 2005 all conditionally released persons were supervised by probation officers ("Sprawozdanie z sądowego wykonywania orzeczeń wg właściwości rzeczowej w 2005 r. — statystyka Ministerstwa Sprawiedliwości," cited in P. Lelental, *Kodeks karny wykonawczy. Komentarz* (Warszawa, 2010), p. 648.

e) refraining from overuse of alcohol or use of narcotic drugs,
f) subjection to treatment, especially addiction treatment or rehabilitation, or thera-
    peutic influences,
g) participation in corrective and educational actions,
h) refraining from any specific contact with the wronged party or other individuals or
    access to the wronged party or other individuals,
i) vacation of the dwelling occupied jointly with the wronged party, and specification
    of methods of contact between the offender and the wronged party,
j) monetary provision up to the amount of PLN 60,000 towards the Fund for Assis-
    tance to Victims and Post-Penitentiary Aid,
k) vindictive damages,
l) ban on driving vehicles of a specific type for the period up to 2 years.

In addition, under art. 100 CrimC, the court may adjudge forfeiture of objects, their monetary equivalent, and economic gains obtained through criminal activity.

Most probably, the compensatory nature of amends of damage in whole or in
part does not require any commentary. It need only be restated that the possibility to adjudge the duty to redress follows only partially from the criminal law
character of this institution and the general principle that the criminal law response to an offence is merely to realise objectives set forth in art. 53(1) CrimC.
Objections may also be raised by the omission in art. 67(3) CrimC of the obligation to compensate non-economic loss; however, in light of the considerations
made in the section pertaining to damage in criminal law, it should be concluded
that loss ought to be understood broadly, and the wording of art. 67(3) CrimC
does not preclude an imposition of the duty to amend non-economic loss (harm)
on the offender. As for the previously discussed judicial obligation to take into
consideration a settlement reached by the parties (art. 53(3) CrimC), such possibility is especially important if the offender pledges in the settlement to pay
such atonement.

Another crucial question is the obligatory character of the imposition of the
obligation to redress damage in connection with the institution of conditional
discontinuation of criminal proceedings. The *ratio legis* of this solution could
probably be tracked down to the desire of the legislator to eliminate instances
in which the person guilty of a punishable act could avoid responsibility and
in which the wronged party would have to pursue compensation for economic
and non-economic loss solely on his or her own, in a separate civil procedure.
It ought to be underlined that the duty to repair damage which complements
conditional discontinuance of proceedings may only be awarded where, as a
result of crime, damage has been caused and the damage is still present at the
time of adjudication of conditional discontinuance, which means that by that

time it has not been repaired whether by the offender or any third party.[52] If the offender has remedied the damage in part, the court must consider whether it is satisfactory or the discussed duty ought to be imposed.[53] The court should, in my opinion, recognise partial redress of loss as sufficient only if this manner of resolving the conflict follows from the settlement concluded between the offender and the wronged party, and the freedom of their consent poses no doubts. Most obviously, where the grounds for conditional discontinuance are provided by prior and full redress of the damage by the offender (art. 66(3) CrimC), the imposition of the obligation to repair becomes baseless. However, when the offender has already undertook to redress damage (e.g. in mediation settlement) but has not carried out that obligation up to the date of adjudication, some controversies arise over the question of whether the duty to carry it out should be awarded. As a result of the lack of direct enforceability of a settlement, as discussed above, the imposition on the offender of the probative duty to redress damage in the amount specified in the settlement seems necessary in order to ensure the fullest possible protection of the wronged party's rights.[54] At the same time, it should be borne in mind that a judicial decision concerning the amount of redress may, at least in theory, diverge from arrangements made by the parties, which would thwart the sense of the settlement having been reached.

Among other probative duties, special regard ought to be shown also to apologies to the wronged party.[55] They are sensible only if made in public. Yet, the duty to apologise cannot be considered manifestation of restorative justice, in view of which the real asset is the offender's understanding of the negative consequences of his or her conduct and authentic penitence, not mere apologies, especially if they are insincere. Much better conditions for authentic apologies are offered by mediation.

---

52 See the S.C. judgment of 16 May 2002, III K 189/02, Prok. i Pr. 2002, No. 12, item 5.

53 B. Kunicka-Michalska in G. Rejman (eds.), *Kodeks karny. Część ogólna. Komentarz* (C.H.BECK 1999), p. 1087.

54 Such position has been presented, e.g., by B. Kunicka-Michalska in G. Rejman (ed.), *Kodeks karny. Część ogólna. Komentarz* (C.H.BECK 1999), p. 1080; contrary stance has been taken, e.g., by M. Kalitowski in O. Górniok, P. Hoc, M. Kalitowski, P. Przyjemski, Z. Sienkiewicz, J. Szumski, L. Tyszkiewicz, A. Wąsek, *Kodeks karny. Komentarz, t.1* (Gdańsk 2005), p. 613.

55 J. Skupiński, *Warunkowe skazanie w prawie polskim na tle porównawczym*, Warszawa 1992, p. 286-287; E. Bieńkowska in G. Rejman (eds.), *Kodeks karny. Część ogólna. Komentarz* (C.H.BECK 1999), p. 1131.

The rule of art. 67(3) CrimC sets forth legal grounds for the reinforcement of other declarations made by the offender in his or her settlement with the wronged party. Pursuant to art. 74 CrimC,[56] applicable in the discussed context, the duration and manner of performance of the adjudged duties is defined by the court upon hearing the opinion of the offender. For the sake of better reassurance of the implementation of settlements, it might be postulated that the cited provision be supplemented by the need not just to hear the opinion of the offender but also to heed any of the promises he or she previously made to the wronged party. From the point of view of restorative justice, it may be also admitted that the gamut of duties prescribed in art. 67(3) CrimC is exhaustive, rather than open like in art. 72 CrimC,[57] which is yet to be discussed below. Opening the catalogue could enable the inclusion of other duties incurred by the offender in the settlement amaong probation conditions not expressly envisaged by the lawmaker. The repetition of some settlement provisions in the judgment, this time as probative duties, allows for their more efficacious enforcement by the wronged party. On the other hand, opening up the catalogue could threaten the principle of specificity and the safeguarding function of criminal law.

Art. 68 CrimC provides obligatory and optional grounds for the institution of criminal proceedings in the event of unsuccessful probation. From the point of view of performance of settlement provisions, the most crucial criteria are the optional grounds prescribed in art. 68(2 CrimC and their relatively obligatory variation of paragraph (2a).[58] Non-compliance with any of the duties or punitive measures imposed in the judgment (or court order) of conditional discon-

---

56 *Art. 74(1) Time and manner of execution of the imposed obligations, specified in Art. 72 shall be determined by the court after hearing the convict; the imposition of the obligation specified in Art. 72(1) item 6 shall require additional consent from the convict.*

    (2) If educational or general care considerations warrant such solution, the court may, during the probation period, institute, extend or modify the obligations imposed on a convict sentenced to imprisonment with conditional suspension of its execution, as mentioned in Art. 72(1) items 3-8, or release him from these obligations, except for the obligation specified in Art. 72(2), and, likewise, either place the convict under supervision or release them from the aforesaid.

57 The obligations related to conditional suspension of the execution of the penalty are listed in Art. 72(1) of the Criminal Code, which shall appear in extenso below. The last point allows for the obligation of the convict to engage in other appropriate conduct during the probation period if it may prevent commission of a further offence.

58 *Art. 68(1) The court shall resume the criminal proceedings, if the perpetrator has, during the probation period, committed an intentional offence, for which he has been validly and finally sentenced.*

tinuance of proceedings may result in their resumption. The consequences are similar in the case of non-performance of the obligations provided in the settlement with the wronged party. This makes an additional security measure for the latter's interests, as they are important from the point of view of the wronged party.[59] On the other hand, however, M. Kalitowski rightly emphasises the impact of the wronged party on the performance of the settlement. This author argues that when deciding to resume the proceeding the court should take into consideration any "possible degree of contribution of the wronged party to restrictions relating to the offender's ability to comply with obligations following the concluded settlement."[60] It seems clear that resumption of process is always justified when the settlement's conclusion was the basis of conditional discontinuance under art. 66(3) CrimC, and its non-performance may be attributed to the offender.[61]

The other probative measure that may be awarded in connection with, inter alia, a settlement entered into between the offender and the wronged party is

---

(2) The court may resume the criminal proceedings if the perpetrator, during the probation period, flagrantly infringes the legal order, and in particular if he commits an offence other than that specified in paragraph (1), evades supervision, does not perform the obligations or penal measures imposed, or if he does not fulfil the settlement concluded with the wronged party.

(2a) The court shall resume the criminal proceedings if circumstances specified in paragraph (2) occur after the perpetrator has received a written reminder by a professional probation officer unless this should be contradicted by special reasons.

(3) The court may resume the criminal proceedings if, after the decision on conditional discontinuance was rendered but before it became final and binding, the perpetrator flagrantly infringes the legal order, and in particular if he commits an offence within that time.

(4) Criminal proceedings which have been conditionally discontinued may not be resumed any later than 6 months after the expiration of the probation period.

59 A. Zoll highlights that non-performance of these duties must be chargeable; a mere objective ascertainment of their non-performance is insufficient. Only such a violation of the terms of probation, in the opinion of this author, may be interpreted as proof of a misled evaluation of the offender's personality. (A. Zoll in A. Zoll (eds.) *Kodeks karny. Część ogólna. Komentarz, t.1, Komentarz do art. 1-116 Kodeksu karnego* (Zakamycze 2007), p. 847.)

60 M. Kalitowski in O. Górniok, P. Hoc, M. Kalitowski, P. Przyjemski, Z. Sienkiewicz, J. Szumski, L. Tyszkiewicz, A. Wąsek (eds.), *Kodeks karny. Komentarz, t.1* (Gdańsk 2005), p. 624.

61 A. Zoll in A. Zoll (ed.) *Kodeks karny. Część ogólna. Komentarz, t.1, Komentarz do art. 1-116 Kodeksu karnego* (Zakamycze 2007), p. 847.

conditional suspension of penalty. It constitutes a sentence imposed on the offender, yet the punishment (imprisonment up to two years, restriction of liberty, or a fine) is not executed in the event of successful expiry of the probation period. Concord between the offender and the wronged party, however, cannot be viewed as a prerequisite for applying this institution, yet the fact of reaching the settlement may be taken into account in the evaluation of requisites formulated in art. 69(1) and (2) CrimC.[62] In the first place, the court is to take into account the offender's attitude, his or her properties and personal conditions, and his or her lifestyle and demeanour to date since the perpetration of the offence. Without any doubt, participating in mediation, signing a settlement, reconciling with the wronged party, and, finally, redressing the damage widely conceived have an impact on the assessment of the factors indicated in the provision of law cited. Moreover, the court is to see to the realization of the purposes of punishment, the participation of the parties in well-executed mediation (or another form of restorative justice) that concludes with the settlement being signed and with the dissolution of conflict which fulfils, often to a satisfactory degree, the restorative and preventive functions, the threat of execution of the conditional sentence, which itself takes a part in criminal process, and finally the duties imposed in the probation period, which can be a sufficient form of punishment.

The probation period related to conditional suspension of penalty amounts to between 2 and 5 years, depending on the specific situation. As is the case with conditional discontinuance of criminal proceedings, in the course of its duration the court may order measures which, if properly selected, may support execution of the settlement. This catalogue strays in some measure from the one presented above, although the principal obligations are the same as the ones at the court's disposal in situations where the proceedings are conditionally discontinued.[63]

---

62 Art. 69(1) The court may conditionally suspend execution of the penalty of imprisonment of up to 2 years or the fine adjudicated as a one-off penalty if such conditional suspension is regarded as sufficient to attain the objectives of the penalty with respect to the perpetrator, and particularly to prevent him from relapsing into crime.

  (2) While suspending the execution of a penalty, the court shall primarily take into account the attitude of the perpetrator, his personal characteristics and conditions, his way of life to date and his conduct after the commission of the offence.

63 Art. 72(1) In suspending the execution of a penalty, the court may obligate the convict to:

  1) inform the court or the probation officer about how the probation period is going,

  2) apologise to the wronged party,

  3) carry out a duty incumbent upon him to provide support for another person,

  4) perform remunerated work, pursue an educational activity or train himself for an occupation,

The most significant difference from the point of view of restorative justice is the facultative character of imposing the obligation to redress damage on the offender. This follows from the fact that in the event of sentencing the offender (including an award of conditionally suspended penalty), the court has at its disposal not only probative duties but also punitive measures, among which there is the duty to redress economic or non-economic loss.[64] This punitive measure becomes obligatory when the wronged party or other entitled person submits a respective motion.

In the context of conditional suspension of sentence, one should also address the possibility to deliver a decision imposing a different probation duty from the ones set forth in the Criminal Code. The non-exhaustive character of the catalogue allows for the inclusion in the judgment of specific obligations incurred by

---

5) *refrain from abusing alcohol or using other intoxicating substances,*

6) *submit to medical treatment, particularly drug withdrawal or rehabilitation programs*

6a) *participate in correctional and educational activities,*

7) *refrain from frequenting specified community circles and places,*

7a) *refrain from contacting the wronged party or other persons in a certain way or from approaching the wronged party or other persons,*

7b) *vacate a dwelling shared with the wronged party,*

8) *engage in other appropriate conduct in the probation period, if it may prevent the commission of a further offence.*

(1a) By imposing the obligation specified in paragraph (1) item 7b on the perpetrator of the offence committed with the use of violence or with the threat to the next of kin, the court specifies methods of contact between the perpetrator and the wronged party.

(2) The court may obligate the convict to redress the damage in whole or in part, unless it has adjudicated a penal measure as specified in Art. 39(5), or a payment of consideration as specified in Art. 39(7).

Art. 73(1) While suspending the execution of a penalty, the court may, in the probation period, place the convict under the supervision of a probation officer or a person of public trust, association, or community organization whose activities include ensuring education, preventing demoralization or providing convicts with assistance.

(2) Placement under supervision is mandatory with respect to a young perpetrator of an intentional offence, to the perpetrator specified in Art. 64(2), and also to a perpetrator of an offence related to sexual preference disorder.

64 *Art. 46(1) In case of conviction, upon the motion by the wronged party or another party so entitled, the court shall impose the obligation to redress the damage caused by the crime in whole or in part or to compensate for wrong suffered. Civil law provisions on claim limitation shall not apply.*

(2) Instead of the obligation specified in paragraph (1) the court may decide upon a vindictive damage to the wronged party.

the offender in settling with the wronged party. This possibility seems especially significant in the case of this probative measure, since non-performance of the settlement is not a premise for execution of the suspended sentence, as will be discussed below. On the other hand, opening up the catalogue and the possibility to adjudge measures of a repressive character which have not been enumerated in the Code may constitute an encroachment on the safeguarding function of criminal law, including especially the principle *nulla poena sine lege*. In addition, it seems important that the time and manner of implementation of the obligations imposed is ascertained with the offender's involvement.[65]

A probation period may also come jointly with a specific penalty in the form of an extra fine, whose purpose is to remove any sense of offender's impunity.[66] With a view to protecting the wronged party's rights and to the obligations owed to him or her by the offender, such an extra fine should not be awarded in situations when, for example, economic pain deriving from the imposition of this measure could hamper the offender's performance of the probation duties encumbering him or her, such as an alimony obligation or a duty to redress damage.[67] Certain guarantees are offered to the wronged party by the Executive Penal Code of 6 June 1997 (EPC),[68] which states in art. 25(3) that civil claims to the convict's assets which are intended to redress economic or non-economic loss enjoy priority over fines.

The last issue related to conditional suspension of penalty is the set of premises for ordering its execution in the event that probation fails.[69] As has been

---

65 Art. 74 CrimC cited above.

66 *Art. 71(1) In suspending the execution of the penalty of liberty deprivation, the court may impose a fine of up to 270 times the daily rate; if its imposition is not provided for on another basis, in suspending the execution of the penalty of restriction of liberty, the court may impose a fine of up to 135 times the daily rate.*

(2) In ordering the execution of the penalty of imprisonment or restriction of liberty, the fine adjudicated under paragraph (1) shall not be subject to execution; the penalty of imprisonment or restriction of liberty shall be reduced by the number of days equal to the number of daily rates of fine paid, rounded up to the nearest full day.

67 See M. Kalitowski in O. Górniok, P. Hoc, M. Kalitowski, P. Przyjemski, Z. Sienkiewicz, J. Szumski, L. Tyszkiewicz, A. Wąsek, *Kodeks karny. Komentarz, t.1* (Gdańsk 2005), p. 643; A. Marek, *Komentarz do kodeksu karnego. Część ogólna* (Warszawa 1999), p. 222.

68 Dziennik Ustaw 1997, No. 90, item 557, as amended.

69 *Art. 75(1) The court shall order execution of penalty if during the probation period the convict commits an intentional offence similar to the one for which he had previously been sentenced to imprisonment by a final and binding judgment.*

discussed above, mere non-performance of the settlement with the wronged party does not constitute even an optional premise for ordering execution of the suspended penalty. The situation differs with respect to punitive measures and probation duties whose non-performance may cause the execution of a conditionally suspended sentence, especially when the offender has already been admonished by the probation officer.[70] Obligatory grounds for ordering the execution of the suspended sentence also include, among other things, repeated acts of domestic violence in relation to a close relation with whom the offender abides during the probation period;[71] this premise may frequently be connected with infringement of obligations imposed by settlement.

The impact of a settlement that has been reached between the wronged party and the offender on extraordinary sentence mitigation and penalty imposition forbearance.

Other institutions that may be applied by the courts in connection with concord between the offender and wronged party are extraordinary sentence mitigation and penalty imposition forbearance. These institutions are forms of conviction of the offender, even though the court applying them either refrains

---

(1a) The court shall order execution of penalty if the person convicted for a crime that was committed with the use of violence or with a threat to a close relation or another minor sharing a dwelling with the perpetrator in the probation period has flagrantly infringed legal order, again with the use of violence or with a threat to a close relation or another minor sharing a dwelling with the offender.

(2) The court may order execution of penalty if in the probation period the convict flagrantly infringes legal order, and in particular, if he commits an offence other than those specified in paragraph (1), or fails to pay a fine, avoids supervision, or fails to fulfil the obligations or penal measures imposed.

(2a) The court shall order execution of penalty if circumstances specified in paragraph (2) occur after the convict has received a written reminder by professional probation officer, unless the opposite is justified by special objectives.

(3) The court may order execution of penalty if, after the sentencing decision has been rendered but before it has become final and binding, the perpetrator flagrantly infringes legal order, and, in particular, if he commits an offence within that time.

(4) The order to execute a penalty may not be issued any later than 6 months after the end of the probation period.

(5) If the convict has been placed under supervision or has been obligated to perform duties in the probation period, the motion for execution of penalty may also be filed by a professional probation officer, or also a person of public trust, association, institution or social organization specified in Art. 73(1).

70 Under the relatively obligatory legal basis of art. 75(2a) CrimC.

71 art. 75(1a) CrimC.

from imposing any penal measures or resigns on penalties and settles for punitive measures, or awards punishment that is lower than specified by statutory provision for a given crime.[72] These solutions are optionally chosen by courts with a view to fulfilling the aims of punishment set forth in art. 53 CrimC, that is the objectives related to distributive justice which have been discussed below. However, particular attention ought to be paid to art. 60 CrimC, which in paragraph (2) expressly invokes concord between the offender and the wronged party as well as reparation of damage.[73]

The formulation of art. 60(2) CrimC, and especially the use of the expression "in particular" implies that the list included in that provision is only exemplary, rather than exhaustive. Z. Ćwiąkalski rightly observes that, in the opinion of the lawmaker, the situations mentioned in this provision produce a high probability of incommensurate punishment in relation to the severity of the offence, when the penalty is imposed at the lower bracket of statutory range.[74] While awarding extraordinarily mitigated punishment, the court must pay attention not only to premises of art. 60(2) CrimC and statutory brackets of art. 60(6) and (7) CrimC[75]

---

72 This refers to institutions of art. 58(3), art. 59, art. 60, art. 61 CrimC.

73 *Art. 60(2) The court may also apply an extraordinary mitigation of penalty in particularly justified cases when even the lowest penalty stipulated for the offence in question would be incommensurate, and particularly:*

1) if the wronged party and the perpetrator have been reconciled, the damage incurred has been redressed, or the wronged party and the perpetrator have agreed as to the manner of redressing the damage.

2) taking into account the attitude of the perpetrator, particularly if he attempted to redress the damage or prevented the damage from occurring,

3) if the perpetrator of an unintentional offence or someone close to him has suffered a major detriment in connection to the offence committed.

74 Z. Ćwiąkalski in A. Zoll (eds.), *Kodeks karny. Część ogólna. Komentarz, t.1, Komentarz do art. 1-116 Kodeksu karnego* (Zakamycze 2007), p. 749.

75 *Art. 60(6) The extraordinary mitigation of a penalty shall consist in the imposition of a penalty below the lower statutory level, or the imposition of a penalty of lesser severity, in accordance to the following principles:*

1) if the act in question constitutes a felony with at least 25 years of imprisonment, the court shall impose a penalty of not less than 8 years,

2) if the act in question constitutes another felony, the court shall impose a penalty of not less than one-third of the lower statutory level,

3) if the act in question constitutes a misdemeanour, and the lower statutory bracket of penalty is not less than one year of imprisonment, the court shall impose either a fine or the penalty of imprisonment or restriction of liberty,

but also general and specific directives of the level of sanction.[76] According to art. 60(2) CrimC, the court should thus consider extraordinary mitigation of punishment when the wronged party has reconciled with the offender, damage has been repaired or the wronged party and the offender have agreed on the manner of redressing the damage. Requisites designated in this article resemble premises discussed above with respect to conditional discontinuance of proceedings. However, the use of a different conjunction by the legislator has given rise to variations in interpreting these requisites. In the opinion of the prevailing majority of academics, reconciliation cannot be said to constitute an independent premise and must be coupled by repair of damage or determination of the manner of such repair.[77] This remark loses significance as a consequence of the non-exhaustive character of the situations listed. Although one should acknowledge that the lawmaker contemplated reconciliation along with redress of damage and agreement as to the means of redress, the possibility still exists that the court may recognise as particularly justified a reconciliation in which the damage is not remedied, or a redress which was not preceded by reconciliation. With respect to reconciliation and redress of damage, all comments made above in reference to the requisites of conditional discontinuance retain their validity.

Also, at this point there appears a certain dissonance between the assumptions of restorative justice and the overtone of criminal law norms. In light of this, separate commentary must be given to the second requisite. It opens up the possibility of applying extraordinary mitigation to a penalty imposed on an offender who only "attempted to redress the damage or prevent its occurrence." Z. Sienkiewicz rightly argues that "the excessively broad interpretation of this premise is justified by the value judgement that a given situation is «particularly

---

4) if the act in question constitutes a misdemeanour, and the lower statutory bracket of penalty is less than one year of imprisonment, the court shall impose either a fine or the penalty of restriction of liberty.

Art. 60(7) If the act in question is subject, alternatively, to the penalties specified in Art. 32 items 1-3, the extraordinary mitigation of penalty shall consist in renouncing the imposition of penalty and the imposition of a punitive measure as specified in Art. 39 items 2-8; the provision of 61(2) shall not apply.

76 See Z. Ćwiąkalski in A. Zoll (eds.), *Kodeks karny. Część ogólna. Komentarz, t.1, Komentarz do art. 1-116 Kodeksu karnego* (Zakamycze 2007), p. 750.

77 K. Buchała in K. Buchała, A. Zoll, *Komentarz do k.k., t.1, Kodeks karny. Część ogólna. Komentarz do art. 1-116 Kodeksu karnego* (Zakamycze 1998), p. 441; J. Wojciechowska in G. Rejman (eds.), *Kodeks karny. Część ogólna. Komentarz* (C.H.BECK 1999), p. 941; Z. Ćwiąkalski in A. Zoll (ed.) *Kodeks karny. Część ogólna. Komentarz, t.1, Komentarz do art. 1-116 Kodeksu karnego* (Zakamycze 2007), p. 753.

justified», and even the lowest penalty envisaged for the crime would be disproportionately severe."[78] Still, it must be added that art. 60(2) item 2 CrimC, despite its rehabilitative and equitable significance, does not bear a compensatory function towards the wronged party and, in earnest, it has little in common with restorative justice. This role may only be attributed to item 1 of the provision discussed, which has the potential to act in a mobilising way for the offender, so as to make the latter strive for the liquidation of the negative consequences of his or her action and for the attainment of concord with the wronged party.

The significance of settlement between the wronged party and the offender for the level of sanction expressed in particular penalties and punitive measures.

In deciding to impose on the perpetrator a penalty without conditional suspension or a punitive measure, the court should also take into consideration the positive effects of mediation between the wronged party and the offender or settlement between the two, reached in proceedings before the court or prosecutor. There crops up the question of whether the catalogue of penalties and punitive measures provided in the Criminal Code[79] enables such a solution. As a rule,

---

78 Z. Sienkiewicz, in O. Górniok, P. Hoc, M. Kalitowski, P. Przyjemski, Z. Sienkiewicz, J. Szumski, L. Tyszkiewicz, A. Wąsek, *Kodeks karny. Komentarz, t.1* (Gdańsk 2005), p. 558.

79 *Art. 32. The penalties are:*
   1) fine,
   2) restriction of liberty,
   3) imprisonment,
   4) life imprisonment for 25 years,
   5) life imprisonment.
   Art. 39. The penal measures are:
   1) deprivation of public rights,
   2) interdiction on holding specific posts, performing specific professions, and engaging in specific business activities,
   2a) interdiction on any activities related to the upbringing, medical treatment, education or care of minors,
   2b) obligation to refrain from frequenting specific circles and places, interdiction on contacting specified persons, interdiction on approaching specified persons and interdiction on vacating a specific dwelling without the permission of the court,
   2c) interdiction on attending mass events,
   2d) interdiction on entering gambling facilities and on participating in gambling,
   2e) obligation to vacate a dwelling shared with the wronged party,
   3) interdiction on driving vehicles,
   4) forfeiture of items,
   5) obligation to redress damage or to compensate for wrong,

within the system of restorative justice, the room for punishment understood as an implement of state repression amounting to repayment for the offence committed is quite limited. It must be admitted that among directives of the level of sanction of penalties and punitive measures, assumptions of restorative justice are not central factors. This does not, however, contradict the fact that the penalty adjudged may to a varying degree promote or at least allow the realisation of the assumptions behind the said idea.

It is very difficult to reconcile restorative justice with unconditional imprisonment, even though it is not impossible to consider the settlement which would accompany the awarding of such a punishment. The offender who goes to prison for a couple of months or years will definitely have problems with fulfilling some declarations made to the wronged party or local community, if only because of the difficulties prisoners often have finding payable employment, or because of the mere fact of separation from the environment of that party or community. The Criminal Code, when regulating the penalty of imprisonment, does not enable the court in any specific way to account for the settlement concluded between the wronged party and the offender.[80] However, this should be no surprise since under art. 58(1) CrimC, "where the statute leaves leeway as to the choice of the type of punishment, the court shall adjudge the penalty of unconditional imprisonment only when other penalty or punitive measure cannot achieve the aims of punishing." Settlement or another positive effect of mediation should provide additional incentives not to impose the penalty of unconditional imprisonment. Simultaneously, persons wronged by the most severe crimes, as well as their perpetrators, should not be deprived of the opportunity of amicably resolving the conflict. Even if fulfilment of the settlement is impeded by incarceration of the convict, it is not impossible per se, since any agreement may prove valuable for both parties.

It would be difficult to speak of the restorative character in reference to fines. A fine is a financial penalty and it is awarded to the State Treasury. Its amount is not directly correlated to the size of damage, and does not follow from any

---

6) *vindictive damage,*

7) *pecuniary consideration*

8) *making the sentence publicly known.*

80 Executive regulations are not conducive to restorative justice as well; although mediation settlement has been mentioned in Art. 162 of the Executive Penal Code in relation to release on parole, this regulation is vague enough to be criticized even by supporters of mediation. (Compare to E. Bieńkowska, "Mediacje w sprawach karnych: analiza obowiązującej regulacji prawnej," Jurysta No. 3/2008, p. 7).

arrangements with the offender. In consequence, even in the case of a crime to the detriment of the State Treasury, the role of the fine is not compensatory. Hence, it does not fulfil the assumptions of restorative justice. Moreover, a fine imposed on the offender in an imprudent way may impair his or her performance of obligations owed to the wronged party. While it is the case that, according to art. 58(2) CrimC, "a fine is not adjudged if the offender's incomes, his or her financial standing or earning capacities justify the conviction that the offender is not going to pay the fine and it will be impossible to garnish it by means of execution," this provision still does not refer directly to compensatory obligations. A certain solace is offered by the Executive Penal Code and its art. 25(3), cited above, which gives restorative claims priority over fines in execution. Nevertheless, the efficacy of this enactment is dubious.[81]

Among all penalties provided in the Criminal Code, the best chances for fulfilment of the idea of restorative justice are offered by the punishment of restriction of liberty, which resembles punitive measures and even probative measures somewhat, in terms of its character. Pursuant to art. 34 CrimC, award of the penalty of restriction of liberty is geared to three requirements:

a) ban on change of the place of residence without judicial consent;
b) duty to carry out, free of charge, controlled work for social purposes;
c) duty to provide information on the service of sentence.

The most important of these, from the point of view of the penalty of restriction of liberty, and the one most strictly connected with the conception of restorative justice, is the obligation to undertake unpaid, controlled work for social purposes. Pursuant to art. 35 CrimC, it may assume two forms:

a) actual work for social purposes;
b) confiscation of remuneration for work for a social purpose indicated by the court.[82]

---

81 See W. Zalewski "Sytuacja pokrzywdzonego przestępstwem w świetle ostatnich nowelizacji prawa karnego" in T. Dukiet-Nagórska (eds.), Zagadnienia współczesnej polityki kryminalnej (Bielsko-Biała 2006), p. 112.
82 *Art. 35(1) Non-remunerated, supervised work for community purposes shall be performed for 20 to 40 hours per month.*
    (2) With regard to a person who is employed, the court may decide that, instead of the obligation specified in Art. 34(2)(2), between 10 and 25 percent of his monthly remuneration shall be deducted for the community purpose selected by the court; while serving the punishment, the convict may not terminate his employment without permission of the court.

The latter variation may be adjudged only with respect of individuals already employed and should be applied in exceptional situations, since actual labour has not only been destined as pain inflicted on the offender but also provided with a view to its rehabilitative function. In the case of confiscation of a part of the earnings, this aspect is lessened. The possibility to devote a proportion of the offender's earnings to social purposes designated by the court has a compensatory element *sensu largo*. The basic form of the duty to work boils down to the performance of unpaid, controlled labour for social purposes indicated by the court in an appropriate workplace, health care facility, social welfare institution, charitable organisation or institution acting to the benefit of the local community. The social usefulness of the labour performed makes it so that the local community may receive the efforts of the offender as sui generis amends for infringement of the legal order, which gives the penalty of restriction of liberty another compensatory dimension. An interesting remark referring to the rehabilitative function of the penalty of deprivation of liberty has been made by R. Giętkowski, who recommends this choice of unpaid labour or deductions against remuneration so as to highlight its link with the legal interest encroached upon by the offence.[83] This principle must, however, be constrained by the protective function of criminal law. For example, referring a person convicted for abusing the elderly to work to the advantage of such persons would be risky, at the least. The hour, place and start time of the work is specified by a professional probation officer who supervises the convict. Art. 57(1) EPC imposes on the probation officer the obligation to hear the convict's opinion.[84] This opens up the possibility of accounting for any potential obligations incurred by the offender through settlement with the wronged party. However, it has been rightly pointed out by M. Szewczyk that this work must not be adjudged directly to the benefit of the victim of the crime,[85] and this constitutes a definite restriction. On the other hand, it guarantees certain protection for the wronged party.

---

83 R. Giętkowski, *Kara ograniczenia wolności w polskim prawie karnym* (Oficyna a Wolters Kluwer business 2007), p. 54.

84 *Art. 57(1) The professional probation officer, 7 days after delivering the decision shall call upon the convict and instruct him of his rights and obligations as well as consequences resulting from evasion of service of the penalty. This professional probation officer shall also, upon hearing the convict, specify the type, place and date of commencing employment, and immediately inform the appropriate municipal authority and the prospective employer.*

85 M. Szewczyk in M. Melezini (eds.), *System prawa karnego. Kary i środki karne. Poddanie sprawcy próbie*, (Warszawa 2010), p. 248.

The basic sanction of the penalty of restriction of liberty may be accompanied by other obligations. Under art. 36 CrimC, the court is free to award to the convict the obligations listed in art. 72 CrimC.[86] The importance of these measures for implementing the settlement between the wronged party and the offender has already been discussed above. One can only add that these obligations are imposed upon hearing the convict, and if they are justified by rehabilitative motives, the court may assign, broaden or modify them in the period of execution of the punishment.[87] It seems that, to a certain degree, this allows the settlement reached between the offender and the wronged party to be considered once the judgment sentencing the offender to restriction of liberty has become final and binding. Since under art. 69(1) CrimC, it is possible to conditionally suspend the punishment of restriction of liberty, there arise questions about the grounds for imposing respective duties. M. Szewczyk remarks:

> In reaching a decision to award duties based on the provision of art. 36(2), the court should have already considered the possibility of conditionally suspending the punishment of restriction of liberty and, depending on the resolution of this query, should then decide whether and which obligations envisaged in art. 72 are to be imposed on the convict as a part of "ordinary" punishment and which as a part of conditional suspension. First, the court ought to resolve the case in a manner which does not double the measures imposed and, second, so as to decide about the consequences of non-compliance of the convict with the adjudged duties. Each time, one must bear in mind that non-performance of obligations imposed under art. 36(2) CrimC (...) will implicate the need to impose a replacement penalty (generally the replacement penalty of imprisonment[88] – D.B.) On the other hand, non-compliance with the obligations

---

86 *Art. 36(2) While imposing the penalty of restriction of liberty, the court may decide to impose on the convict the obligations specified in art. 72(3).*

   (3) Art. 74 shall apply as appropriate.

87 *Art. 61(1) EPC: If it serves educational objectives, the court may, during the service of punishment of imprisonment institute, extend or modify the obligations specified in Art. 36(2) of the Criminal Code or the court may relieve the convict from such obligations.*

   (2) Due to the same reasons, the court may reduce the previously determined number of hours to work per month or the amount of deductions from monthly remuneration, but no more than to the lower statutory limit specified in art. 35(1) and paragraph (2) of the Criminal Code.

   (3) A complaint may be filed against orders delivered under paragraph (1).

88 *Art. 65(1) PEPC: If the convict evades the service of penalty of restriction of liberty or other obligations imposed, the court shall order the execution of a substitutive penalty of imprisonment. If the convict has already served some part of the penalty of restriction of liberty, the court shall order execution of the substitutive penalty of imprisonment for*

awarded within the framework of conditional suspension of penalty would result in revocation of the suspension.[89]

It seems that the court suspending execution of the punishment of restriction of liberty should integrate all the imposed duties into the period of probation so that their non-performance results in an order of execution of the suspended sentence. Regardless of this, when needed, corresponding duties may be imposed at the stage of execution, in accordance with the provision mentioned above, that is art. 61(1) EPC.[90] This assures, among other things, the fullest possible security for the convict's obligations owed to the wronged party. From the point of view of restorative justice, importance of art. 83 CrimC must also be stressed. The reduction of the penalty of restriction of liberty provided for in this chapter may not be effected if the convict has not fulfilled the obligations imposed on him or her, including non-compliance with various restorative duties in the event of which this relief would not be possible. This solution also secures the interests of the wronged party.

Punitive measures are a form of response from criminal law which may, in specific situations, prove to be an important instrument for the implementation of agreements between the wronged party and the offender. They may accompany principal penalties or be awarded independently in the event that punishment is not imposed. Their catalogue has already been cited above. Punitive measures are unlike penalties in that sanction is not their essential purpose. Instead, they bear protective and rehabilitative functions.[91] Some punitive measures may be applied in order to give positive support to obligations the offender incurred in relation to the wronged party. This may refer especially to measures such as:

---

the reminder of the sentence, ordering one day of substitutive penalty of imprisonment for each two days of restriction of penalty.

89 M. Szewczyk in A. Zoll (ed.), Kodeks karny. Część ogólna. Komentarz, t.1, Komentarz do art. 1-116 Kodeksu karnego (Zakamycze 2007), p. 544.

90 The convict might be relieved from such obligations, and that might be assessed in two ways. See the part on restorative justice in the executive stage, p.

91 While analyzing the nature of penal measures, M. Szewczyk notes, "Even if the core of sanctions defined as penalties is assumed to be repression, which is not obvious at all, and their protective and compensatory functions are assumed to be of secondary importance, whereas "penal measures" are to be understood to be the opposite, the difference between penalties and penal measures is about the the point of gravity among their components, not in the mere fact of their existence or non-existence." (M. Szewczyk in A. Zoll (eds.), Kodeks karny. Część ogólna. Komentarz, t.1, Komentarz do art. 1-116 Kodeksu karnego (Zakamycze, 2007), p. 565.)

1) duty to abstain from staying in specific environments or places, prohibition of contacts with specific individuals, interdiction on approaching specific individuals and leaving a particular location without judicial consent,
2) order of vacating a dwelling shared with the wronged party,
3) forfeiture,[92]
4) duty to redress economic or non-economic loss,[93]
5) vindictive damages,
6) monetary provision.[94]

And additionally, in especially justified cases:

1) interdiction on activities related to the upbringing, treatment, or education of minors or the provision of care to minors,
2) interdiction on holding a specific position, the performance of a specific profession or carrying on specific business activity,
3) interdiction on entry to a mass event,
4) interdiction on entry to game centres and participation in gambling,
5) interdiction on driving vehicles.

It seems imaginable that the offender may incur obligations within the above range.

The biggest obstacle in imposing punitive measures as a part of realisation of the assumptions of restorative justice is, just as in the case of penalties, their undoubted criminal law character. They have to be awarded in consideration of, among other things, the level of social noxiousness of the act and the restraining impact of the degree of guilt of the offender.[95] Moreover, on many occasions, the provisions which relate to the application of particular punitive measures restrict their applicability to precisely defined situations pertaining to the violation of specific norms of criminal law. The Criminal Code also envisages instances of obligatory imposition, entirely independent of the parties' accord. Even though the court is still obligated in applying penal measures to

---

92 This refers only to the regulation of Art. 44(5) of the CrimC, according to which forfeiture of objects derived from a crime or objects serving in the commission of a crime shall not be decided if they are to be returned to the wronged party or another entitled entity.
93 This is discussed in the section devoted to damage.
94 Vindictive damages and monetary provision are not paid to the wronged party but are used for social purposes defined in statutory provisions. However, commitments of this type may also be found in mediation settlements.
95 Art. 53 § 1 CrimC, cited above.

take settlements or other positive effects of mediation into account, mandatory provisions may attenuate that impact significantly. It would not be reasonable to criticise this state of affairs, and one may only stress that assumptions of the program of restorative justice do not always come hand in hand with objectives of the force of criminal law.

Complementary remarks

At the end of these deliberations on the current impact of settlement between the wronged party and the offender on the level of sanction, one has to name certain institutions of the Code of Criminal Procedure which modify somewhat the potential of criminal law reaction, and likewise exhibit some connection with the concord between the accused and the wronged party. This refers to the institution of conviction without trial and voluntary submission to punishment.[96]

---

96 *Art. 335(1) The prosecutor may attach to the indictment a motion to convict the accused for a misdemeanour imputed to him, subject to a penalty not exceeding 10 years of imprisonment without conducting a trial if circumstances surrounding commission of the misdemeanour do not raise doubts, and the conduct of the accused indicates that the objectives of proceedings will be achieved.*

(2) If the conditions for filing the motion referred to in (1) occur, and if in light of the evidence collected the explanation of the accused does not raise doubts, all subsequent evidentiary actions in preparatory proceedings may be abandoned. Actions which have a risk of not being conducted in a trial shall still be taken in preparatory proceedings. (3) The indictment may be filed solely on the basis of the circumstances referred to in paragraph (1).

Art. 387(1) Until the conclusion of the first examination at the first-instance hearing, the accused who has been charged with a misdemeanour may file a motion for a verdict sentencing him to a specified penalty or penal measure without carrying out evidentiary proceedings; if the accused has no defense counsel of his choice, the court may, on his motion, assign a counsel.

(2) The court may allow the motion of the accused to issue a verdict convicting the latter only when the circumstances surrounding the offence do not raise doubts and the objectives of the proceedings are to be achieved in spite of the hearing not being conducted in full. It is only possible to consider consider such a motion when there is no objection from the prosecutor, and the wronged party is properly notified about the date of the hearing and properly instructed about the possibility that the accused might file such a motion.

(3) The court may make the allowance of the motion conditional on introducing into it an amendment by the court. The provision of Art. 341(3) shall apply accordingly.

(4) When allowing the motion, the court may regard the evidence specified in the indictment, as well as documents submitted by a party, as revealed.

The conviction of an offender by a court without a trial may take place only upon the prosecutor's request. This request offers the court wider possibilities to adjudge an extraordinary mitigation of penalty, as well as its conditional suspension or replacement by mere punitive measures from the Criminal Code itself.[97] In literature of the field, it is emphasized that one of the important grounds for the formulation of such a request by the prosecutor should be a positive outcome of mediation or a settlement concluded in another way by the wronged party and the offender, even though the Code does not expressly provide for such requisite.[98] A similar or even more significant role may be played by a settlement between the wronged party and the offender on the occasion of the court's examination of the defendant's motion for voluntary submission to liability. In accordance with art. 387(2) CCP, "the allowance of such a motion is possible only when it is not opposed by the prosecutor or the wronged party, who has been duly informed about the date of the trial and instructed about the possibility that the accused will file said motion." The absence of objection on the part of the wronged party will be better grounded if preceded by a resolution of the conflict emerging in connection with the punishable act. S. Waltoś, while commenting on the enactments of art. 335 and 387 CCP, strongly emphasized that "the

---

(5) If the motion has been brought before the hearing, the court shall examine it at the hearing.

97 *Art. 343(1) When allowing the motion referred to in Article 335, the court may apply an extraordinary mitigation of penalty, conditionally suspend execution of the penalty, or adjudicate mere penal measures referred to in Art. 39, items 1-3, 5-8 CrimC*

(2). In the event described in paragraph (1):

1) Extraordinary mitigation of penalty may also occur in some other cases provided for in Art. 60 items 1-4 CrimC,

2) Conditional suspension of execution of penalty may occur independently from percepts referred to in Art. 69 items 1-3 of the CrimC, and it shall not apply to the penalty of imprisonment exceeding 5 years, whereas the probation period may not be longer than 10 years,

3) Reduction of the judgment to adjudication of a penal measure may occur if the statutory range of penalty for a misdemeanour the accused is charged with does not exceed 5 years of imprisonment.

98 See E. Bieńkowska, "Mediacje w sprawach karnych: analiza obowiązującej regulacji prawnej," *Jurysta No.* 3/2008, p. 5-6.; D. Kużelewski, "Wpływ prawa karnego materialnego na mediacje między pokrzywdzonym i oskarżonym – wybrane aspekty" in Z. Ćwiąkalski, G. Artymiuk (eds.), *Współzależność prawa karnego materialnego i procesowego w świetle kodyfikacji karnych z 1997 r. i propozycji ich zmian* (Warszawa 2009), p. 355-357.; D. Wójcik in A. Marek (ed.) *System prawa karnego. Zagadnienia ogólne* (Warszawa 2010), p. 398-400.

condition of reasonable concord, which weighs out the interests of the accused and the wronged party, is previous mediation between the accused (suspect) and the wronged party."[99]

In the spirit of furthering the adversarial (contradictory) character of the process that is strengthening the wronged party's position, what also ought to be discussed here is the amendment which will enter into force on July 1, 2015, to the currently widely understood criminal law. The most significant modification from the point of view of the present study is the introduction to the Criminal Code of art. 59a and the changes to enactments relating to conditional discontinuance of the proceedings.[100] Art. 59a CrimC provides grounds for discontinuing proceedings at the stage of investigation or in-court procedure at the wronged party's request. This novelty constitutes another exception to the principle of legality in Polish law. Upon fulfilment of quite a vast number of prerequisites, discontinuance becomes relatively obligatory. This means that if a perpetrator of an offence under the threat of a penalty of up to 3 years of imprisonment (5 years in the event of misdemeanours against property and medium health impairment) who has not been so far convicted for an intentional crime involving violence manages to repair economic and non-economic loss before the opening of the trial, and if the wronged party should consider it satisfactory and file the respective motion, the process must be discontinued.

---

99   P. Waltoś, "Wizja procesu XXI wieku," *Prokuratura i Prawo* 2002, No 1, p. 19.

100   *Art. 12. In the Act of 6 June 1997—the Criminal Code (Dziennik Ustaw No. 88, item 553 as amended) the following amendments shall be added:*

1) following Art. 59, Art. 59a is worded as follows:

Art. 59a(1) If, prior to the commencement of the judicial proceeding of the first instance, the perpetrator who has not been punished before for a commission of intentional offence with the use of violence redresses the damage and compensates for the harm inflicted, the criminal proceedings for misdemeanour, for which the statutory penalty range does not exceed 3 years of imprisonment, or for misdemeanour against property, for which the statutory penalty does not exceed 5 years of imprisonment, as well as for the misdemeanour specified in art. 157(1), shall be discontinued on the motion of the wronged party.

(2) If the commission of the act inflicted damage on more than a single wronged party, the provision of paragraph (1) may be applied on the condition that the damage is redressed by the perpetrator and the harm is compensated for to all wronged parties.

(3) Provisions of paragraph (1) shall not be applied if there is a special circumstance which serves as evidence that discontinuing the proceedings would preclude the achievement of the objectives of the penalty.

Pursuant to art. 59a(3) CrimC, the only justification for continuing the process is a special circumstance which indicates that discontinuing the proceeding would contradict the realisation of the objectives of punishment. This planned resolution may cause mediation and settlement (also when concluded outside mediation) to become false alternatives for criminal proceedings with regard to minor crime, and it may cause aims generally attributed to penalty to be achieved by other methods drawn from the program of restorative justice.[101] It is worth emphasising that the combination of the requisite to redress economic and non-economic loss (in whole), supplemented by the conferral onto the wronged party of the initiative to submit the motion, protects the latter's interest in large measure. At the same time, paragraph (3), as mentioned above, gives the prosecutor and the court an instrument of control, preventing automatic decisions on discontinuance and minimising, as might be expected, any risk of undue influence on the wronged party. As a result, the goals of the penalties enumerated in art. 53(1) CrimC will have an overriding role and will constitute a prism through which an evaluation will be made of the legitimacy of discontinuance of process. Negative verification of the wronged party's motion will lead to continuance of the proceeding, much as does the non-fulfilment of any of the premises prescribed in art. 59a(1) and (2) CrimC, and the offender's endeavours will be taken into consideration in the terms applied thus far. In consequence, only at this stage will the directives of the level of sanction be fully applicable, obviously including the ones set out in art. 53(3) CrimC. This solution may trigger the popularisation of mediation at the stage of preparatory proceedings (investigation), as has been long postulated by prosecutors. It ought to be underlined that the final wording of art. 59a CrimC accounts for many proposals put forward by academics specialised in the field of criminal law, presented during discussions on the draft amendment, yet it still arouses much controversy.[102] From the point of view of the idea of restorative justice, it definitely makes a step in the right direction, although, unfortunately, an isolated one. This amendment has only been followed by a modification to

---

101 See E. Bieńkowska, "Mediacja w projekcie nowelizacji kodeksu postępowania karnego," *Prokuratura i Prawo* 2012, No. 11, p. 57-58 (http://www.iep.krakow.pl/wydawnictwo/prokuratura/pdf/2012/11/3bienkowska.pdf)

102 See I. Sepioło, "Pojednanie pokrzywdzonego ze sprawcą jako podstawa do umorzenia postępowania w świetle projektu Komisji Kodyfikacyjnej prawa Karnego," *Ruch prawniczy, ekonomiczny i socjologiczny*, 2013, No. 2, p. 113-122. (https://repozytorium.amu.edu.pl/jspui/bitstream/10593/7901/1/11.%20IWONA%20SEPIO%C5%81O%20RPEiS%202_2013.pdf)

art. 66 CrimC, in pursuance of which the possibility of applying conditional suspension of the proceeding is expanded to all misdemeanours threatened by a penalty of imprisonment up to 5 years on terms applicable hitherto, without any reference to reconciliation or redress of damage.[103]

Conclusions

An analysis of the impact of settlement between the wronged party and the offender on the level of sanction leads to the conclusion that the progressive assumptions adhered to by proponents of the introduction of elements of restorative justice into criminal law are not easy to integrate into the repressive statutory framework. Despite the virtual saturation of the general part of the Criminal code with compensatory elements, and even institutions directly referring to restorative justice, the implementation of obligations incurred by the offender in relation to the wronged party is rarely supported by instruments of criminal law (all the more that criminal law does not back the wronged party's obligations towards the offender, even though such stipulations may as well form a part of the settlement). Attempts to render the offender's declarations within the framework of punitive measures bring only limited effects, especially if they are additionally taken into account at the stage of execution. Many of the aims of punishment may be successfully reconciled with the idea of *restorative justice*: the dissolution of conflict in a manner that is satisfactory to both parties perfectly complements the restorative, rehabilitative or even general preventive function. On the other hand, it seems that the classical dimension of criminal punishment, which is understood as a sanction imposed on the perpetrator of a crime by a court in the name of the state, may not be solely dependent on the agreement between the offender and the wronged party or local community. That criminal sanctions

---

103 *Art. 12. In the Act of 6 June 1997—the Criminal Code (Dziennik Ustaw No 88, item 553, as amended) the following changes shall be inserted:*

2) Art. 66 shall be worded as follows:

Art. 66(1) The court may conditionally discontinue criminal proceedings if the guilt and social noxiousness of the act are not significant, the circumstances of its commission do not raise doubts, and the attitude of the perpetrator, not punished previously for an intentional offence, his personal characteristics and his way of life to date provide reasonable grounds for the assumption that even in the event of discontinuance of the proceedings, he will observe the legal order, and, particularly, that he will not commit an offence.

(2) Conditional discontinuance shall not be applied to the perpetrator of an offence for which the statutory penalty exceeds 5 years of imprisonment.

interfere in individuals' (offenders') rights does not permit a resignation of the guarantees safeguarded by substantive criminal law, such as the principle *nullum crimen sine lege, nulla poena sine lege*. It may be that the new provision of art. 59a CrimC will offer a good solution, since in view of it, the abandonment of punishment does not deprive state authorities of control over the realisation of punishment objectives.

Olga Sitarz

Active Repentance at the Stage of Preparation for or Attempt at an Offence and Restorative Justice

Terminology

It should be mentioned at the start that the very term "active repentance," which is not normative in the Polish system, raises some doubts and is not always used by legal doctrine. In fact, the offender's conduct does not have to be active in its character and it does not have to result from repentance (understood as remorse), as will be discussed below. The term's non-normativity and its scope are very controversial in Polish literature. On one hand, there are supporters of an understanding of the term as broadly encompassing the institutions specified in the general part of the Criminal Code (art. 15, 17, 23 CrimC[1]) which refer to punishable forms of conduct preceding the perpetration of an offence and to forms of redressing the damage after the offence, which have been included by the lawmakers in certain crime definitions (e.g. art. 295, 307[2]).[3] In

---

1   Art. 17(1) Any person who intentionally resigns from an act and, in particular, who has destroyed the tools prepared or has prevented their use in the future, shall not be liable for punishment for the preparation. In the case of conspiring with another person so as to commit a prohibited act, any person who furthermore engaged in substantial endeavours intended to prevent the act shall not be liable for punishment.
      Art. 15(1) Any person who intentionally resigns from committing an act or prevents a consequence which constituted a feature of a prohibited act shall not be liable to suffer a penalty for an attempt.
      Art. 23 (1) A co-offender who has intentionally prevented the prohibited act from being committed shall not be liable for punishment.
2   Art. 295 (1) The court may apply an extraordinary mitigation of penalty or even refrain from imposing it against a perpetrator of the offence defined under art. 278, 284-289, 291, 292 or 294 who has voluntarily redressed the damage in its entirety or who has returned the vehicle or the thing which has a particular importance for the culture in an undamaged condition.
      Art. 307 (1) The court may apply extraordinary mitigation of penalty or even refrain from its imposition against a perpetrator of the offence defined under art. 296 or 299-305 who has voluntarily wholly redressed the damage. (translation by E. Małkiewicz-Łozińska).
3   Example: D. Gajdus, *Czynny żal w polskim prawie karnym* (Toruń: Wydawnictwo Uniwersytetu Mikołaja Kopernika, 1984), p. 54, L.Wilk in T.Dukiet-Nagórska (eds.),

its narrow sense, on the other hand, active repentance is limited to punishable behaviour that precedes the perpetration of the offence (that is preparation and attempt), conduct attributable to an instigator and accomplice,[4] or even to one of the types of conduct mentioned in art. 15, on the prevention of consequences.[5] In effect, commentators of the special part of the Criminal Code, which includes related provisions, sometimes refer to quasi-active repentance, specific active repentance,[6] withdrawal,[7] or exemption from criminal liability.[8] Merely historical importance may be ascribed to the perspective which limits active repentance to actions taken after perpetration of the offence;[9] however, it must be remembered that, chronologically, this was the first definition of the concept. In 1902, E. Krzymuski wrote that "active repentance is voluntary redress to the crime by the offender before the authorities learn about the offence, and this redress consists in making the crime harmless in material terms, or in compensating for the economic damage inflicted."[10] Ultimately, M. Klepner, noting that it is

---

Prawo karne część ogólna, szczególna i wojskowa (Warszawa: LexisNexis, 2012), p. 162, K. Tkaczyk, *Instytucja czynnego żalu w prawie karnym w ujęciu prawnoporównawczym* (Przemyśl: Wyższa Szkoła Prawa i Administracji, 2008), p. 22.

4   Example: D. Gajdus, *Czynny żal w polskim prawie karnym*, p. 55-56; W.Wróbel, A.Zoll, *Polskie prawo karne. Część ogólna* (Kraków: Znak, 2010), p. 374-375; Ł.Pohl, *Prawo karne. Wykład części ogólnej* (Warszawa: LexisNexis, 2012), p. 191-193, 204-205.

5   See, for example, J. Makarewicz, *Kodeks karny z komentarzem* (Lwów: Wydawnictwo Zakładu Narodowego Imienia Ossolińskich, 1932), p. 84; L. Tyszkiewicz, *Współdziałanie przestępne i główne pojęcia z nim związane w polskim prawie karnym* (Poznań: Uniwersytet im. Adama Mickiewicza w Poznaniu, 1964), p. 129; A. Krukowski, *Odstąpienie od przygotowania w kodeksie karnym*, Palestra 3 (1972), p. 15; W.Świda, *Prawo karne*, (Warszawa: Wydawnictwo Prawnicze, 1978), p. 200; I. Andrejew, *Polskie prawo karne w zarysie* (Warszawa: Państwowe Wydawnictwo Naukowe, 1971), p. 167; A. Marek, *Prawo karne. Zagadnienia teorii i praktyki* (Warszawa: Państwowe Wydawnictwo Naukowe, 1997), p. 42; A. Marek, *Prawo karne* (Warszawa: C. H. Beck, 2011), p. 193.

6   M. Fleming, J. Wojciechowska in A. Wąsek (eds.), *Kodeks karny. Część szczególna. Komentarz. Tom I*, (Warszawa: C. H. Beck 2004), p. 126.

7   See e.g. M. Kalitowski in O. Górniok (eds.), *Kodeks karny. Komentarz* (Warszawa: 2004), p. 737.

8   M. Bojarski in O. Górniok (ed.), *Kodeks karny. Komentarz*, p. 737; B. Michalski in A.Wąsek (ed.), *Kodeks karny. Część szczególna. Komentarz. Tom I*, p. 381.

9   Codification Commission justification of the Criminal Code quoted after: D. Gajdus, *Czynny żal w polskim prawie karnym*, p. 52.

10   E. Krzymuski, *Wykład prawa karnego ze stanowiska nauki i prawa austriackiego* (Kraków: Krakowska Spółka Wydawnicza, 1902), p. 148.

impossible to agree on the scope of the term "active repentance" in a single piece of legislation, suggests that the term should be used very carefully (as one should avoid using terms not defined by law).[11] Still, it seems that the concept of active repentance is well established in the Polish literature, and, at the same time, the terminological differentiation between the offender's conduct that prevents damage (either withdrawal or so-called "counteraction") and his or her conduct liquidating the damage seems unjustified.

Active repentance before committing the offence

This part deals with the question of active repentance shown before perpetrating the offence, that is, at the stage of preparation or attempt. Polish criminal law distinguishes *de jure* three types of active repentance preceding the crime: active repentance connected with preparation,[12] attempt[13] and joint participation.[14] It must be noted, however, that this division is not logical, but rather results from certain legislative choices. The functional classification of active repentance preceding perpetration of the offence (understood as commission of its final stage rather than punishable preparation or attempt, which can be "committed" as well) is de facto divided into two categories, that is active repentance connected with preparation and active repentance connected with an attempt (in each case the act leading to repentance may be committed by one or more individuals). Another type of active repentance, whose scope of dissimilarity will be verified in further discussion, relates to the stage following commission of the crime (as

---

11 M.Klepner, *Klauzule bezkarności w polskim prawie karnym*, Palestra, 9-10 (2001), p. 38-39.

It should be noted that some authors do not use the term *active repentance*; instead to name the instrument described under Art. 15 the term *unpunishable attempt* is used (though in other sources the notion of active repentance occurs in relation the issues considered) – W.Wróbel, A.Zoll, *Polskie prawo karne*, p. 236-239, 374-375.

12 *Art. 17(1) Any person who intentionally resigns from an act and, in particular, has destroyed the tools prepared or has prevented their use in the future, shall not be liable to punishment for the preparation. In the case of conspiring with another person so as to commit a prohibited act, any person who furthermore took up material endeavours intended to prevent the act shall not be liable to punishment.*

13 *Art. 15(1) Any person who intentionally resigns from committing an act or prevents a consequence which constituted a feature of a prohibited act shall not be liable to suffer a penalty for an attempt.*

14 *Art. 23 (1) A co-offender who has intentionally prevented the prohibited act from being committed shall not be liable for punishment.* (translation by E. Małkiwiecz-Łozińska)

many forms of repentance after the offence are *de facto* active repentance undertaken before the real damage has taken place and are aimed at preventing it).

At the beginning, it should also be stated that active repentance preceding the crime is not restricted to any specific types of offence: legislators does not deny the benevolence of active repentance to any offender, even in the case of the most serious crimes. In this sense, active repentance has a universal character and it is solely the offender who decides whether or not he or she wants to take advantage of it. All the forms of active repentance mentioned above are characterized with regard to their normative shape by the same constitutive elements (prerequisites):

- the offender's conduct is different from (contrary to) the prohibited conduct; exceptionally, additional activity may be required by law, e.g. influencing an accomplice or accomplices;
- the intended act has basically not yet been perpetrated;
- the offender's action is voluntary.

Fulfilment of all the above conditions, according to Polish criminal law, results in obligatory and unconditional impunity, despite the fact that the prohibited act has been committed in the form of (punishable) preparation or attempt.

A special role of the second of the above elements—of the act not yet being perpetrated—must be underlined here. Should the first or third condition not be met, that is, either there is no conduct contrary to the prohibited behaviour or the offender's action is not voluntary, active repentance cannot not come into question. However, if the second prerequisite is not fulfilled, that is, to put it simply, the damage has been done, active repentance can still be taken into account, but only in the form known as ineffective active repentance.[15] Its legal consequence might be extraordinary mitigation of penalty. Even where the offence has been committed, sometimes it is still possible for the offender to avoid punishment. The second requirement is not absolute in the case of preparation by more than one person (this issue will be further developed below).

As it seems *prima facie*, active repentance may become an important element in the model of restorative justice. However, an appropriate assessment of the features of active repentance must be based on a careful analysis of its prerequisites.

---

15 *Art. 15(2) The court may apply extraordinary mitigation of penalty in relation to an offender who has intentionally tried to prevent the consequence which constitutes a feature of a prohibited act.*

   Art. 23(2) The court may apply an extraordinary mitigation of penalty towards a co-offender who has intentionally tried to prevent the prohibited act from being committed.

The analysis must be preceded by the general statement that whether in the case of preparation or attempt, damage broadly conceived is done to a particular wronged party and to society—in the sense that it causes anxiety and fear about crime, and also lowers the sense of security. In other words, the prohibited act's not yet being perpetrated does not mean that the damage is not present, that conflict is non-existent and that there is no room for restorative justice. This reservation made, it is possible to consider active repentance as a mechanism of restorative justice, and the particular elements of active repentance will be scrutinised from this angle, apart from views and doubts expounded on by experts that cannot have any influence on the assessment of active repentance as one of mechanisms of restorative justice.

Requirements with regard to the conduct of the perpetrator of the prepared or attempted act

There are three prerequisites for applying the impunity clause, and they basically exclude one another: withdrawal from committing the crime, preventing the consequences of a crime, and restraining an accomplice from committing the crime. In the literature they are often unjustifiably said to be alternatives. In fact, it is the situation (created by the offender) that somehow forces him or her to behave in a specific manner. Thus, in some circumstances it is sufficient to desist from a criminal act (which means that the prohibited behaviour is not continued, for instance the offender walks away from the door which he or she tried to force open in order to commit theft). In other situations counteraction is undertaken (for example the perpetrator stops the bleeding after the victim is hurt), which in some cases will require influencing accomplices, whether effectively or not. The ultimate criterion for evaluating the right substantive prerequisite concerning the offender is the absence of perpetration of the crime.

Polish legislation does not stipulate any required (strictly specified) conduct that would meet the criteria of active repentance. In the case of active repentance undertaken at the preparation stage by a sole perpetrator, he or she must voluntarily desist from preparation, which is generally indicated definitively.[16] As an example of behaviour manifesting the intention to withdraw from the offence, the legislators provides the destruction of the tools prepared or the prevention of their future use (Art. 17(1) CrimC). In this respect, it is highlighted

---

16 A.Zoll in A.Zoll (ed.), *Kodeks karny. Część ogólna. Komentarz. Tom I. Komentarz do art. 1-116 k.k.* (Warszawa: C. H. Beck, 2007), p. 234.

in the commentaries that the offender's behaviour must be real and easily seen by others.[17] What is more important, however, is that neither doctrine nor case law requires that any information about the withdrawal from preparation must reach the victim or the persons who learned about the commission of punishable preparation.

In the case of an attempt made by a sole offender, the offender's conduct must consist either in withdrawing from the perpetration of an offence or preventing the consequence prescribed in a definition of a particular crime. The legislators did not give any examples of any specific behaviour in this case. It should be assumed that what was meant was any behaviour due to which the wrongful act was actually not performed. It must be emphasised at this point, as it is particularly valid from the perspective of restorative justice, that both in legal doctrine and in case law it is assumed that prevention of consequences does not have to be achieved personally by the offender. In accordance with Art. 15(1) of the Criminal Code, it is sufficient when the consequences are prevented by third parties if their action was initiated by the offender attempting the crime (for example, when a victim's life is saved by a doctor who has been called in by an offender attempting murder of the victim). It also seems an essential observation that, in the case of active repentance at the stage of attempt at prohibited act, the law does not require that the withdrawal, or even the prevention of consequences, be noticed by the victim. It must be emphasized that the requirement of directness with regard to attempt (i.e. that only behaviour aimed directly at committing the crime may be recognised as attempt) does not counteract the victim's lack of awareness about becoming the object of attack and, subsequently, about the offender's subsequent active repentance. Directness is not connected with space. What is more, even if the victim is aware of the attack aimed at him or her, it is not necessary that he or she know about the perpetrator's active repentance (that the offence was not perpetrated as a result of the offender's change of mind and not, for example, as a result of intervention by third parties). Therefore, an offender will not be punished if he or she takes action on the first step of stealing food in a shop, putting the products into his or her pockets, and is spotted by the owner, but then changes his or her mind and puts the goods back onto a different shelf three aisles away, but is not spotted this time by the owner.

Polish penal law does not limit the time during which the perpetrator should embark on active repentance. However, punishment is avoided only

---

17 Example: R. Zawłocki in M. Królikowski, R. Zawłocki (eds.), *Kodeks karny. Część ogólna. Tom I. Komentarz do artykułów 1-31* (Warszawa: C.H.Beck, 2010), p. 635.

on the condition that the prohibited act is not committed, and particularly when the effects of crime are prevented. Therefore, even though the counter-action taken by the offender attempting the crime does not have to be taken immediately, it must prevent the perpetration of the crime. If the offender's active repentance is "delayed," he or she may be held fully responsible for the prohibited act.

In the case of offences committed jointly by more than one person, the re-quirements stipulated for active repentance are different, and, interestingly enough, they are diversified (probably unjustifiably[18]) according to the stage at which the joint action took place. At the stage of preparation, under art. 17(1) CrimC, in the case of conspiring with another person so as to commit a prohibited act, any person who took up material endeavours intended to pre-vent the act is not liable to punishment. Therefore, the offender's efforts put into preparation do not have to be effective, and the fact that the act has been committed does not preclude impunity, provided that an accomplice took es-sential efforts. It has not been specified in statutory law what kinds of efforts these might be. Examples have likewise not been provided. In the end, it is a question for competent authorities (whether prosecutor or court) to decide in each individual case. At the stage of attempt, however, pursuant to Art. 23 (1) CrimC, a co-offender who has intentionally prevented the prohibited act from being perpetrated is not liable to a penalty. Experts and commentators, when comparing active repentance at the stage of attempting an offense committed by a sole perpetrator and jointly by co-offenders, emphasise that prerequisites concerning the latter are more stringent, since an accomplice is required to have taken effective measures which have resulted in preventing perpetration of the prohibited act.[19] It should be noted, however, that this is not true, as the require-ments concerning active repentance at the stage of attempt are always the same regardless of the way of committing (or contributing to) the crime. Prevention of the crime being perpetrated is necessary in each case, which stems from the very function of active repentance. Yet, the truth is also that preventing the prohibited act might, but does not have to, be more difficult in the case of the involvement of more than one offender. One should agree with the position of

---

18 However, A. Zoll argues that the different requirements relating to the active repent-ance of co-offenders taking part in preparation and attempt result from the remote-ness between the preparation and perpetration of an offence. A. Zoll in A. Zoll (ed.), *Kodeks karny. Część ogólna. Komentarz. Tom I. Komentarz do art. 1-116 k.k.*, p. 277.

19 P.Kardas in A.Zoll (ed.), *Kodeks karny. Część ogólna. Komentarz. Tom I. Komentarz do art. 1-116 k.k.*, p. 442.

the Supreme Court that in some situations, even in the case of a joint act, withdrawal itself prevents perpetration of the crime.[20] For example, the perpetrator in charge, the one who has ordered others to commit a prohibited act, resigns and withdraws from it, an action which turns out to be enough to prevent the perpetration altogether.

Subjective aspects of active repentance: requirements relating to voluntariness

One of the main issues concerning active repentance is voluntariness as a condition of exemption from punishment by the offender guilty of preparation or attempt. Z. Kubec underlined the significance of this notion by saying that it is the most important and the most difficult problem,[21] while A. Marek stated that it is the essential element of the impunity clause.[22] It is basically the only criterion that allows for a distinction between punishable preparation or attempt barred by third party (punishable as an actually perpetrated act) on one hand, and desistance of criminal conduct (not punishable), on the other. As S. Budziński pointed out, "there are two reasons to stop actions once initiated: the offender either does not want to continue or is unable to do so."[23]

The lawmakers did not specify the criteria or prerequisites of voluntariness. In the literature of the field and in case law, there are many interpretations of this notion, which A. Spotowski classified into two main groups: psychological and normative constructions. According to the psychological conceptions, the motive for withdrawal from an attempt to commit a crime is of no significance; what matters is that the offender could have committed the act, in his or her own mind, but did not want to do so. In the case of normative constructs, the notion of voluntariness is very specific and strictly connected with an assessment of the motives for withdrawal.[24] Leaving aside the issue of the accuracy of this

---

20 Cf. P.Kardas in A.Zoll (ed.), *Kodeks karny. Część ogólna. Komentarz. Tom I. Komentarz do art. 1-116 k.k.,* p. 443 and A.Wąsek, as quoted by P.Kardas.

21 Z. Kubec, *Kilka uwaga na temat odstąpienia od usiłowania,* Państwo i Prawo 3 (1969), p. 565.

22 A. Marek, *Prawo karne,* Warszawa 2011, p. 194.

23 S. Budziński, *Wykład porównawczy prawa karnego* (Warszawa: 1988), p. 174, after: A.Stefański, *Dobrowolne odstąpienie od usiłowania,* Prokuratura i Prawo 4 (1996), p. 112.

24 A. Spotowski, *O odstąpieniu od usiłowania,* Państwo i Prawo, 6 (1980), p. 91-93

At the same time, it should be pointed out that the normative theory was significantly developed in German law by C.Roxin, who is even considered this theory's

terminology, it must be said that that in its essence this division has retained its validity up to the present day. The psychological frame is aptly illustrated by R. Frank's well-known formula, in pursuance of which voluntariness can be stated when the perpetrator says, "I don't want to achieve my goal, even though I am able to," while the sentence, "I couldn't reach my goal even if I wanted to" indicates the lack of voluntariness.[25] There is no doubt that the majority of criminal law specialists share this view, along with the judiciary. W. Wolter, for instance, remarked that "the statutory requisite is minimalistic," as it is sufficient for the perpetrator that he or she did not want to perpetrate the crime any longer.[26] W. Radecki's viewpoint should probably also be labelled under this group. On the basis of what he called "grammatical interpretation," the author believes that the word "voluntarily" contains moral judgement, with the sole reservation that this is not an evaluation of the motives (or at least it does not always refer to the motives), but rather an estimation of to what extent what happened depended on the offender's will, as this, in the author's opinion, is also a matter of moral judgement. Then, quoting E. Krzymuski, W. Radecki adds that for criminal law it does not matter whether a person avoids becoming a criminal thanks to his or her beliefs or because of fear; it does not matter whether the perpetrator withdrew from committing the crime because of remorse or because of fear of punishment.[27] The reasoning of the Krakow Court of Appeals might be a contemporary illustration of the courts' current approach on this issue:

> Any person who, being able to continue an attempt, resigns from it because he or she does not want to achieve the previously intended goal, desists from the attempt. In determining the voluntariness of desisting from an attempt, the motivation behind such behaviour is of no significance. The perpetrator does not have to understand the culpability of his or her behaviour or the harm done, etc., in order to voluntarily desist from an attempt (emphasis mine). Judicial practice knows various motives for such behaviour, from the most noble, though morally neutral, to most doubtful situations. In each of these cases, the applicability of art. 15(1) CrimC seems appropriate and specifically

author – K.Tkaczyk, *Instytucja czynnego żalu w prawie karnym w ujęciu prawnoporównawczym*, p. 55.

25 In: A.Spotowski, *O odstąpieniu od usiłowania*, p. 92.
    As K.Tkaczyk indicates, it is R.Frank's concept of voluntariness that is quoted in most works on active repentance. – K.Tkaczyk, *Instytucja czynnego żalu w prawie karnym w ujęciu prawnoporównawczym*, p. 50. In the Polish doctrine it was first mentioned by Śliwiński, *Prawo karne materialne*, p. 308.

26 W. Wolter, *Nauka o przestępstwie* (Warszawa: Państwo Wydawnictwo Naukowe, 1973), p. 273.

27 W. Radecki, *Prawne i moralne oceny czynnego żalu*, Palestra, 12 (1976), p. 22-25.

pertinent since it helps to alleviate the harm suffered by the victim and encourages other offenders to follow its example, benefitting victims in turn.[28]

M. Szerer presents a different view on the subject, stating that in the wording of the provision on active repentance, there is nothing that justifies associating the decriminalization of voluntary desistance from an attempt with expedience. He emphasized that, in terms of criminal law and policy, it would be nonsense if the perpetrators of serious crimes (like rape) were legally granted impunity in each case that they refrain from the attempt by their own will.[29] Z. Papierkowski underlined that the *ratio legis* of active repentance "is based on moral subjectivism concerning the offender's guilt and the postulate of objective public interest." In his opinion active repentance should be based on remorse similar to penitence, and may take place only when objective social damage has not been done.[30] A. Spotowski believes that the law should not reward immoral behaviour and indicates that it is quite possible, with the provision being formulated as it is, to add elements of motive evaluation to the definition of the concept of voluntariness, which is so laconic as to fail to indicate unequivocally any particular direction of interpretation, while the general assumptions of our criminal law seem to encourage, in Spotowski's view, a normative interpretation connected with the assessment of the prognostic significance of the offender's behaviour after the withdrawal. For this reason, he claims that the criterion of voluntariness should be any conduct of the offender that shows his or her will to observe the law.[31] It must be noted that all normative suggestions have one fundamental drawback: they result from a narrowing interpretation. This type of interpretation concerning circumstances exempting from penal liability will always act to the disadvantage of the offender. That is why it should be concluded, to paraphrase the above quotation by M. Szerer, that in the wording of Art. 15 (1) of the Criminal Code, there is nothing that allows a narrowing interpretation of this provision. The crucial argument here is that the legislator's main goal is to act in the best interest of the victim, while the "justice" of the solutions offered is less important.

A completely different problem is how to determine whether a particular behaviour in a particular situation is voluntary or not. Z. Kubec remarked that

---

28 Judgment of the Court of Appeal in Kraków of 15 April 2009, II AKa 45/09, Lex No. 527435.

29 M.Szerer, „*Dobrowolne*" *odstąpienie od usiłowania*, Nowe Prawo, 5 (1977), p. 627.

30 Z.Papierkowski, *Glosa do wyroku z dnia 14 września 1967 r., (V KRN 599/67)*, Nowe Prawo, 7-8 (1968), p. 1236. Rejman Has criticised this view – G.Rejman, *W kwestii dobrowolnego odstąpienia od usiłowania*, Nowe Prawo 3 (1969), p. 436-439.

31 A. Spotowski, *O odstąpieniu od usiłowania*, p. 94.

determining whether withdrawal from attempt was voluntary would always be a difficult question of fact, and the decision will depend on determining what was decisive: the offender's will or external circumstances.[32] The following ruling shows how difficult such an assessment can be. In the opinion of the Supreme Court,

> there are no grounds for the assumption that the convict desisted voluntarily from committing the act if the court's findings show that the abandonment of a further attack by the attacker was caused first by the victim's unhesitating defence and then by her promise to testify that she was attacked by somebody else, in a situation in which the victim gripped the knife and pulled it out of the attacker's hand, the attacker then pulled the victim's hand with the knife in his direction, and then, after the victim's promise concerning her testimony, further actions were taken, that is, the police were called and the knife was washed.[33]

Additionally, it seems that, in the case of rape, the problem of assessing voluntariness is particularly difficult. W. Radecki, aware of the potential consequences, wrote in 1974 that if it was the offender's fear of venereal disease that made him refrain from the act, his desisting should be assessed as involuntary. The author argued that fear of punishment (a factor not considered as excluding voluntariness by most authors[34]) is different from the fear of physical side effects of the crime.[35] In W. Radecki's opinion, the offender's physical incapacity is also treated as involuntary desistance, while an offender who refrained from rape because he

---

32 Z. Kubec, *Kilka uwaga na temat odstąpienia od usiłowania*, Państwo i Prawo, 3 (1969), p. 565-567.

33 S. C. decision of 24 November 2011, V KK 274/11, Lex No. 1103635.

34 Cf. S. Śliwiński, *Polskie prawo karne materialne* (Warszawa: Gebethner i Wolff, 1948), p. 309.

35 Cf. W Radecki, *Usiłowanie zgwałcenia w świetle przepisów kodeksu karnego*, Nowe Prawo, 12 (1974), p. 1619. Cf. also: A.Gubiński, *Glosa do wyroku z 5 I 1973, III KR 258/72*, Państwo i Prawo, 1 (1974), p. 175 and J.Warylewski in A.Wąsek (ed.), *Kodeks karny. Część szczególna. Tom I. Komentarz do artykułów 117-221*, (Warszawa: C.H.Beck, 2006), p. 859-860, who commented positively on the thesis of the Supreme Court that fear of venereal disease does not preclude voluntariness because the motive for withdrawal from an attempt does not have to be morally positive in order to apply active repentance.
    The widest catalogue of the circumstances that do not preclude voluntariness in relation to rape was presented by Leszczyński. In his opinion, having in mind the aim of active repentance (preventing the crime) the circumstances include: fear of punishment, fear of being discredited, fear of venereal disease, and sudden revulsion toward the person being raped as a result of this person being dirty, menstruating, having

feared that his wife or his minor victim's parents might learn about his actions can be exempted from liability.[36] Then, a Supreme Court ruling reads that when the withdrawal is caused by a third party's disapproval, it is considered voluntary.[37] In this context, an intriguing question arises: does lack of "courage" make such behaviour involuntary?[38] This brief review of standpoints allows for the conclusion that despite their declarations authors quite often fail to distinguish between the notions of irrelevant motivation and relevant voluntariness. And yet, it is not just any kind of motivation which counts as voluntariness. An apt illustration of this distinction is an example given by S. Śliwiński, who wrote: "The revulsion that an offender felt when he faced the intended act may also exclude voluntary desistance, but only if the revulsion was so strong that the offender could not overcome it. If he was able to do so, but decided otherwise, the desistance is considered voluntary."[39] This position was also expressed by the Supreme Court when it stated that voluntariness is at play in cases when "the offender did not have to succumb to the above-mentioned influence, which in the light of life experience was not the decisive reason for his resignation but only one of the factors that made him desist from the crime."[40] Thus, making catalogues of factors excluding and not excluding voluntariness is not justifiable.[41] Each and every one of these factors must be assessed in the context of a particular offender and a particular situation. To put it briefly, one must answer the question of whether the offender could resist a given factor (whether it be lack of courage, fear of punishment, repulsion, other people's presence, etc.). It seems then that Gubiński was right in saying that it is impossible to determine any general rules for the assessment of voluntariness in desisting from an attempt. In each case it must be assessed individually in the light of the unique circumstances of a particular situation.[42] A tempting solution was proposed by the Supreme Court 80 years ago: "'voluntary desistance from

dermatitis, or being soiled with urine or excrements. J. Leszczyński, *Z problematyki usiłowania i dokonania przestępstwa zgwałcenia*, Nowe Prawo, 9-10 (1975), p. 1450.

36 W Radecki, *Usiłowanie zgwałcenia w świetle przepisów kodeksu karnego*, Nowe Prawo 12 (1974), p. 1619-1620.

37 S. C. judgment of 5 January 1973, III KR 258/72, OSNKW, 7-8 (1973), item 92.

38 W. Makowski, *Kodeks karny. Komentarz* (Warszawa: Księgarnia W.Hoesicka, 1937), p. 123, quoted after: S. Śliwiński, *Polskie prawo karne materialne*, p. 307.

39 S. Śliwiński, *Polskie prawo karne materialne*, p. 307.

40 S. C. judgment of 5 January 1973, III KR 258/72, OSNKW, 7-8 (1973), item 92.

41 Cf. D. Gajdus, *Czynny żal w polskim prawie karnym*, p. 62.

42 A. Gubiński, *Glosa do wyroku z 5 I 1973, III KR 258/72*, Państwo i Prawo, 1 (1974), p. 175.

the act' is not the case if external circumstances affected the offender's will in such a compulsory manner that, judging by everyday life experience (emphasis mine), these external circumstances removed the incitement that had created his intent to commit a crime."[43] However, an assessment of the offender's free will based upon the experience of the assessing person might prove unreliable, which is illustrated by the above-mentioned motives for withdrawal from committing sexual crimes. Yet, it is obvious that considerable subjectivity and variation comes into play in assessments of the degree of something's influence on a person's will in various spheres of life: what is repulsive to some people might be quite acceptable to others.[44] In assessing voluntariness, one must not, in my opinion, rely on the model of the so-called ideal citizen, so often used in criminal law. This person must inevitably prove unreliable in describing emotional reactions under threat,[45] and in the same way the impact of external circumstances is always individual, depending on psychological features, the hierarchy of values held by a particular person, and his or her needs.

A good summary of the present deliberations on voluntariness is the Supreme Court's ruling of 27 January 1966, which states that voluntariness is awareness of the possibility of continuing the crime, coupled with a conscious and free will to resign from achieving the intended goal.[46]

Bearing in mind the aim of this work, it should be emphasised that Polish criminal law does not preclude impunity in cases when active repentance is undertaken at the victim's request, but active repentance caused by a sense of pity towards the victim is treated by the law in the same way as any other voluntary active repentance.

The legal consequences of active repentance

The legal consequences of active repentance and, most importantly, its mechanism are of great importance for assessing its place in the model of restorative justice. According to the regulations quoted above (arts 15(1), 17(1) and 22(1)

---

43 Judgment of the Supreme Court of 4.06.1934 r., (3 K. 573/34), Zbór Orzeczeń SN. Orzeczenia Izby Karnej XII/34, item 305, p. 534

44 An example may be the attitude of an offender attempting rape at all costs, who consents even to "languish" in prison.

45 Cf. M. Szafraniec, *Przekroczenie granic obrony koniecznej w polskim prawie karnym* (Kraków: Zakamycze, 2004), p. 139.

46 S. C. judgment of 27 January 1976, IV KR 322/75, unpublished, qtd. in: A.Stefański, *Dobrowolne odstąpienie od usiłowania*, p. 111.

CrimC), preparation and attempt are exempted from punishment in the presence of effective active repentance. The victim's will, his or her view on the matter, and forgiveness or absence of forgiveness have no impact on the offender's impunity. Impunity is guaranteed even if the wronged party bears all the negative consequences (but the intended act was not committed), unless these consequences meet the statutory criteria of another crime, since in such a situation we speak about qualified attempt with a possible full penal liability.[47] If effective active repentance has been undertaken, anxiety, pain, and loss of confidence or trust on the part of the victim (generally speaking, damages done), do not become the subjects of a separate legal assessment, setting aside the disputes among experts concerning the scope of punishable conduct in spite of active repentance.

Unconditional impunity in the case of active repentance before the crime means that after active repentance has been confirmed there is no possibility of instituting criminal proceedings, and that if the proceedings have already commenced, they should be discontinued (art. 17 item 4 CCP). The only entitlement that the prosecutor or the court has in this respect is to examine whether the prerequisites for impunity were actually fulfilled, that is if the fact that the crime was not perpetrated was actually the result of the offender's (free) decision. It must also be noted that the formulation "is not liable to penalty" (found in arts 15 (1), 17 (1) 1 and 22 (1) CrimC) means that no punitive or other penal measures may be imposed on the offender.[48] The legal consequence of active repentance preceding a crime is absolute exemption from criminal *liability*. At the same time, by discontinuing the proceedings on the grounds of exemption from punishment, the court can decree the forfeiture of property mentioned in art. 39 item 4 and art. 100.[49] As K. Tkaczyk notes, a resolution concerning the evidence (art. 323

---

47 For instance, prevention of the victim's death by the offender does not exempt the offender from punishment for the detriment to health suffered by the victim and caused by the act.

48 It should be noted that if it has been determined once cour proceedings have started that prerequisites of the impunity clause have been fulfilled through active repentance, the defendant cannot be convicted or acquitted. The judgment can only confirm that the defendant cannot be punished. Cf. K. Tkaczyk, *Instytucja czynnego żalu w prawie karnym w aspekcie prawnoporównawczym*, p. 183.

49 A. Sakowicz in K. T. Boratyńska, A. Górski, A. Sakowicz, A. Ważny (eds.), *Kodeks postępowania karnego. Komentarz*, (Warszawa: C. H. Beck, 2012), p. 81. See also P. Hofmański, S. Zabłocki, *Elementy metodyki pracy sędziego w sprawach karnych* (Warszawa, Zakamycze 2006), p. 30.

§ PCPP) is the only negative consequence which might affect an offender show-ing active repentance.

However, it must be stated categorically that the absence of punishment does not mean impunity in the popular understanding of the word. Impunity in the Polish language (according to the PWN Dictionary[50]) refers to situa-tions in which the offender gets away with what he or she did, that is he or she remains unpunished despite the will of legislators and law enforcement bod-ies. The term refers to offenders who have not been identified or who cannot be punished because of a lack of evidence of the crime being committed. On the other hand, in situations where the punishment can be imposed but the court decides to spare the offender, the absence of such a penalty may become a strong incentive to reach some specific aims. My belief is that even the most far-reaching decision by a legislator of the offender's non-liability for punish-ment, or by a court to refrain from imposing a penalty, should be viewed as a manifestation of the rule of law and the criminal justice system. That is why some functions of criminal law can be performed by penal procedure itself (even in a reduced form), through the court's decision to discontinue the pro-ceedings, and first of all through the disclosure of the offence and of the ot-fender's identity.[51]

The functions of active repentance

A few words should be devoted to the functions of active repentance, so that later on they can be juxtaposed against the function of restorative justice. The pres-ence of active repentance in Polish law is usually justified by the function it is supposed to perform. As D. Gajdus indicates, active repentance has the following functions: a justice-seeking function, a preventive function, an educational function, a compensatory function and a decriminalising function.[52] It seems,

---

50 M. Szymczak (ed.), *Słownik języka polskiego. Tom I* (Warszawa: Państwowe Wydawnictwo Naukowe, 1978), p. 144. Examples: „Bezkarni chuligani. Bezkarne ko-rzystanie z cudzych osiągnięć" (Impunity of hooligans. Impunity of making use of another's achievements).

51 Cf. O. Sitarz, *Czynny żal jako instrument polityki kryminalnej i karnej*, Archiwum Kryminologii, Vol. XXXI (2009), p. 167.

52 D. Gajdus, *Czynny żal w polskim prawie karnym*, p. 69.
    In this context, a question asked by Lubelski at a conference on restorative justice must sound quite intriguing: What is the relation of the compensatory function of criminal law to the justice-seeking function? Does the former supplement the latter or do they compete? The author was in favour of the former conception. M. Lubelski,

however, that although the result of effective active repentance is the offender's impunity, it is hard to agree that one of the functions at play here could be decriminalisation. As adopted by legislators, decriminalisation (either complete, or partial in the case of ineffective active repentance) is merely an instrument if we stress the preventive, compensative or educational functions, or merely a consequence, if we stress the justice-seeking function, but from the legislators' point of view it is not an aim in itself.

In D. Gajdus's opinion, in view of a mixed justification (legal, political and criminal) for active repentance in the Polish law, it follows that active repentance serves justice through the so-called justice-pursuing correction (which modifies the extent of criminal liability by reacting to change of intent and prevention of consequences). In this context, the impunity clause arouses some doubts, in D. Gajdus's opinion, as it breaks all connections between the offence committed, guilt, and the punishment understood as a normative effect of crime. The author adds, although it is hard to agree with him, that it is the social sense of justice that should not allow active repentance to decriminalize a given act.[53]

At a basic level, the preventive function of active repentance does not arouse any controversies, since these regulations on active repentance are intended to prevent perpetration of the prohibited act, to prevent the damage being done (the assumption being that criminal law can affect human conduct positively and is a stimulus for socially responsible behaviours). Still, the author herself spots a demoralising feature in this institution. In D. Gajdus's opinion, the provisions on active repentance (as inadequately shaped) may provide encouragement for committing crimes. As the author explains, a strictly objective approach to active repentance does not allow an assessment of the offender's change of attitude, so the offender could still remain a "potential criminal."[54] Yet, it seems that the "negative element" of the impunity clause (or extraordinary mitigation of penalty) mentioned above undermines not the preventive but the corrective function. The preventive function means that a specific damage intended by the offender has been prevented, and, in this sense, effective active repentance always fulfils this function.

With regard to the educational function, what raises doubts in the view of D. Gajdus is the specific form of active repentance in which the law requires denunciation, because it might be difficult to deem as morally positive the attitude

---

Głos w dyskusji przeprowadzonej w dniu 17.05.2002 r. na temat sprawiedliwości naprawczej, Czasopismo Prawa Karnego i Nauk Penalnych, 2 (2002), p. 239.

53 D. Gajdus, *Czynny żal w polskim prawie karnym*, p. 79-80.

54 *Ibid.*, p. 69-71.

of an offender who discloses a crime, his or her accomplices' attitudes, and all the surrounding circumstances. Ultimately, however, the author notes that active repentance actually substitutes and replaces punishment, educates the offender, exposes him or her to moral dilemmas, stimulates desirable attitudes, and models adequate behaviours.[55] In my opinion, the assessment of an offender who reports on his or her accomplices does not involve any moral doubts. It is hard to agree with C. Beccaria's claim that active repentance is a situation in which "a nation approves of a treachery despised even by wrongdoers."[56] Wrongdoers, as can be presumed, despise not betrayal by itself, but the betrayal of their secrets. At the same time, however, the educational function of active repentance before a crime should not be overestimated. It seems that in reality a situation opposite to the one described by D. Gajdus is the case, and that active repentance is a result of the offender's moral dilemmas, change of attitude, and self-correction. In other words, active repentance is the effect, not the cause of the offender's self-improvement. The last of the considered functions, the compensatory function of active repentance, can according to D. Gajdus be divided into two spheres, namely material compensation and moral compensation, but the author claims that material compensation is present both before and after committing a crime.[57]

Today, the moral compensation of active repentance should be stressed, since it has (similarly to the offence itself) an individual aspect (the satisfaction of the wronged party) and a social dimension (the clear signal of giving up crime). It is worth noting that active repentance (at the stage of preparation or attempt) can minimise victimisation, prevent material damage, minimise fear caused by commission of the crime, and, as a result, prevent conflict or, in a wider sense, minimize this conflict. The wronged party, thanks to the offender's behaviour, may feel particular satisfaction when seeing the activities undertaken to prevent the damage. The benefits of active repentance on the part of the offender are

---

55 *Ibid.*, p. 74-76.
56 C. Beccaria, *O przestępstwach i karach* (Warszawa: Wydawnictwo Prawnicze, 1959), p. 192.
57 D. Gajdus, *Czynny żal w polskim prawie karnym*, p. 78.
    However, A. R. Światłowski claims that the "compensatory function becomes significant in situations in which the redress of damage by the offender is to be rewarded." He believes that a wider understanding of the compensatory function, that is one which accounts for the prevention of damage, is inadequate because it blurs the difference between the compensative and preventive functions. A. R. Światłowski, *Kompensacyjna funkcja czynnego żalu w Kodeksie karnym z 1997 r.*, Czasopismo Prawa Karnego i Nauk Penalnych, 2 (2002), p. 151.

evident: avoidance of punishment and stigma, but even more important, avoidance or serious minimization of potential conflict with the wronged party. These features may translate into benefits for the whole system of justice, such as serious reduction or lack of need whatsoever for criminal proceedings, and benefits for society as a whole, such as potential absence of conflict or its diffusion, and minimization or total elimination of the feeling of insecurity caused by crime. Among social benefits, I would also place the fact that the offender autonomously assumes responsibility for his or her actions, and that he does so before the institutionalised response, since what takes place is effective (and almost immediate) social reintegration.[58]

It should be emphasised that the voluntariness of active repentance, or to be more precise the changing of one's original intent, even if it does not mean true contrition, reflects a critical evaluation by the offender of his or her own act, in which he or she recognizes it as blameworthy and socially unacceptable.

These features of active repentance lead to a clear conclusion, that active repentance is an institution focused on the wronged party and the protection of his/her best interests, even though the Criminal Code contains *de facto* only information about benefits on the part of the offender.

Nevertheless, all of these benefits of active repentance do not mean that active repentance fulfils the objectives of the model of restorative justice.

Active repentance and restorative justice

It is time now to answer the question of whether active repentance is *de lege lata* an element of the restorative justice model. In other words, can it be said that even traditional criminal law pursues the objectives of restorative justice, even if only through selected instruments such as active repentance before an offence?

In order to answer the question, one must review the elements of active repentance from the viewpoint of restorative justice.

1) Active repentance certainly implements one of the main objectives of restorative justice, which is restitution, that is redress of damage (in the widest sense of the word),[59] in the form of the prevention of loss intended originally by the

---

58 Cf.: M. S. Umbreit after D.Wójcik *Rola mediacji między pokrzywdzonym a sprawcą przestępstwa* in A.Marek (ed.), *Zagadnienia ogólne. System prawa karnego. Tom I* (Warszawa: C. H. Beck, 2010), p. 353.

59 Cf. J. Consedine, *Sprawiedliwość naprawcza – kompensacyjna praktyka prawa karnego*, Mediator, 3 (2005), p. 18.

offender and minimising the harm resulting from punishable preparation or from the attempt to commit a crime.

2) The exclusive aim of active repentance is the additional protection of the wronged party's legal interests (even though the offender's active repentance benefits not only the wronged party and the offender, because exempted from punishment, but also society at large and the system of justice).

3) The institution of active repentance does not ensure the wronged party, nor even offer him or her, anything except for the prevention of damage *sensu stricto* and the potential redress of damage *sensu largo* (if general anxiety caused by an attempt is treated as damage). The wronged party does not even have to know about active repentance, does not have the possibility of expressing his or her emotions concerning victimisation, and cannot listen to the offender to learn why it was he or she who would become a victim. The wronged party does not have the possibility of forgiving the offender. In such circumstances there might be lacking what J. Consedine wrote about the transformation from victim to survivor (by breaking free form the anger and pain of victimisation, among other ways).[60]

4) Active repentance expressed by the offender does not ensure his or her contrition—that he or she takes on responsibility and admits the wrong done. This kind of motivation can be the cause of active repentance but it does not have to be, and the law does not require it to be. On the other hand, even the most positive attitude of the offender does not manage to obtain the victim's forgiveness. The offender gains only "impunity," but there is no place for those emotions that could influence his or her life.

5) Unconditional impunity and its significance for criminal proceedings (a negative prerequisite for court proceedings, meaning that the proceedings are not instituted or are discontinued) lead to a situation in which there is no place for legal proceedings and thus no place for rapprochement between the wronged party and the wrongdoer. Active repentance could improve the relationship, but there is no possibility of assessing whether this has actually happened or, in the case of negative diagnosis, of making joint efforts to improve this relation. In other words, penal consequences of active repentance end the legal (and only legal) dispute (through discontinued criminal proceedings), *de facto* making it impossible to solve a potential conflict, as there is no place for any mediation in criminal cases once the proceedings have been discontinued.

---

60 *Ibid.*, p. 18.

What then is active repentance from the point of view of restorative justice? It is automatic forgiveness expressed by the state, without checking whether the wronged party is satisfied and the conflict has been settled (and, in cases of active repentance at the stage of preparation when conspiring with others, even if the damage has been done). This means that although the institution of active repentance is of great significance to the wronged party, it cannot be de lege lata seen as an element of restorative justice. Therefore, it does not even matter that active repentance preceding the crime is expressed so early that there is no space for (more or less formal) mediation; what matters is that the constitutive elements of restorative justice are not present in this form of active repentance, so it cannot be seen as a mechanism of this model.

It is worth mentioning that there is a place for restorative justice in the case of ineffective active repentance and active repentance resulting in a qualified form of attempt, but this is the case only because in these situations the offence has been perpetrated, as it were, "by chance," and the offender must be punished, which opens the way to settling or minimizing the conflict, either through mediation or through restorative conferences (and criminal proceedings concern not the prevented damage but the damage done, although the very mediation may also cover the issue of attempt at the originally intended act).

The question must be asked of whether active repentance before perpetration of a crime that does not fulfil de lege lata the objectives of restorative justice could be modelled in such a way as to actually pursue the objectives of this new model of criminal liability.

First of all, it is the subjective aspect of active repentance that should be modelled differently. Some experts, although only few, claim that certain consequences could be subject to a morally positive attitude that results from the offender's remorse or regret.

A restorative model would also call for different forms of the penal consequences of active repentance. Impunity would have to be optional and dependent on reconciliation with the wronged party, and perhaps also conditioned by the wronged party's consent. Active repentance shaped in accordance with these postulations would fit well into the existing procedural—"consensual"—institutions, which would constitute a copestone for previous mediation (this is how mediation was supposed to function[61]). Therefore, it would be the offender's active repentance that would open the way to the development of

---

61 A. Murzynowski, *Instytucja mediacji jako czynnik humanizacji w stosowaniu prawa karnego w Polsce*, Mediator, 1 (2004), p. 6-7.

dialogue between the wronged party and the offender, giving hope for potential future impunity.

This formula, however, would necessarily limit the effectiveness of active repentance as preventive measure, since impunity would not be guaranteed to the perpetrator (optional impunity is a weaker inducement to refrain from the crime, perhaps not even "worth a try"), and this negative consequence could affect the safety of the wronged party. Because of this, it must be remembered that active repentance modelled in this way would enhance the restorative model and the corrective function of criminal law but, at the same time, it would weaken its preventive function. Yet, there are certainly no doubts that it is the preventive function that should be prioritised, and if there is a choice of measures to be taken, they should be selected in such a way as to prevent damage, and thereby prevent victimization, rather than to compensate for the damage done.

Summa summarum, it seems that the institution of active repentance demonstrated before a crime is perpetrated should remain as it has been currently regulated by legislators, because it has a great role to perform in the present (retributive) legal model into which it has been incorporated. On the other hand, the restorative model—an extremely important and even indispensable model—should be pursued by means of different mechanisms.

Olga Sitarz, Leszek Wilk

Post-Perpetration Active Repentance and Restorative Justice

The question we will attempt to answer in the following chapter is whether active repentance that is expressed after the perpetration of a crime meets the assumptions underlying the restorative justice model both *de lege lata* and *de lege ferenda*. Please note, however, that the following chapter exclusively discusses general and military penal law as covered by the Criminal Code, whereas a different issue will be addressed in another part of this study: whether an institution extremely extensive and common in criminal fiscal law, namely active repentance following the perpetration of either a crime or a tax offence, might be considered in the context of restorative justice.

At this point, however, it is necessary to note that so-called "post-perpetration active repentance" is not defined in general terms: Polish lawmakers have offered the benefits of active repentance only in several cases precisely specified in the CrimC. The perpetrators of other crimes who have prevented the infringement of interests protected by law or who have redressed damage caused, are held liable under general provisions in light of which the court is to take into account the offender's manner of conduct after the perpetration of the crime (art. 53(2) CimC). Also, when even the lowest penalty stipulated for the crime in question would be incommensurate, the court might also apply extraordinary mitigation of penalty if the damage has been redressed (art. 60 para 2 item 1).

With respect to the terminological difficulties related to the term "active repentance" discussed in the previous chapter, it is essential to note at this point that post-perpetration active repentance, as defined by the lawmaker in a special part of the Code,[1] is conduct by the offender that prevents the occurrence of

---

1 Another significant problem is the possibility of applying regulations which refer to forms of pre-perpetration active repentance (art. 15(1) and art. 17(1)) to regulations that criminalize both preparation of a crime and attempts to perpetrate a crime (also known as preliminary crimes) and treat them as commission of a crime (regardless of the existence of a pertaining regulation the special part). In the Polish doctrine, there is no consent in this regard. More on that in: Z. Ciopinski, *Typizacja przygotowania*. Studia Iuridica, 10 (1982), p. 121-124; A. Liszewska in R. Dębski (ed.), *Nauka o przestępstwie. Zasady odpowiedzialności, System Prawa karnego. Tom 3* (Warszawa: C.H. Beck, 2013), p. 820-821.

damage or reduces it; lawmakers relate such conduct to particular mitigating consequences in criminal law (thus, the term does not cover any conduct by an offender occurring after perpetration of a crime that, in light of article 60 para 2 item 1 and 2 of the CrimC, might induce the court to apply extraordinary mitigation of penalty under general provisions).

Prior to analysing and evaluating regulations related to post-perpetration active repentance, it must be pointed out that active repentance is not homogeneous in nature, and that its forms on multiple occasions appear to have been established *ad casum*. The general pattern of these forms, however, is quite alike; the crucial dissimilarity between them, both in terms of their assumptions and their implications for criminal law, if justified, in fact boils down to the value of the offender conduct that amounts to active repentance related to the protection of a specified interest protected by law. All the types of active repentance analysed here are expressed after the perpetration of a prohibited act: after all the statutory elements of a crime, as defined in the CrimC, have been established. What is essential, however, for assessing the nature of active repentance is the lawmaker's decision of what to make the subject of criminalization: is it an infringement of a legal interest or a peril thereto? Hence, there is a distinction between active repentance expressed prior to the infringement of interest and after infringement of interest. To some degree, this distinction is a matter of agreement, as it is based on the notion of interests that are protected by law but are not easy to define precisely.[2] For example, the voluntary averting of an impeding

---

2   One can cope fairly well with the term "interest protected by law" if it is of physical nature, such as health and life. Therefore, in light of the Criminal Code, the common use of wrongs to health and life as illustrations for the theory of interests protected by law is not a matter of coincidence. Such interests are easy to evince and their infringement and causal relations are easy to determine. However, in addition to these, normatively defined individual interests, such as respect, can be easily understood as interests protected by law. For a long time, both community and universal interests that were violated in cases of high treason, espionage and corruption were considered interests protected by law. What has happened recently and made the phrase less clear is that both case law and literature keep naming new non-individual interests, such as "the institution of subsidy or credit," "the social use of insurance zone," "water, air, soil," etc. As illustrated by the above examples, the problem is mostly related to future-oriented sectors such as economy and environment protection. This ongoing process of forming new interests is possible because, as has been pointed out, no other basic phrase in criminal law offers such a diversity of unsubstantiated definitions as the concept of an "interest protected by law." Thus, "business," "values," "states," "assumptions," "objects," "social relations," "socially important areas," and "functional

danger to the life or health of a human being, after the offender has exposed that human being to that danger, might be used as an illustration of active repentance shown after perpetration of a crime but before the actual infringement of interest (article 160 CrimC), whereas voluntary redress in full for any damage after a crime against property (i.e. theft) has been committed (art. 295 of the CrimC) is an example of active repentance following both the perpetration of a crime and the infringement of the protected interest.

The above distinction has not allowed, however, the formation of homogenous types of active repentance. Within the type of active repentance which precedes the infringement of interest, there are not only subtypes aimed at preventing damage, but also functionally dissimilar subtypes aimed at supporting law enforcement authorities in detecting criminal offences (i.e. active repentance related to corruption offences). The second type of active repentance is, likewise, not homogenous in nature. There appear to be three subtypes whose formation is of substantial significance for the implementation of restorative justice postulates. The first subtype refers to active repentance forms demonstrated after infringement of interest but aimed at *preventing further essential damage* (active repentance related to evasion of alternative military service, art. 146, detention of hostage, art. 252(4) and (5); and desertion, art. 340). These forms are functionally related to post-perpetration but pre-infringement active repentance. The second subtype covers active repentance aimed at *facilitating the work of law enforcement authorities* (related to money laundering, art. 299(8)), and it is functionally related to active repentance in corruption offences. What constitutes the

---

beings" are mentioned in this context. Therefore, what constitutes an actual subject of legal protection in any case appears to be dependent on free mental speculation. This speculation, however, is supported by knowledge of criminal law theory, according to which each type of prohibited act must have a particular object to protect, a social interest to be protected by a specifically tailored regulation of law; otherwise criminal prohibition would be an empty norm, and it would be impossible for any specific criminal conduct to match its description. There arises a question, however, about the use of such a dematerialized, non-individual interest. For example, with regard to economy, what is the meaning of terms such as "an instrument to control economy by the state and to reach political and economic objectives," "the way the public is affected by effective support of economy by the state," "proper functioning of insurance institutions." More on that in: H. J. Hirsch, *W kwestii aktualnego stanu dyskusji o pojęciu dobra prawnego*, Ruch Prawniczy Ekonomiczny i Socjologiczny, 1 (2002), p. 1-19; M. Prengel, *Dobro prawne – centralne pojęcie prawa karnego*, Jurysta, 5 (2002), p. 5; W. Cieślak, *Niektóre zagadnienia przedmiotu prawnokarnej ochrony*, Państwo i Prawo, 11-12 (1993), p. 65.

third subtype are "standard" forms of active repentance aimed at *redressing the damage* (selected offences against property and business transactions, art. 295 para 1, art. 296 para 5, art. 297 para 3, art. 299 para 8, art. 307 CrimC).

All the above forms of active repentance, as far as their normative shapes are concerned, are characterized by identical constituent assumptions: material and personal requirements. There are material requirements such as desisting from certain activities, preventing certain consequences (damage),[3] and sometimes revealing the commission of a crime or redressing the damage. Without any doubt, these measures enable the avoidance of any further escalation of the conflict caused by commission of the crime, satisfy the needs of the wronged party as far as redress of damage is concerned, and in this sense they also serve some of the functions assigned to the program of restorative justice. Simultaneously, the offender's conduct after the perpetration of a crime is of essential importance to the authorities responsible for the detection and prosecution of crimes, if the bottom line is to reveal a crime and its circumstances. Colloquially, denunciation has rather a pejorative overtone. It is especially negative in the underworld, where the term is understood as betrayal.[4] Despite such negative connotations, denunciation might play, and actually does play, a role in combatting various crimes, such as organized crime, tax delinquency, and corruption. Thus, one can say that in some respects denunciation satisfies needs held by the community aggrieved by the crime, as denunciation might be perceived as a natural repayment of an outstanding debt to society as a whole rather than a specific wronged party.[5] Furthermore, as self-denunciation or pleading guilty to the commission

---

3 For doubts related to the assumption of preventing a specified consequence, see: Ł. Pohl, *Charakterystyka i prawnokarne konsekwencje czynnego żalu według art. 298 § 2 kodeksu karnego* in B. Janiszewski (ed.), *Nauka wobec współczesnych zagadnień prawa karnego w Polsce. Księga pamiątkowa ofiarowana Profesorowi Aleksandrowi Tobisowi* (Poznań: Wydawnictwo Poznańskie, 2004), p. 202-203.

4 D. Gajdus, *Czynny żal w polskim prawie karnym*, (Toruń: Wydawnictwo Uniwersytetu Mikołaja Kopernika 1984), p. 154 and the sources cited there.
Still, one cannot agree with this author that the introduction of "voluntariness" as a requisite of active repentance corresponding to denunciation, as proposed by D. Gajdus, will lead to the reduction of moral objections (p. 163).

5 Arguments about interpretation of the term "revealing" should be left aside. A brief review of doctrinal stances and court rulings on the subject has been made by J.Paśkiewicz, *Problematyka wybranych klauzul niepodlegania karze* in T. Bojarski, K. Nazar, A.Nowosad, M. Szwarczyk (eds.), *Zmiany w polskim prawie karnym po wejściu w życie Kodeksu karnego z 1997 roku* (Lublin: Wydawnictwo Uniwersytetu Marii Curie-Skłodowskiej, 2006), p. 68.

of a crime are sometimes required, these actions might be seen as the offender taking responsibility for his or her act, and might serve the purpose of his or her social rehabilitation. Some forms of post-perpetration active repentance also involve a time frame which, if not precisely formulated, might reduce the impact of the regulation (e.g. in art. 229(6): "prior to reporting to authorities"), and thus a different phrase to express the deadline, "prior to the first hearing in the case,"[6] has been proposed in the literature.

As far as the personal aspect is concerned, what is generally required is that the offender's conduct is voluntary, but the lawmaker does not always account for this condition, which is of paramount significance from the viewpoint of restorative justice.[7] Simultaneously, it should be noted that there is no reason for a different understanding of voluntariness as it relates to post-perpetration and pre-perpetration[8] active repentance. Therefore, it is appropriate to cite again the thesis of the Supreme Court that precisely captures the core concept of voluntariness while referring the reader to the previously discussed problem of voluntariness. As the Supreme Court has stated, voluntariness occurs if a person is aware of the possibility to perform a prohibited act[9] at the moment when he or she makes a conscious decision not to pursue his or her intended goals any further, doing so independently of any pressure from all external factors; or, let us add, voluntariness refers to a conscious and unaffected will to restore the state prior to the perpetration of the prohibited act.

Meeting these requisites renders to the offender a bonus of its own kind that is precisely specified in the regulations. In the case of post-perpetration active repentance, the lawmakers provide various "benefits" for the offender, from optional extraordinary mitigation of penalty to unconditional impunity. It should

---

6   K. Tkaczyk, *Instytucja czynnego żalu w prawie karnym w aspekcie prawnoporównaw-czym*, (Przemyśl: Wyższa Szkoła Prawa i Administracji, 2008), p. 238.

7   Voluntariness is not required for active repentance related to the interception of a vessel (art. 169(3) CrimC) or the detention of a hostage (art. 252).

8   J. Paskiewicz noticed some discrepancies concerning active repentance as it relates to money laundering when she argued that voluntariness is not the case if the offender divulges information out of fear of punishment. The authors have also claimed that there is no voluntariness in situations in which evidence collected within procedures instituted against the offender explicitly point to his or her guilt, and he or she is aware of this – J.Paśkiewicz, *Problematyka wybranych klauzul niepodlegania karze*, p. 64, 78.

9   The Supreme Court's Judgment of January 27, 1976, IV KR 322/75, unpublished, cited after: A. Stefański, *Dobrowolne odstąpienie od usiłowania*, Prokuratura i Prawo 4 (1996), p. 111.

also be noted that if a person is not liable for a penalty, instituting criminal proceedings is not allowed (and procedures that had already been instituted must be discontinued), whereas a decision to extraordinarily mitigate the penalty, and even refrain from imposing the penalty, is always made after the completion of court proceedings.

The crucial dissimilarity between the discussed types of active repentance boils down to functions attributed to each of them. Obviously, it should be repeated once again after D. Gajdus that active repentance serves the following functions: retributive, preventive, corrective, compensatory, and depenalising;[10] the function of supporting law enforcement authorities in crime detection might be also added. The function that is of leading importance, however, is determined by the type of active repentance.

Beyond all doubt, active repentance demonstrated prior to the infringement of interests protected by law predominantly serves the preventive function. The *ratio legis* of introducing regulations of the first type is to prevent damage. The lawmaker gives up (totally or partially) the *ius puniendi* even if the offender has already committed a crime as long as he or she has prevented the infringement of the legally protected interest. It should be emphasized now that this form of active repentance refers exclusively to the situation in which acts preparatory to the commission of crime, or more precisely, preparatory to the infringement of protected interests, become punishable as for perpetration of a crime. This includes predominantly concrete and abstract offences involving exposure to danger, with preparation and attempt being treated as commission or infringement of dematerialized interest (a concept so abstract that is sometimes referred to as "pre-infringement interest"). That is what causes post-perpetration but pre-infringement active repentance to functionally resemble stadial active repentance (as discussed in detail in the previous chapter of this study). Therefore, in this form also (as in active repentance expressed at the stage of punishable preparation or attempt), active repentance can potentially minimize primary victimization, prevent economic damage, minimize fear caused by commission of crime, and thereby prevent or greatly mitigate conflict. On multiple occasions, the wronged party might derive particular satisfaction from watching the conduct of the offender that is aimed at the prevention the damage. On the other hand, the offender's benefits from this form of active repentance are also obvious: there is no punishment (and consequently no stigmatization) or there is a chance to reduce the punishment, and above all there is an opportunity to

---

10 D.Gajdus, *Czynny żal w polskim prawie karnym*, p. 69.

avoid or to substantially minimalize the conflict with the wronged party. These benefits translate into advantages gained by the judicial administration system, such as the absence or substantial reduction of criminal proceedings, and advantages gained by society at large, in the form of absence or resolution of conflict and elimination or reduction of a sense of endangerment caused by commission of crime. There is another social benefit: the offender, independently of any pressure, takes responsibility for his or her act even prior to an institutionalized response, an act which is followed by successful (and almost immediate) social rehabilitation.[11] At this point, it is worth stressing that voluntariness of active repentance, even if it does not always equal sincere repentance, is still an expression of the offender's critical assessment of their own act and a partial acknowledgement of the blameworthy, socially unacceptable nature of that act. These features of active repentance lead to the unquestionable conclusion that active repentance demonstrated after the commission and prior to infringement of a legally protected interest is an institution aimed at the wronged party and at legal protection of the latter's interests.

Another form of active repentance consists in reporting the acceptance of or offering of a financial benefit. Regardless of the potential question of whether this form belongs to the type of active repentance that precedes the infringement of a legal interest or follows it, it is characterized by certain features that allow the creation of a *de facto* separate, third type. What makes this type distinct from the others is neither the absence of an individual wronged party (as both parties have entered the "transaction" on a voluntary basis) nor even the rather morally questionable obligation of denunciation, but the mere function of underlying regulations. Even though revealing corruption and its circumstances enables the prevention of a person holding a public office from making an unfair and partial decision, and thus prevents the occurrence of as of yet unspecified damage, still its primary objective is to support the law enforcement authorities. As argued by D. Gajdus, anticipated impunity is not a symptom of leniency towards a briber; it is merely a manner of turning such person into assistants in the prosecution of deeply immoral criminals.[12] These regulations are aimed at breaking solidarity between the person who offers and the person who accepts benefits, the same solidarity that effectively hinders the detection and prosecution of corruption. Therefore, this form of active repentance not only does not use the concept of individual wronged party, and

---

11 C.f. M. S. Umbreit after D. Wójcik, *Rola mediacji między pokrzywdzonym a sprawcą przestępstwa* in A. Marek (ed.), *Zagadnienia ogólne. System prawa karnego. Tom I* (Warszawa: C. H. Beck, 2010), p. 353.

12 D. Gajdus, *Czynny żal w polskim prawie karnym*, p. 153-154.

does not require prevention of infringement of his or her interest, but also, even in broader a sense, it serves neither the preventive nor the compensatory function. Active repentance related to money laundering (art. 299(8) CrimC) appears to be an example of this special type of "procedural" origin.[13]

Due to the same variation discussed above, active repentance expressed after the infringement of an interest protected by law also serves various functions. Thus, active repentance demonstrated after infringement of legal interest but aimed at preventing further essential damage (active repentance in detaining a hostage, art. 252(4) and (5)) is functionally close to post-perpetration but pre-infringement active repentance and primarily fulfils the *preventive function*. The second subtype is active repentance aimed at facilitating the work of law enforcement bodies (related to money laundering, art. 299(8)) and it is functionally related to active repentance in corruption offences. What constitutes the third subtype are "standard" forms of active repentance aimed at redressing damage (selected crimes against property and business transactions, art. 295(1), art. 296(5), art. 297(3), art. 299(8), art. 307 CrimC). This subtype of active repentance predominantly serves the compensatory function (in a standard, narrow understanding of this word)[14] or the restitutive function (in a broader sense): not until the condition to redress the damage is met or restitution of some other kind is available does the offender acquire specific rights. Thus, active repentance expressed after infringement of interests protected by law is also an institution oriented toward the wronged party, not by virtue of protection of the latter's interests, however, but by virtue of their restitution. It also seems that this form of active repentance might somehow serve the corrective function (unlike pre-infringement active repentance, as discussed earlier), by shaping the desired moral attitude in the offender.

The functions of particular forms of active repentance as envisaged by the lawmaker could be either strengthened or weakened through legislative measures. In reference to the aforementioned penal and legal consequences of active repentance expressed by the offender, there is a need to emphasize that optional benefits (extraordinary mitigation of penalty or refraining from imposition of

---

13 See for example J. Długosz in R. Zawłocki (ed.), *Przestępstwa przeciwko mieniu i gospodarcze. System Prawa Karnego. Tom 9* (Warszawa: C.H.Beck, 2011), p. 608.

14 A. R. Swiatlowski, *Kompensacyjna funkcja czynnego żalu w Kodeksie Karnym z 1997 r.* Czasopismo Prawa Karnego i Nauk Penalnych 2 (2002), p. 153. He does not share D. Gajdus's view that the compensatory function concurs with prevention of damage, because such a broad understanding of the compensatory function of active repentance obscures the difference between the compensatory and preventive functions.

penalty) make prevention less effective (as they might portray commission of a crime as rewarding, since the highest price to pay would be nothing other than the repair of the damage),[15] whereas they also bolster compensation and, above all, the rehabilitative impact. This relation is not symmetrical, since compulsory mitigation or exclusion of liability to penalty makes prevention more effective without weakening compensation, but surely it has negative effects on the corrective function. Furthermore, both personal and material requirements defined by the lawmaker might strengthen or weaken the predicted function of active repentance. Any additional material or personal requirement weakens the preventive or compensatory function, but if properly formulated such a requirement might boost the rehabilitative function. For example, a lack of voluntariness facilitates the decision to exercise active repentance; therefore, the opportunity to redress the damage is increased and the opportunity to rehabilitate the offender is decreased (thus, the exceptional waiver of voluntariness is allowed). This finding gives rise de lege ferenda to the selection of both the requisites of active repentance and its criminal law consequences so as to enable the selected models of active repentance to fully serve their predicted functions. In other words, so as to cause the normative shape of active repentance expressed prior to the infringement of a legal interest to serve the preventive function, and to cause active repentance shown after infringement of a legal interest to serve the compensatory function.

It should next be considered whether post-perpetration active repentance might be placed within the system of restorative justice instruments, and whether post-perpetration active repentance

> allows for the avoidance of the further escalation of conflict, facilitates the prompt transformation of the offender into a member of society again, fulfils the needs of the wronged party, restores the meaning of socially important values, successfully teaches the society about binding norms and values, and provides procedures in case of violation of binding rules.[16]

Based on the above analysis, the conclusion might be reached that post perpetration, but pre-infringement (i.e., before the infringement of interests protected by law) active repentance cannot be an instrument of restorative justice for the reasons identical to the ones indicated with regard to stadial active repentance.

---

15 K. Tkaczyk, *Instytucja czynnego żalu w prawie karnym w aspekcie prawnoporównawczym*, p. 243, and first of all D. Gajdus, *Czynny zal w polskim prawie karnym*, p. 159.

16 M. Płatek in M. Płatek, M. Fajst (eds), *Sprawiedliwość naprawcza. Idea. Teoria. Praktyka* (Warszawa: Liber, 2005), p. 95.

At the heart of the issue, there is no room for the process of resolving the conflict between the offender, the wronged party, and the society once the imposition of penalty is unconditionally refrained from. And even in a case where forms of pre-infringement active repentance from the special part of the Criminal Code are different from the model of pre-perpetration active repentance that is related to preparation and attempt of crime (especially with regard to the type and nature of criminal law consequences), there is a need to postulate that these forms should resemble stadial active repentance as much as possible (for example through the introduction of unconditional impunity), since stadial active repentance has been the best model in service of the preventive function. Thus, even from the viewpoint of the wronged party, successful prevention is a better solution than compensation. A similar finding should be applied to post-perpetration and post-infringement active repentance that is nevertheless aimed at preventing the infringement of another interest (e.g., the voluntary release of a hostage). In such a situation, the particular preventive nature of this solution dictates the omission of the postulates of restorative justice.

As the additional type of active repentance related to corruption and money laundering has been delimited, this type should also be analysed from the viewpoint of aims set by restorative justice. As previously established, the *ratio legis* of such solutions is to support law enforcement, and therefore fulfilment of the preventive and compensative functions, as they are traditionally understood, is hard to imagine. Obviously, it might be assumed that cooperating with law enforcing authorities to a certain degree certifies the offender's assumption of responsibility for the prohibited act and signals a rehabilitation of its own kind, but these forms of active repentance are predominantly determined by the procedural objective assumed by the lawmaker, and there is no room for restorative justice either *de lege lata* or *de lege ferenda*.

There is no doubt that active repentance expressed after the infringement of an interest protected by law and related to redressing the damage is deeply compensatory in nature; however, this does not automatically mean that it fulfils the assumptions of restorative justice. Instead, several issues should be discussed. First, there arises the question of whether perpetrators of crimes without individual victims can take part in restorative justice (*de lege lata* such offences are against neither a local community, the state, the justice system, nor a defensive power). Without any doubt, mediation in such cases must be ruled out for obvious reasons (although restorative conferencing cannot be). Furthermore, the requirement of voluntariness does not, *de lege lata*, mean a morally positive attitude in the form of active repentance; plus, such voluntariness is, *de lege lata*, not always required. Simultaneously, it should be noted that additional, occasionally required substantive conditions that enable mitigation or reduction of punishment, such as denunciation, do not obscure the rehabilitative model, although denunciation is still ethically and morally questionable. On the other hand, the previously discussed statutory deadlines for expressing active repentance, for example, by the time of reporting to law enforcement authorities, by the commencement of legal procedure, and by the time of entry of judgment, might obstruct the restorative process for no valid reason. Also, it should be noted that references to the notion of damage in the current provisions, in combination with the problem of understanding the scope of this term, make the institution of active repentance a weaker instrument of restorative justice (a thief must redress damage in full to embrace the benevolence of extraordinary mitigation of penalty, and he or she has no certainty about what the term denotes). What seems especially significant, however, is that the position of the wronged party on whether his or her expectations have been met is of no legal relevance in any form of post-infringement active repentance.[17]

Simultaneously, it should be stressed that consequences set out by criminal law, wherever they are either optional or compulsory, but where they exclusively refer to extraordinary mitigation of penalty, create a genuine opportunity to apply the process of conflict resolution (there are no formal obstacles to criminal procedures, including mediation) and to meet thereby the needs of both the wronged party and the offender. This opportunity, however, is not derived from active repentance itself; rather it is merely possible to state that the specified legal consequences of active repentance do not make such a resolution impossible (since the process is not concluded).

There also arises the question of whether the list of forms of post-perpetration active repentance, especially post-infringement active repentance as the one that exclusively suits the principles of restorative justice, is not too short (in the first place, the "special" form of active repentance related to all offences against property and business transactions appears to be missing, as well as the form of active repentance related to traffic offences, and to other sectors), especially in the light of postulates that restorative justice should be general in nature and available to all.

In reaching a conclusion, it should be repeated that active repentance expressed before perpetration (stadial) and after perpetration but before actual

---

17 A.R. Światłowski without any doubt considers the position of the wronged party in this respect non-binding on the court – A.R.Światłowski, *Kompensacyjna funkcja czynnego żalu w Kodeksie karnym z 1997 r.*, p. 161.

infringement of any tangible interest, as they are functionally the same, from the viewpoint of restorative justice, means forgiveness expressed by the state without verifying whether the wronged party is satisfied or whether the conflict is extinguished (and in relation to active repentance shown by the offender who cooperates with authorities during the stage of preparation, even if the damage occurs). This signifies that, despite its tremendous significance to the wronged party, the institution of active repentance cannot be *de lege lata* perceived as a strand of restorative justice. It is missing constituent elements of restorative justice, making it impossible to consider this form of active repentance an instrument thereof.[18]

Without any doubt, post-perpetration and post-damage active repentance *de lege lata* fits more easily into the framework of restorative justice.[19] Moreover, post-perpetration active repentance that would start (rather than close) the process of conflict resolution in the system of Polish penal law could also, facing impunity as an alternative, make the offender less likely to deny commission of the prohibited act and allow him or her to maintain a civilized interaction with the wronged party or even to restore a previous relationship (in light of the principle that "penalty is an enemy of truth").[20] However, what makes this form of active repentance *de lege lata* an effective one from the viewpoint of restorative justice is that it does not exclude the latter: it opens the door to the process of resolving the conflict. In order to briefly formulate the postulates *de lege ferenda* (as they make a separate, extensive issue), it is necessary to note that the model of post-damage active repentance in accordance with the concept of restorative justice would have to stem from a morally positive attitude, without imposing excessively burdensome time frames, and would have to be a component of a conflict resolution process in which the position of the wronged party is considered. It seems that for this form of active repentance there is a place both in the traditional, standard, retributive criminal law and the penal law of the new paradigm, as an alternative for the former. It is also worth stressing that, irrespective of findings in another part of this study, this form of active repentance is of much stronger compensatory impact than the obligation to redress the

---

18 This problem is discussed in detail in the section on stadial active repentance.
19 See W. Zalewski, *Sprawiedliwość naprawcza. Początek ewolucji polskiego prawa karnego?* (Gdańsk: Arche, 2006), pp. 286-287.
20 Therefore, to optimize this outcome, M. Wright suggests giving victim the opportunity to go to a mediation centre instead of the police. M. Wright, *Naprawa krzywd w społeczeństwie czy sprawiedliwość przyszłości?* Mediator, 4 (2005), p. 18, 25.

damage imposed on the offender. The introduction of potential new forms of active repentance must be also considered.[21]

In the end, one can only point out that all the controversies about regulations related to post-perpetration[22] active repentance that are present in the doctrine undoubtedly lessen the impact of these rules. Since the regulations are of an exceptional nature, their ineffectiveness strongly impacts both the wronged party and the offender.

---

21 We cannot share the view of J. Paśkiewicz, who underlines that new, subsequent clauses of impunity may be introduced only if such introduction is justified by suitable empirical research on the frequency of the application of certain provisions regulating instances in which an offender is exempt from a penalty. J. Paśkiewicz, *Problematyka wybranych klauzul niepodlegania karze* in T. Bojarski, K. Nazar, A. Nowosad, M. Szwarczyk (eds.), *Zmiany w polskim prawie karnym po wejściu w życie Kodeksu karnego z 1997 roku*, p. 80.

22 See for example: B. Michalski, *Przestępstwa przeciwko mieniu. Rozdział XXXV Kodeksu karnego. Komentarz* (Warszawa: C.H.Beck, 1999), p. 308; A. R. Światłowski, *Kompensacyjna funkcja czynnego żalu w Kodeksie karnym z 1997 r.*, p. 156-162; Ł. Pohl, *Charakterystyka i prawnokarne konsekwencje czynnego żalu według art. 298 § 2 kodeksu karnego* in B. Janiszewski (ed.), *Nauka wobec współczesnych zagadnień prawa karnego w Polsce. Księga pamiątkowa ofiarowana Profesorowi Aleksandrowi Tobisowi*; J.Paśkiewicz, *Problematyka wybranych klauzul niepodlegania karze* in T. Bojarski, K. Nazar, A. Nowosad, M. Szwarczyk (eds.), *Zmiany w polskim prawie karnym po wejściu w życie Kodeksu karnego z 1997 roku*, Lublin 2006, *passim*; R. Zawłocki, *Naprawienie szkody jako podstawa uchylenia albo złagodzenia karania za przestępstwa gospodarcze* in Z. Ćwiąkalski, G. Arytmiak (eds.), *Karnomaterialne i procesowe aspekty naprawienia szkody w świetle kodyfikacji karnych z 1997 r. i propozycji ich zmian*, (Warszawa: Zakamycze, 2010), p. 156-166.

Anna Jaworska-Wieloch

Selected Aspects of Enforcement of Judicial Decisions Awarding Redress of a Damage

Although conflict caused by criminal behaviour should ideally be resolved in the course of fact-finding proceedings, the court's freedom to enforce a settlement or another type of agreement between the wronged party and the offender, in combination with the likelihood that the terms agreed upon are implemented only after the judgment becomes final, may postpone the moment of conflict dissolution to the stage of executive proceedings. At this stage, realising the principles of restorative justice is more difficult since the role of criminal executive law is to ensure the enforcement of the final judgment with all its components, both those agreed upon under a settlement and those originating from the court. It is important also for the reason that legal provisions envisage uniform consequences or their absence in the event of the non-performance of specific duties imposed on the convict, regardless of the grounds of their inclusion in the criminal judgment. In the same way, the executive court's area of interest merely covers the execution of judgment. As far as the settlement between the wronged party and the offender is concerned, the court ought generally to supervise its performance. However, where accord has not been enforced by the court on the merits, its realisation will fall outside the scope of executive proceedings. The limited range of this procedure triggers a focus on the possibility of supervising verdicts requiring the redress of damage, although one has to remember that the resolution of conflicts spawned by crime may require other types of behaviour on the part of the convict, as well as changes to the living situation of the convict or the wronged party, and on the notion of attempting to reach agreement at the stage of executive proceedings.

The offender's failure to repair the damage inflicted by his or her crime does not necessarily imply a will to breach the agreement concluded previously with the wronged party. The same result may as well follow from objective reasons unintended by the convict (for example, termination of employment, health impairment). It is safe to assume that due presentation of his or her life situation to the wronged party might have an alleviating impact on the conflict originated by criminal offence, or at least prevent its exacerbation despite a delay in the reparation of damage. Even if the need to enforce the judgment prevents the following in executive proceedings of the principle of equality of arms vested in the wronged party and the offender and the full observation of their agreement, recognizing the wronged party's role at this stage is also a clear asset. In consequence, it should be deemed alarming that executive provisions have been shaped so as to minimise his or her position. The wronged party is no longer a party to the proceedings; he or she may neither submit motions nor challenge the court's decisions. Apart from strictly delimited situations,[1] he or she is not instructed about the course of execution. Not only has the wronged party been removed from the centre of attention, in fact he or she has been ousted entirely from the proceeding. This creates negative consequences not only for the wronged party as such, and for his or her sense of injustice deriving from the crime, but also for the course of proceedings, since no activeness is expected of the wronged party, even with regard to the demands for remedying the damage. The wronged party is under no obligation to inform the court even about such rudimentary information as a change in place of residence. Often, this brings about far reaching problems for a convict who wants to redress the damage but does not know how to achieve that end.[2] As a result, one may argue for de lege ferenda the strengthening of the wronged party's position so that the latter could become a party to the proceeding, which could have positive consequences to the process of extinguishing the conflict caused by the offence, and could also increase efficiency of executive proceedings with respect to its controlling function.

Bearing in mind the fact that the stage of executive proceedings cannot fully respect agreements made between the convict and the wronged party, one should consider the role attributable to the court from the perspective of restorative justice. The aim of the system of judicial administration is to guarantee the execution of a final judgment, and also the reparation of damage. In the phase of proceedings analysed, the reason for including the resolution on the repair of damage (i.e., whether it follows from an agreement between the parties) is of little importance. The court should supervise the redress, even if this obligation does not involve enforcing the settlement. Indemnification will always have great value, even when it results from a decision made ex officio, without actual

---

1   Some rights have been envisaged, e.g., in art. 168a EPC.

2   Filing a motion to the executive division of a court to receive the contact information of the wronged party appears to be the best solution in such a case; if the contact data turns out to be out of date, the only solution is to deposit the object of redress with the court in accordance with Art. 467(1) of the Civil Code: (*Apart fom the cases defined in other provisions, the debtor may deposit the object of redress with the court if, due to circumstances he is not responsible for, he does not know who the creditor is or he does not know the place of residence or the seat of the creditor.*)

concord between the parties (although this manner of conflict resolution is always most desired). A redress of damage which does not stem from this agreement is not merely confined to compensation. It may lead to the extinguishing of conflict between parties, which seems crucial from the point of view of restorative justice.

An analysis of the provisions on executive proceedings which confer on the court supervisory functions over the verdict stipulating repair of damage necessitates references to the diverse legal bases of judicial rulings imposing such duties, because the criminal law consequences of these verdicts are not the same. Ideally, all convicts should strive for redress of damage on their own initiative; however, their readiness in this respect may be determined by the consequences pending in the event of non-compliance with the obligation. A properly framed model of executive proceedings should be aimed at encouraging the convict to satisfy the wronged party's needs and providing the court with due control mechanisms so as to extinguish the conflict caused by criminal offence.

Problems with the execution of compensation awarded under art. 415 CCP

Damages awarded in a civil action within criminal proceedings may derive from an agreement between the parties, since the wronged party may seek this form of indemnification (for instance, due to the possibility of adjudging interests). Compensation awarded in criminal proceedings does not forfeit its civil law character, with all its advantages and disadvantages. The satisfaction of the wronged party is conduced by preserving the possibility to commence coercive execution right up to the date of limiting the execution of the claim, that is for a period of 10 years from the day on which the judgment became final and binding (art. 125(1) CivC).[3] In addition, the lapse of the limitation period may be interrupted if the creditor applies for an execution clause or for the institution of executive proceedings.[4] The court's resolution in this respect is enforceable on

---

3 *Art. 125(1) CivC: A claim ascertained by the final judgment of a court or of any other authority entrusted with the adjudication of particular actions or by an award given by arbitrators, as well as a claim recognized by a settlement concluded before a court or before arbitrators or a settlement concluded before a mediator and confirmed by the court, shall be statutorily barred after ten years even if the period of limitation for such claims is shorter.*

4 See A. Jedliński in A. Kidyba (eds.), *Kodeks cywilny. Komentarz lex* (Warszawa, 2012), p. 768.

the date when the judgment becomes final and binding, which seems beneficial to the efficiency of efforts to redress the damage as well as to the extinguishing of conflict caused by crime.

The convict's readiness to repair the damage is not bolstered by threatening criminal consequences in the event of the wronged party's non-satisfaction, since the penal law system does not provide for any sanctions in the event of failure to redress damage, regardless of the penalty imposed. Even in the case of an award of a probative measure, there are no legal grounds for unsuccessful termination of probation, just as there are no respective provisions explicitly specifying reasons for resuming criminal process or execution of penalty.[5]

This solution adopted by the lawmaker should not be evaluated negatively, since the pursuance of compensation in criminal proceedings or the award of damages ex officio does not change the character of this provision, which makes an exclusively civil law claim. Art. 415 CCP is there only to keep from having to participate in two judicial proceedings rather than turn the claim into a specific criminal law remedy. In consequence, compensation awarded in criminal proceedings does not constitute an element of penal law reaction to the crime that has been committed, and authorities carrying on investigations may not interfere in the performance of the adjudged provision. As a result, this solution does not vest any controlling functions in the court, leaving compliance with the duty to compensate outside the scope of interest of criminal law. If the wronged party strives for such indemnification deliberately, he or she ought to be aware of the necessity to independently seek the execution of the awarded compensation if the convict neglects his or her compensatory duty.

Performing of the duty to redress damage, awarded as punitive measure

For the court, the prospect of realising controlling functions at the stage of executing the punitive measure of the duty to redress damage could be a source of serious doubts. At the beginning, it ought to be pointed out, however, that although no provision provides directly for the moment of enforceability of this punitive measure, doctrinal writers have accepted that its penal law character, its lack of any requirement to hear the accused's opinion before its imposition, and, consequently, the insignificance of the latter's views as to the legitimacy of the awarded measure enable the conclusion that in accordance with art. 9(2)

---

5 Such was the position of the SC in the judgment of 01 April 2011, III KK 58/11, OSNKW 2011/8/70, p. 36.

EPC[6] it becomes enforceable at the moment when the court judgment becomes final and binding.[7] This thesis seems all the more legitimate since, under art. 196(1) EPC,[8] the judgment is enforceable with regard to the redress order on the date of its validation (becoming final and binding). This judgment makes up an execution title regarding compensation. As a result, it is unnecessary to appoint the deadline to carry out this punitive measure.[9] One of the consequences of this rendition of the time of enforceability is the possibility for the wronged party to claim the interests accrued after the date when the ruling has become final and binding, as this is the very moment at which the claim becomes due. Such a solution favours the interests of the wronged party, which gains the right to claim interests quite quickly. However, one may as well question the justice of the convict's obligation to repair damage already at the time when the judgment becomes final and binding, since failure to meet the deadline may result not only in negative civil law effects (higher interests) but also criminal law consequences. *De lege ferenda*, it seems recommendable to assign a more realistic deadline for reparation of damage, so as to level the positions of convicts obligated to redress damage under both the awarded punitive measure and the probation requisite.[10]

Court competences with regard to control of the duty to repair damage have been made dependent on the penalty imposed. Where a punitive measure has been adjudged as an independent response to the offence (yet the court refrains from imposing a penalty or mitigates it extraordinarily), or where it comes in conjunction with an independent fine or unsuspended imprisonment, the court has no possibility to impose negative consequences on a convict who is defiant of the adjudged punitive measure, and, correspondingly, it is futile to take any controlling measures in this respect.

---

6   *The judgment and orders delivered under art. 420 CCP are enforceable upon their validation unless a statutory provision provides otherwise* (art. 9(2) EPC).

7   M. Siwek, "Glosa do wyroku Sądu Apelacyjnego w Lublinie z dnia 27 września 2000 r., II AKa 180/00," *Palestra* 7-8 (2003), p. 260.

8   *In the event of adjudication of the duty to compensate economic or non-economic loss, vindictive damages or monetary provision to a person who did not participate in the process, the court shall, ex officio and without charging any fees, send the execution title to the wronged person or other entitled party* (art. 196(1) EPC).

9   Such was the opinion of the Court of Appeal in Katowice in the judgment of 21 December 2000, II AKa 338/00, Prok. i Pr. - wkł. 2001/10/20, p. 12.

10 If the convict is obligated to redress the damage in the form of probative measure, the court sets the deadline for redressing the damage, upon which the obligation becomes chargeable – for more see subsection 4 of the present chapter.

This solution should not be considered correct. While in the case of unsuspended imprisonment, especially long-term sentences, the chances of repairing the damage are small, in the event of imposing this punitive measure as an independent reaction to the offence or an element accompanying independent fine, the legal system should envisage instruments inducing offenders to redress the damage. It might be objected that the absence of such consequences results from the civil law character of the relevant measure, yet one should not neglect the fact that in the case of penalties other than the ones indicated above (as pointed out below), the law prescribes such criminal consequences. Moreover, since the obligation to repair damage has been built into the system of penal measures, it would be unwise to accept the awarded punitive measure completely without any negative effects for non-compliance. This resolution not only attenuates the functions of penal measures but also cannot be said to promote the realisation of principles of restorative justice, since the court has no controlling power in this respect, and the convict is not incited to redress damage by any legal instruments which might increase the wronged party's chances for satisfaction.

In the case of the imposition of penalties other the one indicated above and the duty to redress damage, the court should remain in control of their execution since it is so significant for the applicability of other legal institutions. Should the offender be sentenced to restriction of liberty, redress of damage will be of essence in the event of his or her release from the rest of the penalty under art. 83 CrimC[11] (the requisite for applying this institution is fulfilment of the imposed punitive measures). Reparation of damage, however, is of no relevance to the potential imposition of imprisonment as a replacement penalty, as art. 65(1) EPC[12] does not provide, among prerequisites for its adjudication, evasion of the awarded punitive measures. Even though this solution might seem inaccurate and *de lege ferenda* calls for legislative reform, in the present statutory framework any interpretation to the contrary seems illegitimate because this provision alone

---

11 Art. 83 CrimC: *A person sentenced to the penalty of restriction of liberty who has completed at least half of the adjudged sentence, observed the legal order and diligently performed the work ordered by the court, and has also fulfilled the obligations imposed on him, may be relieved by the court from the rest of the penalty, as if it were fully served.*

12 Art. 65(1) EPC: *If the convict evades service of the penalty of restriction of liberty or other obligations imposed, the court shall order the execution of substitutive penalty of imprisonment. If the convict has already served some part of the penalty of restriction of liberty, the court shall order the execution of a substitutive penalty of imprisonment for the reminder of the sentence, ordering one day of substitutive penalty of imprisonment for every two days of restriction of liberty.*

regulates grounds for imposition of a replacement penalty, and comparisons of its content with legal rules governing, inter alia, the resumption of criminal proceedings or the ordering of the execution of a previously suspended sentence clearly indicate its dissimilarity in this regard. As a consequence, ordering the execution of imprisonment as a result of evading the awarded punitive measure would amount to inadmissible application of law *per analogiam* to the detriment of the convict.

In the case of conditional discontinuance of criminal proceedings or conditional suspension of the execution of a sentence, evading the adjudged punitive measures constitutes a premise for negative termination of probation (art. 68(2) CrimC,[13] art. 75(2) CrimC[14]); for this reason the court is obliged during the period of probation and in the subsequent six months to make sure the offender has repaired the damage, and if not, it is necessary to ascertain if this was a result of evasion of the awarded punitive measure (if the convict demonstrated bad will in this respect, or in other words if he or she could have redressed the damage but was unwilling to do so).

Under art. 46(1) CrimC,[15] civil law provisions on the limitation of claims and the possibility of awarding annuity do not apply to the duty to redress damage. The introduction of this regulation in the CrimC was justified by shorter limitation periods in civil law than in criminal law concerning the punishability of offences.[16] Although at the time of entry into force of the CrimC of 1997, this argument was legitimate, as the Civil Code limitation period for claims arising out of felonies and misdemeanours was 10 years old (art. 442(2) CivC), it may not be overlooked that as of 10 August 2007 the lawmaker introduced art. 442[1] to the Civil Code, whose paragraph (2) prescribes a twenty-year limitation period

---

13 *Art. 68(2) CrimC: The court may resume criminal proceedings if during the probation period the perpetrator flagrantly infringes the legal order, and in particular if he commits an offence other than that specified in paragraph (1), if he evades supervision, does not perform the obligations or penal measures imposed, or if he does not fulfil the settlement concluded with the wronged party.*

14 *Art. 75(2) CrimC: The court may order execution of the penalty if the convict flagrantly infringes the legal order, and in particular if he commits an offence other than that specified in paragraph (1) or if he evades payment of the fine, evades supervision, performance of the duties or penal measures imposed.*

15 *Art. 46(1) CrimC: In the event of conviction, the court may, on a motion by the wronged party or another entitled person, impose the obligation to redress the damage caused by the offense in whole or in part or to compensate for the harm inflicted; the provisions of civil law on statute of limitation of claims shall not apply.*

16 *Nowe kodeksy karne - z 1997 r. z uzasadnieniami* (Warszawa 1997r.), p. 148.

for felonies and misdemeanours.[17] This should not, however, render pointless the exemption under art. 46(1) CrimC of civil law provisions on limitation. In the literature of the field, it has been underlined that this model of regulation is a manifestation of the penal character of the measure which separates it from the basic assumptions of civil law, such as limitation of claims.[18] Since the measure qualifies as criminal a law response to a punishable act, the admissibility of its adjudication ought to be correlated to the limitation of punishability.[19] Even in accepting this argumentation, it is worth noticing that as a consequence, the whole Title VI of Book I of the Civil Code is not applicable to the duty to redress damage. This makes it impossible to allow limitation only by the plea of the defendant or to determine rules concerning the start, suspension, and interruption of the limitation period.[20] This raises doubts as to advantages gained by such a regulation to the interests of the wronged party, who may avail of a broad scope of possibilities in civil proceedings.[21] Even though such an exemption seems necessary, bearing in mind the need to jointly treat the punitive measure (which constitutes a response to the crime) and the execution of the criminal judgment (which shapes the penal liability of the offender), it nevertheless must be considered incongruous with the character of restitution in the context of impeding conceivable satisfaction to the wronged party and placing the latter in the course

---

17 Art. 442¹(2) CivC: If the damage is caused by a felony or misdemeanour, the claim to redress the damage is subject to limitation upon expiry of 20 years since the date of commission of the crime regardless of when the wronged party learned about the damage and the person obligated to redress it.

18 Jerzy Lachowski, Tomasz Oczkowski, ‚Obowiązek naprawienia szkody jako środek karny', Prokuratura i Prawo 9 (2007), p. 42-43.

19 Z. Gostyński, Obowiązek naprawienia szkody w nowym ustawodawstwie karnym (Kraków 1999), p. 224.

20 M. Łukasiewicz, A. Ostapa, ‚Nawiązka i karnoprawny obowiązek naprawienia szkody a roszczenie cywilnoprawne', Prokuratura i Prawo 2 (2002), p. 75; A. Muszyńska, Naprawienie szkody wyrządzonej przestępstwem, Warszawa 2010, p. 401-402; a contrary position has been presented by Z. Gostyński, in whose judgement the exemption of provisions on the statute of limitation of art. 46(1) CrimC is addressed solely to a criminal court, which means that, e.g., rules on interruption of the limitation period are not irrelevant [see Z. Gostyński, Obowiązek naprawienia szkody w prawie karnym, p. 171-172].

21 The limitation period prescribed for an awarded claim may be interrupted by any action before court or another authority resolving disputes or executing claims of a given type taken directly in order to assert, ascertain or secure the claim, which bars limitation of the claim's execution.

of executive proceedings in a worse situation than would be the case in civil proceedings.

The above conclusion should serve as introduction to further investigations regarding issues related to the enforceability of the duty to repair damage in the event of conviction. This problem grows in significance in the light of art. 76(2) CrimC[22] and art. 107(6) CrimC,[23] which leads to the clear conclusion that non-performance of the duty to redress damage does not bar erasure of the corresponding entry in the register of penalties.[24] If this is so, what happens to the awarded punitive measure in the event of the erasure of that entry and the legal cancellation of the criminal judgment? Most doctrinal authors assume that non-performance of the duty to repair damage is to be considered independent of erasure of the entry in the register of penalties, since the execution of the imposed measure may be effected on such occasions under civil law procedures, without criminal law consequences.[25] Such statements must arouse serious doubts such as:

1) there is not a single legal provision that could be considered a basis for trans-forming the awarded criminal measure into a civil law obligation;[26]
2) it would not be clear how long the punitive measure would retain enforce-ability, since civil law provisions on the limitation of claims have been exempt with regard to its execution;
3) a criminal judgment creating the obligation to redress damage is constitutive in character, whereas civil court judgments are declaratory, and this distinction cor-responds to the consequences of limitation and the execution of the adjudicated

---

22 *Art. 76(2) CrimC: If a fine or a penal measure is imposed upon the convict, erasure from the register of penalties may not occur before the execution, remission or limitation thereof; this shall not apply to the punitive measure specified in Art. 39(5).*

23 *107(6) CrimC: If a punitive measure was imposed on the convict, erasure from the register of penalties may not occur before its execution, remission or limitation, subject to Art. 76(2).*

24 As in A. Wąsek in O. Górniok (ed.), *Kodeks karny. Komentarz* (Gdańsk 2005), p. 770; A. Marek, *Kodeks karny. Komentarz*, Warszawa 2006, p. 241; M. Mozgawa, *Kodeks karny. Praktyczny komentarz* (Warszawa 2010), p. 224.

25 As in M. Kalitowski in O. Górniok (ed.), *Kodeks karny. Komentarz* (Gdańsk 2005), p. 652; A. Marek, *Kodeks karny. Komentarz*, p. 193; A. Muszyńska, *Naprawienie szkody wyrządzonej przestępstwem*, p. 389; A. Zoll in A. Zoll (ed.) *Kodeks karny. Część ogólna. Komentarz Lex* (Warszawa 2012), p. 980; G. Łabuda in J. Giezek (ed.) *Kodeks karny. Część ogólna. Komentarz* (Warszawa 2012), p. 517.

26 See M. Łukasiewicz, A. Ostapa, ,Nawiązka i karnoprawny obowiązek naprawienia szkody a roszczenie cywilnoprawne', *Prokuratura i Prawo* 2 (2002), p. 77.

claims, inasmuch as limitation periods in criminal law are fixed and may not be prolonged. Upon the limitation of enforceability of specific resolutions, one is not in a position to claim their implementation. Limitation of enforceability of civil law rulings causes a mere transformation of the obligations ascertained in these decisions into non-actionable obligations which continue to hold;[27]

4) in the case of the erasure of an entry in the register of penalties, the adjudged duty to redress damage loses its raison d'être, since a punitive measure was imposed in the convicting judgment which has been declared non-existent (art. 106 CrimC).[28]

The problems depicted above relating to the execution of the punitive measure that governs the redress of damage clearly point to the fulfilment of restorative justice postulations at this stage. In the first place, it must be stated that consequences threatening the convict for evading performance of the imposed punitive measure are heterogeneous and dependent on the penalty imposed on him or her. Sometimes they are none, which in actuality negates the desirability of awarding the duty to redress damage as a punitive measure. Even though a model convict ought to make efforts to repair the damage inflicted by criminal offence without any external stimuli, the legislator should consider introducing into penal executive law uniform consequences for evasion of judicial decision in this respect, since one of the reasons behind the inclusion of damage repair in the system of penal measures was to enable law-enforcing authorities to induce the convict to compensate the loss. Such a resolution would enable to a fuller extent an account of the interests of the wronged party, and it would give the courts controlling functions, which would increase the likelihood of the judgment being enforced in its entirety. Another problem counteracting the realisation of the idea of restorative justice is the threat of the awarded duty being cancelled relatively fast (such is the case in the event of erasure of entry in the register of penalties). This solution does not favour the resolution of conflict caused by the crime, as it places the wronged party in a difficult situation. Although the legislative framework is of no significance to a convict who, irrespective of the judicial ruling, wishes to compensate

27 M. Łukasiewicz, A. Ostapa, ,Obowiązek naprawienia szkody - wybrane zagadnienia', *Prokuratura i Prawo* 9 (2001), p. 58.

28 Similar opinion is presented by M. Łukasiewicz, A. Ostapa, ,Nawiązka i karnoprawny obowiązek naprawienia szkody a roszczenie cywilnoprawne', *Prokuratura i Prawo* 2 (2002), p. 76.

Art. 106 CrimC: From the moment of erasure of entry in the register of penalties, the sentence is considered non-existent; the penalty is deleted from the register of convicts.

the damage anyway, the awareness that legal consequences for failure to redress are missing may hinder the convict's willingness. As a result, the introduction in the CrimC of the duty to repair damage as a punitive measure fulfils neither its compensatory function (since the wronged party is in fact put in a worse position than would be the case in civil proceedings) nor penal functions attributable to punitive measures (despite the existence of an award of the duty to repair damage on behalf of the state as a consequence of the committed crime, its execution falls outside the scope of the competence of public authorities, and proceeds without supervision of the criminal court, at the expense of the wronged party).[29]

The execution of the duty to redress damage, as awarded along with the penalty of restriction of liberty

The problems that arise from the execution of the duty to redress damage frame executive proceedings differently when this duty is imposed in conjunction with the penalty of restriction of liberty. In particular,

1) art. 61(1) EPC[30] provides for the possibility of obligating the convict to repair damage during the whole period of the execution of the penalty of restriction of liberty (as regards other verdicts, it is not possible to adjudge at the stage of execution the duty to redress);[31]
2) art. 61(1) EPC does not preclude *expressis verbis* the release of the convict in the course of the execution of restriction of liberty from the imposed duty to redress damage (rules governing other institutions provide for such a prohibition).[32]

---

29 A. Marek, T. Oczkowski in M. Melezini (ed.) *System prawa karnego. Kary i środki karne. Poddanie sprawcy próbie* (Warszawa 2010), p. 721; see also S. Waltoś, „Od fikcji do sensownego unormowania kompensacji szkody w procesie karnym" (supplemented voice in the penal discussion)', *Czasopismo Prawa Karnego i Nauk Penalnych* 2 (2002), p. 182.

30 *Art. 61(1) EPC: If it serves educational objectives, the court may, during the service of imprisonment, set, extend or amend the obligations specified in Art. 36(2) of the Criminal Code or relieve the convict from such obligations.*

31 With regard to conditional discontinuance of proceedings, conditional suspension of sentence and release on parole, the legislator has expressly precluded this option (art. 67(4) CrimC in conjunction with art. 74 CrimC, art. 74 CrimC, art. 163(2) EPC); it is obvious that a punitive measure or compensation in criminal proceedings may not be awarded in the executive stage.

32 In reference to conditional discontinuance of proceedings, conditional suspension of penalty and release on parole, the lawmaker clearly proscribed such a possibility (Art. 67(4) CrimC in relation to Art. 74 CrimC, Art. 74, Art. 163(2) PEPC), yet there

Unlike in the case of probative requisites, the wording of art. 61(1) EPC is not conclusive about whether in reality during execution of the penalty of restriction of liberty there remains the possibility to impose the duty to redress damage or to relieve the convict of such an obligation. In the opinion of R. Giętkowski, the disharmony presented above ought to be understood in such way that art. 61(1) EPC contains only a general principle authorising the court to modify pending duties during the period of execution of restriction of liberty, made more precise (by specifying which duties and in what way they may be modified) in art. 74 CrimC,[33] which is to be applied under art. 36(3) CrimC[34] to the penalty of restriction of liberty.[35] This thesis is supported by opinions about the impossibility of intervening in the course of executive proceedings in the civil law relationship emerging between the offender and the wronged party at the time when the judgment became final.[36] The contrary stance has been taken by A. Muszyńska, in whose opinion the content of art. 61(1) EPC clearly differs from provisions regulating modifications to the adjudged duty to redress damage in the course of its execution. Moreover, should a different interpretation be adopted, it would

---

is no possibility to relieve the convict from the punitive measure or compensation in executive proceedings.

33 *Art. 74(1) CrimC: The time and manner of execution of the imposed obligations specified in art. 72 shall be determined by the court after hearing the convict; the imposition of the obligation specified in art. 72(1) item 6 shall require additional consent from the convict.*

   (2) If corrective considerations so require, the court may, during the probation period, institute, extend or modify the obligations imposed on a person sentenced to imprisonment, as mentioned in art. 72(1) items 3-8, or release him from such obligations (except the obligation specified in Art. 72(2) and, likewise, either place the convict under supervision or release him from the aforesaid.

   (3) In the case of submitting the convict to supervision or obliging him to perform obligations in the probation period, a professional probation officer, or a person of public trust, association, institution or social organization mentioned in Art. 73(1), may also file a motion for determination of time and manner of performing his duties.

34 *The provision of art. 74 applies accordingly (art. 36(3) CrimC).*

35 R. Giętkowski, *Kara ograniczenia wolności w polskim prawie karnym* (Warszawa 2007), p. 127.

36 It has been argued in the literature that since the ruling by a criminal court obligating the perpetrator to redress the damage leads to the creation of a legal relationship between the convict and the wronged party, even if there is no explicit provision to exclude the possibility of amendments within such an obligation, any modifications of this ruling should be deemed unacceptable (see Z. Gostyński, *Obowiązek naprawienia szkody w nowym ustawodawstwie karnym*, p. 233).

render seemingly futile the amendment to art. 61(1) EPC of 2003[37] allowing for the possibility to modify, in the course of execution of restriction of liberty, all duties grasped in art. 36(2) CrimC (that is the duties rendered in art. 72(1) and (2) CrimC) without limiting them, as was the case previously, to the duties of art. 72(1) items 3-8 CrimC.[38]

It seems that the thesis allowing for the modification of duties also with respect to the repair of damage is favoured by the following arguments:

1) linguistic (literal) interpretations indicate that if the lawmaker clearly prohibited each time the exemption of the convict in the course of executive proceedings from the duty to repair damage, the absence of an analogous preclusion in art. 61(1) EPC, according to the directive proscribing attribution of the same sense to varying provisions, should be interpreted as allowance of modifications in this respect;

2) a rational lawmaker could not amend provisions without valid reasons, which means that the reform of art. 61(1) EPC of 2003 allowing modification to all duties rendered in art. 36(2) CrimC, and not (as previously) only the ones listed in art. 72(1) items 3-8 CrimC, should produce essential consequences;

3) the fact of establishment through criminal judgment of a civil law relationship between the convict and the wronged party does not yet allow for a conclusion about the inadmissibility of interfering in the content of this relationship in the course of executing the sentence, since the legal system already knows a number of similar instances (for example, the order of execution of penalty precludes the offender's duty to repair damage imposed in criminal judgment, and the erasure of an entry in the register of penalties annuls the punitive measure involving the duty to redress);

4) the reference that is made in art. 36(3) CrimC to the appropriate application of art. 74 CrimC may entail a conclusion about applicability of rules found in art. 74 CrimC to the penalty of restriction of liberty, but only in respect to the need to hear the opinion of the convict before modifying the duty and to obtain the convict's consent before awarding the duty to undertake addiction treatment.[39] To accept the contrary interpretation, which would regard art. 74 CrimC as a provision that specifies which duties and to what extent they may be modified while the penalty of restriction of liberty is executed,

---

37 Act of 24 July 2003 amending art. 61(1) EPC as of 1 September 2003 (Dziennik Ustaw 2003, No. 142, item 1380).

38 A. Muszyńska, *Naprawienie szkody wyrządzonej przestępstwem*, p. 379-381.

39 K. Postulski, *Kodeks karny. Komentarz* (Warszawa 2013), p. 328.

would lead one to accept the futility of the introduction to art. 61(1) EPC in
the Code (the reference in art. 36(3) CrimC to the appropriate application
of art. 74 CrimC would authorise the court to modify duties in the course of
penalty execution).

The arguments set out above speak in favour of the need to acknowledge that
in the course of executing the penalty of restriction of liberty, it is permissible both to obligate the offender to redress the damage and to release the latter
from the duty to do so. Is this the right solution? It seems that it is not justifiable to differentiate in this respect between the situations of convicts sentenced
to restriction of liberty and other penalties. On the other hand, the realisation
of the idea of restorative justice within executive proceedings should match its
progress with the current needs of the wronged party and the convict. If, for
example, the wronged party declared that he or she did not want the damage to
be compensated, and considered the conflict caused by the crime to be resolved,
the executive court would be in charge of mechanisms enabling the adjustment
of the ruling to this stance. Similarly, if in the course of judicial proceedings the
wronged party did not seek a resolution concerning compensation because of an
extra-judicial settlement concluded with the offender, which was subsequently
unimplemented by the convict, the court would be in a position in the course of
executive proceedings to adjudge the duty to repair damage. It seems, thus, that
flexibility in this matter speaks in favour of the assumptions of restorative justice. Still, keeping the focus on the coherence of the legal system, it would seem
recommendable to include similar stipulations for other legal institutions aimed
at reparation of damage, and at least for probative measures.

Coming back to the problems of execution of duties to redress damage along
with the penalty of restriction of liberty, one should remember that convicts in
relation to whom this penalty has been conditionally suspended may not apply
to shorten its execution in compliance with art. 83 CrimC, and the remaining
issues pertaining to performance of the duty to redress will be convergent with
the terms of execution of probative requisites.

When the punishment of restriction of liberty is executed, the convict ought
to abide by all the related obligations, especially the main sanction corresponding to the duty to gratuitously perform supervised labour for social purposes or
have specified sums of money set off against the convict's wage. The duty to repair the damage imposed under art. 36(2) CrimC is an accessory to the executed
penalty (as is the case with probative requisites). It remains valid only until the
sentence has been fully served. Failure to compensate may bring the convict the
consequences set out below.

In the first place, the convict has to serve the whole sentence (the full amount of work or set-off awarded) as it is not feasible to shorten its duration based on art. 83 CrimC, whose application is contingent on the fulfilment of the duties imposed by court. Since the verb "fulfilment" leaves little room for interpretation, it ought to be concluded that it is necessary to fulfil the obligations adjudged by court to redress the damage in full. This thesis should not be identified with the need to redress the damage caused by the offence as imposed by the court. Art. 83 CrimC merely requires that the duty awarded by court be fulfilled. As a result, where the court has obligated the convict to compensate the damage only in part, the resolution in this matter must be executed before shortening the duration of execution of the penalty of restriction of liberty.

Next, it seems necessary to consider the possibility to adjudicate in accordance with art. 64 EPC and to decide whether and to what extent the penalty of restriction of liberty may be considered executed in light of achievement of this punishment's goals, despite non-performance of the adjudged amount of work or set-off against the wage received in exchange of labour in full, or nonperformance of other duties related to the penalty of restriction of liberty. This doubt is made all the more serious by art. 64 EPC, which, while providing for the rule shown above, allows for an exception to the duty to compensate for economic or non-economic loss. In consequence, in the opinion of most doctrinal writers, this provision proscribes considering the penalty of restriction of liberty when it is executed in the event of non-performance of the obligation to repair damage.[40] The Supreme Court, showing its approval of this interpretation, held in the justification to the resolution of 25 February 2002 that this interpretation is supported by the wording of art. 74(2) CrimC, which was applied as appropriate to the penalty of restriction of liberty. Although this provision envisages the possibility of release from the duties connected with conditional suspension of execution of the penalty, it makes an exception for the duty to redress damage, which points to the legislator's consequence in this regard. The lawmaker clearly forbids release from only this duty as well as considering the penalty executed without performance of the same obligation.[41]

The opposite position on this issue has been taken by S. Pawela. In the view of this author, art. 64 EPC is a mere exception to the rule that to consider the

---

40 Tak Z. Gostyński, *Obowiązek naprawienia szkody w nowym ustawodawstwie karnym*, p. 245-246; S. Lelental, *Kodeks karny wykonawczy. Komentarz* (Warszawa 2012), p. 313; K. Postulski, *Kodeks karny wykonawczy. Komentarz*, p. 337.

41 See the justification of the SC resolution of 25 February 2002, I KZP 2/02, OSNKW 2002, No. 5-6/30, p. 14.

penalty of restriction of liberty accomplished is to recognise the expiry of the duties connected with this punishment since compensation of damage may be enforced by way of execution procedures under art. 196 EPC.[42] In the opinion of R. Giętkowski, apart from the issue of the emergence of a legal relationship between the obliged and entitled party in pursuance of a court ruling, one must not forget that since the duty to repair damage has become devoid of the criminal law protection in conjunction with probative measures, there are no reasons to argue that non-performance of this obligation in combination with the penalty of restriction of liberty should bar the possibility to consider the penalty executed, since the execution of compensation of damage (even where it has been imposed as a punitive measure) remains to be enforced by the wronged party.[43]

It seems that the position is not correct which depicts the content of art. 64 EPC as forbidding as a rule any consideration of executing the punishment of restriction of liberty in the event of non-compliance with the obligation to repair damage, since the implications of adopting such a stance would stand in opposition with conclusions to be reached by recourse to a systemic and functional interpretation of the discussed provision. This raises the question of how long could the duty to repair damage should be executed in the case of performance in full of the community services or set-off against wage, and whether the failure to compensate the damage should really prolong the period of execution of the penalty at stake. Detailed deliberations in this respect are presented towards the end of the present section. At this point, however, it may be stated that, in spite of the opinion given by the Supreme Court that art. 74(2) CrimC manifests the lawmaker's conclusion to preclude only release from this obligation and consideration of the penalty to be accomplished without execution of this duty,[44] the ban on release from the duty to repair damage stipulated in art. 74(2) CrimC is limited only to the probation period, since resolution on that matter loses its legal relevance upon its expiration. The Court's reference to art. 74(2) seems to have been missed because the issues of release from the duty to redress damage in the context of penalty of restriction of liberty are covered amply in art. 61 EPC, which constitutes *lex specialis* in relation to art. 74(2) CrimC. Coming back to the main topic of the present deliberations, it ought to be pointed out that the lawmaker consequently omits to hinder erasure of entry in the register of penalties on grounds of non-performance of damage resulting from the

---

42 S. Pawela, *Kodeks karny wykonawczy. Praktyczny komentarz* (Warszawa 1999), p. 201.
43 R. Giętkowski, *Kara ograniczenia wolności w polskim prawie karnym*, p. 169-170.
44 As in the judgment of the SC resolution of 25 February 2002, I KZP 2/02, OSNKW 2002, No. 5-6/30, p. 14.

crime (art. 76(2) CrimC, art. 107(6) CrimC). It would be unwise to believe that a rational lawmaker does not mind the absence of redress of damage with regard to the penalty of imprisonment, and, at the same time, this lawmaker should preclude for these reasons any acknowledgement of complete execution of a generically less severe penalty, that is restriction of liberty. The arguments depicted above lead to the conclusion that art. 64 EPC constitutes an exception with regard to the duty to compensate for economic and non-economic loss, stipulating that non-performance of these duties cannot stand in opposition with acknowledgement of completion of the penalty of restriction of liberty. This stance seems consistent with the content of art. 76(2) CrimC and art. 107(6) CrimC, and *de lege lata* it ought to be deemed the correct one, although it is not necessarily accurate on these merits, since it fails to implement the program of restorative justice by marginalising the wronged party's position, removes him or her from the court which supervises execution of the criminal judgement, and omits to support the convict's needs to redress damage by pending legal consequences.

The evasion of the duty to redress damage that is imposed along with the penalty of restriction of liberty constitutes one of prerequisites for ordering replacement punishment of imprisonment based on art. 65(1) EPC. This provision adopts the penalty of restriction of liberty (remaining to be executed) as a conversion of replacement imprisonment, stipulating that one day of replacement imprisonment corresponds to two days of restriction of liberty. In consequence, there has emerged doubt about whether it is possible to order a replacement penalty in the the case that the whole service or set-off against wage imposed is performed and that there is thus a corresponding evasion of duties. The Supreme Court allowed for such a possibility, indicating that art. 65(1) EPC provides for one legal consequence of the evasion of the duty to serve the penalty of restriction of liberty or performance of the duties imposed by court, that is it provides for the commencement of the procedure of substituting the penalty of restriction of liberty for replacement penalty, without explicating further the reasons for this substitution or the degree of completion of the penalty of restriction of liberty. As a result, the "conversion rate" of substituting the penalty of restriction of liberty for the replacement sentence should be the gravity of the duty and its proportion to the total of the burdens following from the penalty of the restriction of liberty, as adjudged in a specific case.[45]

---

45 Justification of the SC resolution of 25 February 2002, I KZP 2/02, OSNKW 2002, No. 5-6, item 30, p. 15-17; see R. Giętkowski, *Kara ograniczenia wolności w polskim prawie karnym*, p. 173-174.

The view presented above has been criticised by K. Postulski, according to whom art. 65 EPC simultaneously makes the level of the replacement penalty dependent on the period of the remaining sentence of restriction of liberty, which bars the possibility of awarding replacement punishment in the event of the execution of all the community labour, and maintains that the duty to repair damage may be executed on such occasions only in civil law execution.[46] This stance ought to be considered correct with regard to the impossibility of awarding a replacement penalty in such situations, because in the case of completion of the prescribed community work or set-off against wage received for labour, the sentence of restriction of liberty has been substantially served, and the conversion provided in art. 65(1) EPC loses its rationale. Moreover, imposition of a replacement penalty would contradict the terms of application of the sanction already suffered towards the adjudged penalties in their entirety (e.g. art. 63 CrimC) and lead to a duplication of the same punishment. In addition, attention out to be paid to the character of the duties envisaged in art. 36(2) CrimC, whose imposition, by reference to art. 72 CrimC, should be effected analogically to probative measures, and so the aim of their adjudication should be to motivate the convict to positively accomplish the period of execution of penalty by creating conditions favouring his or her observance of the law in future. This does not mean, however, that *de lege ferenda* it would not make sense to introduce a separate conversion factor for calculating a replacement penalty in the case of non-compliance of the duty to repair damage in conjunction with the penalty of restriction of liberty. Such a solution would give the criminal court oversight competences that would enable supervision of execution of the sentence as to the compensatory obligation, and would mobilise the convict to redress damage and account to a fuller extent for the legitimate interests of the wronged party.

At the same time, it seems necessary to note how unconvincing the opinion of K. Postulski presented above seems; Potulski considers the failure to redress damage in the case that the adjudged community works or set-off against labour wage have been completed as proper grounds for deferring the start of the period leading to erasure of entry in the register of penalties.[47] This conclusion

---

46 K. Postulski, *Kodeks karny wykonawczy. Komentarz*, p. 342-343; more on this subject in K. Postulski, ‚Glosa do uchwały SN z dnia 25 lutego 2002 r., I KZP 2/02', *Palestra* 1-2 (2003), p. 210 *et seq.*

47 As in K. Postulski ‚Glosa do uchwały SN z dnia 25 lutego 2002 r., I KZP 2/02', *Palestra* 1-2 (2003), p. 211; E. Bieńkowska, ‚Obowiązek naprawienia szkody lub zadośćuczynienia w prawie karnym (kontrowersje i wątpliwości)', *Państwo i Prawo* 8 (2012), p. 56.

is supported by arguments related to systematic interpretation: since the commencement of the period leading to erasure of entry in the register of penalties is not barred by non-performance of the duty to compensate damage imposed as punitive measure (art. 107(6) CrimC), and since a rational lawmaker should not introduce more severe consequences for non-performance of the duty to redress damage adjudged in combination with the penalty of restriction of liberty than in the case of the same obligation accompanying other sorts of penalties,[48] it does not seem possible to accept the above position.

Problems involving the execution of the duty to redress damage awarded as a probation requisite

The duty to redress damage imposed as a probation requisite may constitute an element of conditional discontinuance of criminal proceedings (art. 67(3) CrimC), conditional suspension of execution of a sentence (art. 72(2) CrimC) or release on parole of an imprisoned convict (art. 159(1) EPC in conjunction with art. 72(2) CrimC). All these institutions consist in submitting the perpetrator of an offence to probation, although the decisions to impose each of them are delivered at different stages of the penal proceedings. Whereas a judgment conditionally discontinuing criminal proceedings or awarding a conditionally suspended penalty may be entered into only in proceedings that determine the merits of the case, decisions concerning release on parole of an imprisoned convict may be arrived at exclusively in the course of executive proceedings. For these reasons, it would not be conceivable for the present chapter to skip a discussion of the possibilities for and prerequisites of obliging the offender to repair damage at the time of release on parole, as this problem could not be scrutinised while analysing various aspects of adjudication concerning compensation in fact-finding proceedings.

As a consequence, it must be pointed out that art. 159(1) EPC[49] provides for the possibility of imposing on a convict who has been released on parole

---

48 See E. Bieńkowska, ‚Obowiązek naprawienia szkody lub zadośćuczynienia w prawie karnym (kontrowersje i wątpliwości)', *Państwo i Prawo* 8 (2012), p. 56.

49 *Art. 159(1) PEPC: A penitentiary court may place a conditionally released convict, in the probation period, under the supervision of a probation officer, a person of public trust, association, organization or institution that within the scope of its duties caters for education, prevention of demoralization and provides assistance to convicts. The court may also impose on the convict the obligations specified in art. 72(1) of the Criminal Code, and if the damage caused by the crime committed by the convict has not been redressed, it may adjudge the obligation specified in in art. 72(2) of the CrimC. Placement*

obligations following from art. 72(2) CrimC,[50] in cases in which the damage that was inflicted by a criminal offence for which the offender has been convicted remains unremedied. This is a new solution that was introduced in the EPC in 1997. It entered into force on 1 January 2012.[51] The amendment was justified by the need to cater to the legitimate claims of the wronged party, and by the fact that an arrangement in which the convict benefits from a release on parole should also benefit the victims of his or her crime.[52] Without questioning this thesis, as it favours a fuller realisation of criminal law functions (especially rehabilitative and compensatory), it is necessary to make a number of critical comments.

First, one must not overlook the fact that the only requirement found in art. 159(1) EPC is to redress the damage caused by the crime for which the convict has been imprisoned. This provision does not mention the possibility of awarding to the offender ahead of time, in the judicial fact-finding proceeding, the duty to redress damage. As a consequence, the first question that springs to mind concerns the admissibility of obligating the convict released on parole to repair the damage caused by his or her criminal offence, if that damage continues to persist, and the court has not decided to do so on the merits. It seems that this question ought to be answered in the negative, because otherwise the penitentiary court would encroach upon the competences of the criminal court, increasing the level of sanction of the criminal judgment[53] and, additionally,

---

under supervision is mandatory in the case of a person sentenced for an offence specified in art. 197-203 CrimC, an offence committed in relation to sexual preference disorder, a minor perpetrator of an intentional offence, the offender specified in art. 64 CrimC, and a person sentenced to life imprisonment.

50 Art. 72(2) CrimC: The court may obligate the convict to redress the damage in whole or in part unless it has adjudicated a penal measure specified in art. 39(5) or a monetary provision specified in art. 39(7).
51 Dziennik Ustaw 2011, No. 240, item 1431.
52 This opinion can be found in the justification of the Act amending the EPC of 16 September 2011 [after:] K. Dąbkiewicz, *Kodeks karny wykonawczy. Komentarz* (Warszawa 2012), p. 459; this amendment was approved in the doctrine—see K. Dąbkiewicz, *Kodeks karny wykonawczy. Komentarz*, p. 459; K. Postulski, *Kodeks karny wykonawczy. Komentarz*, p. 646; for criticism related to te usefulness of the introduction of this reform from the perspective of the aims of release on parole rather than practical possibilities to embark on this institution, see S. Lelental, *Kodeks karny wykonawczy. Komentarz*, p. 701.
53 Although the necessity to redress the damage is not a *sensu stricto* legal distress resulting from sentencing, this obligation may bring about important consequences to the

securing the performance of the duty imposed in this manner with the possibility to recall the release on parole. Moreover, the realities of executive proceedings, the bulk of the cases on the roll, and the desired pace of proceedings forestalls the tedious process of evidencing the amount of loss and identity of the wronged party, as such actions should be taken in fact-finding proceedings. In addition, the fact that, in the period of probation that is correlated with conditional discontinuance of criminal proceedings and conditional suspension of execution of penalty, it is not admissible to adjudge this obligation once the judgment becomes final and binding[54] demonstrates that competence in this regard is vested in the criminal courts. The arguments depicted above lead to the conclusion that adjudication of the duty to redress the damage at the moment of release on parole is possible only in the event of previous resolutions included in the criminal judgment as to the need to repair damage.

Next, one may ask the question of whether the possibility to obligate the convict released on parole to redress damage is independent of the legal basis of the respective resolution included in the criminal judgment. The anti-cumulation clause widely accentuated in CrimC and CCP, which excludes not only the possibility to jointly apply provisions of art. 415 CCP, art. 46(1) CrimC and art. 72(2) CrimC but also forbids adjudication on redress of damage in the event of a previous decision imposing compensation in civil proceedings,[55] even if the latter has not been effectively executed,[56] seems to exclude such an option. The aim of introducing anti-cumulation clauses is to prevent the possibility of the parallel existence of two separate execution titles referring to the same damage, while the duty to repair damage ordained in the order of release on parole would actualise the possibility to append this title with the enforceability clause under art. 107 CCP. In consequence, it should be acknowledged that in the case of an award of compensation in the convicting judgment as a result of

---

offender's financial situation, however, and the linkage of the committed offence with the necessity to redress the damage caused might appear to be the primary distress for him or her following from the judgment.

54 Art. 74(2) CrimC permits only imposition of obligations specified in art. 72(1) items 3-8 CrimC in the probation period related to conditional suspension of penalty, and therefore the obligation to redress the damage cannot be imposed within this period. Appropriate application of this provision has also been provided in art. 67(4) CrimC. C.f. A. Muszyńska, *Naprawienie szkody wyrządzonej przestępstwem*, p. 378-379.

55 See the SC judgment of 22 March 2012, V KK 25/12, Lex No. 1157584.

56 Art. 415(5) sentence 2 PCCP does not envisage such distinction—see the judgment of the SC of 16 November 2011, III KK 270/11, Lex No. 1055028.

civil action within criminal proceedings, there is no option to obligate the convict released on parole to redress the damage, since the binding court's verdict in that matter retains validity. It is possible to apply for an enforceability clause and then to carry out civil law execution based on this execution title. However, even where the compensation is barred by limitation of the claim, there are still no grounds for obligating the convict released on parole to repair the damage, since a civil action remains a civil action with all its consequences, including the fact that limitation is not taken into account *ex officio* (even though a debtor might file an anti-execution suit, entering the plea of limitation of enforceability of the judgment, it still must be done on the debtor's initiative). This means that until the moment that the anti-execution action is brought, this execution title remains valid. Moreover, even though compensation awarded in criminal proceedings under art. 415 CCP brings certain benefits to the wronged party (e.g. the possibility to grant to the latter the interests accrued as of the date of the criminal offence), in fact it denotes resignation on the criminal law protection afforded to reparation of loss when adjudged as a punitive measure or probation requisite, which results in the exclusion of the possibility to repeatedly grant at the stage of executive proceedings this kind of protection at the moment of release on parole.

Another problem is the question of the admissibility of obligating the convict released on parole to redress the damage in the event of adjudication in the convicting judgment of the punitive measure of art. 46(1) CrimC. It seems that this query ought to be answered in the negative, since art. 159(1) EPC directly (rather than appropriately) refers to art. 72(2) CrimC, exempting its applicability when the duty to repair damage is imposed under art. 46(1) CrimC. For many years following the time of the judgment's validation, the debtor might remain entitled to apply to append the enforceability clause, since art. 107(2) CCP does not assign any term upon the expiry of which such application would cease to be permissible. Even if the execution of the said punitive measure were barred by limitation (art. 103(1) item 2 CrimC prescribes a fifteen-year-period in this regard), the court would not examine this fact in enforcement clause proceedings,[57]

---

57 Such was the opinion of the CS in the judgment of 20 November 1975, VI KZP 30/75, OSNKW 1976/1/2, p. 3 et seq.; see as well the approving assessment of the cited ruling by Wiesław Daszkiewicz [W. Daszkiewicz, 'Przegląd orzecznictwa Sądu Najwyższego (Prawo karne procesowe – I półrocze 1976)', *Państwo i Prawo* 3 (1977), p. 123]. It is also favoured by systemic arguments—art. 26 EPC ordains the direct (rather than appropriate) application of art. 776-795 CPC, which refers, *inter alia*, to provisions on complaints against the enforceability clause being appended to an execution

leaving to the debtor's discretion the question of who may enter the plea of limitation by bringing an anti-execution action. The above arguments lead to the conclusion that it is impossible to obligate the offender to repair damage along with a release on parole if the punitive measure of art. 46(1) CrimC has previously been awarded.

Since this is the case, when is it possible to impose the obligation envisaged in art. 72(2) CrimC on a convict who has been released on parole? It seems that the only case when such a resolution could be imaginable is that of a prior adjudication to the convict of the duty to repair damage under art. 72(2) CrimC in the proceedings on the merits. In the event of a later order of execution of the penalty, under the conception adopted for the purpose of the present study,[58] the awarded duty is legally annulled. It vanishes and, in the same way, the final and binding ruling of the court with regard to compensation of damage that could otherwise be enforced ceases to exist. This state of affairs allows for a conclusion concerning the non-violation of the anti-cumulation clause. The situation differs significantly, however, from limited claims, which continue to exist, yet only as non-actionable claims, because on such occasions the court resolution obligating the offender to redress the damage is no longer there.

In summary, the imposition of the duty to repair damage that results from a criminal offence on a convict released on parole is admissible if the following prerequisites are jointly met:

1) the convicting judgment contains a resolution obliging the convict released on parole to compensate the damage in pursuance of art. 72(2) CrimC;
2) the penalty imposed in the judgment for the committed crime first took the form of a conditionally suspended imprisonment and then the execution of that penalty was ordered;
3) the damage caused by the crime for which the convict is serving his or her sentence has not been remedied.

If the conditions named above are met, it is possible to obligate the convict released on parole to compensate damage on the basis of art. 159(1) EPC in conjunction with art. 72(2) CrimC. In principle this solution favours the realisation of the idea of restorative justice, since it allows the wronged party to be placed

---

title. In consequence, the system does not envisage any legal situation in which the court would be authorised to review limitation of execution of the awarded punitive measure.

58 This is further elaborated upon in the present section.

back in the centre of the proceeding and accounts for his or her interests, while the convict's willingness to redress the damage will probably be reinforced by his or her urge to positively go through the period of probation.

Coming back to the issue of the execution of resolutions on reparation of damage adjudged as probation requisites (along with conditional discontinuance of criminal proceedings, conditional suspension of execution of penalty and release on parole of an imprisoned convict), attention should be paid to the common elements of these institutions.

The first issue is the moment of enforceability of the duty to repair damage. As opposed to the punitive measure envisaged in art. 46(1) CrimC or the compensation awarded upon allowance of civil action in criminal proceedings, this is not the time when the judgment becomes final and binding but the deadline fixed by the court for the performance of this obligation.[59] Accepting the other conception, i.e. the moment when the judicial ruling becomes final and binding, would deprive the convict of the possibility to repair damage voluntarily, which constitutes one of the criteria for evaluating the criminological and social prognosis. If the criminal court fails to specify the time, deadline and manner of performance of the obligation to repair damage, it is possible at this point to modify the court ruling in executive proceedings.[60] However, if the deadline for performance of the obligation has not been set either in the judgement[61] or in the period of probation, there arises a question about the moment of enforceability of such a ruling. The Court of Appeals in Katowice took the stance that on such occasions the said duty becomes enforceable only upon expiry of the probation period (up to that moment, the wronged party may not apply to append the enforceability clause and refer the case to coercive execution).[62] However, this opinion is not undisputed, as M. Siwek has pointed out that upon expiration of the probation period the duty to redress damage, with the view to its accessory character, forfeits its legal subsistence, and, in the same way, coercive execution is no longer allowed following that point in time.[63] Bearing in mind the stance on the accessory character of the duty to repair damage in relation to the period of

---

59 See the SC resolution of 24 May 2005, I KZP 17/05, OSNKW 2005/7-8/59, p. 10 et seq.
60 See the decision of the Court of Appeal in Katowice of 7 September 2011, II AKz 587/11, Lex No. 1102937.
61 In the event of release on parole by court order.
62 See the order of the Court of Appeal in Katowice of 7 September 2011, II AKz 587/11, Lex No. 1102937.
63 M. Siwek, *Glosa do postanowienia p. apel. z dnia 7 września 2011 r., II AKz 587/11*, Lex/el/2012.

probation (that will be explicated below in more detail), as accepted in the present study, the second of the cited opinions should be considered the right one. This solution does not favour the program of putting into practice the assumptions of restorative justice, because if the court omits to specify the deadline for the performance of the duty to compensate, the convict will be able to redress the damage during the whole probation period, which deprives the wronged party of the right to apply, within this timespan, to append the execution title with an enforceability clause. In addition, upon expiry of the period of probation, the wronged party will remain unable to do so, since at this point the obligation to redress the damage forfeits its legal subsistence. In consequence of this state of affairs, the wronged party becomes entirely devoid of the possibility to seek satisfaction by way of coercive execution, which brings to naught even the compensatory function of criminal law, not to mention any conceivable realisation of restorative justice. Nonetheless, it must be noted that the court retains the option to negatively terminate the probation period within 6 months of its expiry in the event that it ascertains evasion of the obligation to repair damage.

The common issue for all measures submitting the offender to probation is the absence of the possibility to release the offender from the duty to redress the damage (art. 67(4) in conjunction with art. 74 CrimC, art. 74(2) CrimC, art. 163(2) EPC). In the literature, this prohibition has been substantiated by the emergence of a legal relationship between the entitled and obligated parties as a result of the duty to compensate the damage imposed by court in its judgment.[64] In principle, the wronged party ought to know when to apply to append the execution clause to the judgement so as not to be surprised by premature release of the convict from the obligation to perform the resolution. A ban on releasing the convict from the obligation to repair damage may also result from the fact that resolution in the matter constitutes a criterion for verification of the criminological and social prognosis of the convict; also, evasion of the duty to repair damage may be a proof of unsuccessful progress of the probation period. For the reasons put forward in discussing the penalty of restriction of liberty, it must be stated that the allowance of the admissibility of adjudging this duty in the probation period and the respective release of the convict during the same period would realise the idea of restorative justice to a fuller extent, making the gamut of options available to court for modifying the previous verdict more flexible.

---

64 Z. Gostyński, *Obowiązek naprawienia szkody w nowym ustawodawstwie karnym*, p. 232.

The question of the likelihood of the duty to redress damage imposed as a probation requisite in the event of non-satisfaction of the wronged party within the probation period is dubious in the doctrine of law. According to one opinion, in the case of negative conclusion of probation, the probation obligation to redress the damage expires in the unfulfilled part because of its accessory character.[65] This thesis has also been supported by the following arguments:

1) the essence of the probative measures imposed under art. 72(1) and (2) CrimC is the possibility of performing and executing them solely in the probation period,[66]
2) no legal provision gives grounds for transforming after expiry of the probation period the criminal law duty to repair damage into an obligation of civil law character,[67]
3) the non-performance of obligations envisaged in art. 72(1) and 2 CrimC has no influence on erasure of entry in the register of penalties,[68]
4) in case of the resumption of proceedings previously conditionally suspended, art. 551 CCP ordains the reopening of the proceedings *de novo*, and the previously imposed duty to repair damage is legally cancelled.[69]

Other representatives of the doctrine,[70] proponents of the notion of transforming the probation requisite into a civil law obligation upon expiration of the probation period, argue that:

1) the adoption of another position is not possible when the compensatory aims of criminal proceeding are born in mind,[71]

---

65 K. Postulski, *Kodeks karny wykonawczy. Komentarz*, p. 787; as in M. Siwek, ,Glosa do wyroku Sądu Apelacyjnego w Lublinie z 27 września 2000r., II AKa 180/00', *Palestra* 7-8 (2003), p. 261.

66 As in the justification of the SC judgment of 10 December 2008, II KK 106/08, OSN-wSK 2008/1/2530, p. 989.

67 M. Łukasiewicz, A. Ostapa, ,Nawiązka i karnoprawny obowiązek naprawienia szkody a roszczenie cywilnoprawne', *Prokuratura i Prawo* 2 (2002), p. 77.

68 J. Lachowski in M. Królikowski, R. Zawłocki (eds.), *Kodeks karny. Część ogólna. Tom II* (Warszawa 2011), p. 585.

69 T. Kozioł, *Warunkowe umorzenie postępowania karnego* (Warszawa 2009), p. 255-256; such consequences are admitted even by opponents of such statement – see A. Muszyńska, *Naprawienie szkody wyrządzonej przestępstwem*, p. 388.

70 A. Muszyńska, *Naprawienie szkody wyrządzonej przestępstwem*, p. 387 *et seq.*; D. Krzyżanowski, ,Prawnokarne instytucje służące zaspokojeniu roszczeń pokrzywdzonego a dochodzenie roszczeń w prawie cywilnym', *Palestra* 9-10 (2008), p. 45-46.

71 A. Muszyńska, *Naprawienie szkody wyrządzonej przestępstwem*, p. 387.

2) there is no provision that would provide grounds for annulment of the awarded duty,[72]
3) in all other cases, it would be necessary to ascertain that the entitled party does not pursue his or her claims, which would constitute a restriction of his or her rights and a form of expropriation.[73]

It seems clear that the first of the positions presented above ought to be treated as more accurate. In the first place, one should note that probative obligations are accessory to the adjudged probation period. As a result, they may be performed, but also may only be enforced in the probation period.[74] The essence of the application of probation requisites is their annulment upon expiry of the period of probation. Since it is undisputable that the obligation to refrain from overuse of alcohol or undertake addiction treatment dies out upon expiry of the probation period, no provision of law allows a corollary stipulating that the duty to repair damage ought to be treated differently. Secondly, in accordance with the provision of art. 76(2) CrimC, the only punitive measure which does not prevent erasure of entry in the register of penalties is the obligation to redress damage adjudged in pursuance of art. 46(1) CrimC. In the provision under examination the lawmaker does not mention the duty to repair damage adjudged under art. 72(2) CrimC, even if in the compensatory sphere it serves the same function as the punitive measure envisaged in art. 46(1) CrimC. The third argument is supported by systematic reasons, since the well established opinion of doctrinal writers is that, in case of resumption of criminal proceedings which have been previously conditionally discontinued, litigation is to be conducted *de novo* (also with regard to the loss to be ascertained),[75] which means that the previous duty to repair damage does not transform into a civil law claim, and also that there are no legal provisions which would give rise to the conclusion that in respect of other punitive measures this consequence should differ. One could also advance historical

---

72 A. Muszyńska, *Naprawienie szkody wyrządzonej przestępstwem*, p. 387.
73 Tak D. Krzyżanowski, 'Prawnokarne instytucje służące zaspokojeniu roszczeń pokrzywdzonego a dochodzenie roszczeń w prawie cywilnym', *Palestra* 9-10 (2008), p. 45-46 (this opinion may have been expressed by the author in respect of the duty to compensate adjudged as a punitive measure, yet the author referred also to compensatory duties awarded as a probative requisite, p. 45).
74 Such was the justification of the SC judgment of 10 December 2008, II KK 106/08, OSNwSK 2008, item 2530, p. 989; the same position was taken up by A. Zoll in A. Zoll (ed.), *Kodeks karny. Część ogólna. Komentarz lex*, p. 962.
75 T. Kozioł, *Warunkowe umorzenie postępowania karnego*, p. 255-256; A. Muszyńska, *Naprawienie szkody wyrządzonej przestępstwem*, p. 388.

arguments: art. 94(2) CCP of 1969 provided for the possibility to append an execution clause to a ruling imposing the duty to compensate damage if the court ordered execution of a conditionally suspended penalty,[76] whereas art. 107 CCP of 1997 does not introduce any similar restriction. Finally, it must be pointed out that if the contrary interpretation were adopted, there would be no chance at all to obligate convicts to repair damage based on art. 159(1) EPC in conjunction with art. 72(2) CrimC, since this would always lead to violation of anti-cumulation clauses, which in turn would contradict the assumption of the reasonable lawmaker whose intervention modified the cited provision to that end.

Grounds for early negative termination of a probative measure may be provided by the convict's evasion of a previously adjudged obligation to repair damage, however, the criminological and social prognosis may also be determined innacurate on the basis of other factors, such as commission of crime in the probation period. In light of the above, the non-payment of compensation by the convict may be related to other states of affairs.

The first of them is the ascertainment of negative conclusion of a probative measure before the duty to repair damage becomes enforceable. Since the deadline appointed by court to the convict to satisfy the wronged party would not have expired, non-compliance with this obligation could not constitute a basis for negative conclusion of the probation period, and the grounds for a respective court ruling must be provided by other means (for example, commission of a new crime during the period of probation). If one is to adopt the conception of legal annulment of the obligation to redress damage at the end of probation, the wronged party will not be in a position to effectively apply for an enforcement clause, since the court's decision concerning remedy of damage has ceased to exist. The wronged party would also be deprived of the opportunity to apply early for an enforceability clause, since the court resolution becomes enforceable only upon the lapse of the deadline given to the convict by the court to comply with the discussed obligation. This situation is far from advantageous from the point of view of restorative justice, because the procedural position of the wronged party is marginalised. He or she loses the chance to make use of coercive execution of the judicial order to redress damage, which is a failed solution from the point of view of the compensatory function of criminal law. Moreover, the convict's willingness to repair the damage may abate since execution of the previously imposed penalty has been ordered, and non-performance of the obligation to redress does not produce any negative criminal legal consequences.

---

76   Art. 94(2) PCCP of 1969 (Act of 19 April 1969, Dziennik Ustaw 1969, No. 13, item 96).

The other situation refers to the conclusion of the probation period at the time assigned in advance in spite of the failure to repair the damage. It is possible in the event of defective functioning of the system of administration of justice (for instance, it is ascertained too late that the convict has not repaired the damage, or no steps have been taken to determine whether he or she complied with the said duty) or in the case of refusal to interpret the failure to remedy the damage as evasion of the said obligation. The wronged party retains on such an occasion the opportunity to apply for an enforceability clause, but only between the lapsed deadline assigned by the court for remedying the damage and the end of the probation period. Additionally, in such situations the realisation of the idea of restorative justice leaves much to be desired, because the convict is under no threat of criminal law consequences for the failure to redress the damage, and, in the same way, he or she may have no motivation to comply with the duty. In addition, analysis of the convict's conduct (if it may be deemed evasion of the court ruling) concentrates only on the attitude of the offender, which sets aside interests of the wronged party, who is left only with a chance to resort to coercive execution, a chance that is only real if the application for an enforceability clause is submitted between the ending point of the period during which the convict was obliged to repair damage and the end of the probation period.

The third possibility is related to negative conclusion of the probation period once the obligation to repair damage becomes chargeable. The reasons for acknowledgement of failure of the previously formulated criminological and social prognosis may follow from various causes of negative conclusion of the probation period. If the reason is failure to redress damage, it is not sufficient to merely ascertain the absence of satisfaction of the wronged party's claim, because it is necessary to establish that the convict's conduct amounted to evasion of the imposed duty. In the literature of the field, the term "evasion" is understood as a negative mental attitude towards the sanctions adjudged for the probation period (supervision and duties) involving deliberate (intentional) non-compliance with probation requisites even though it is objectively possible to comply with them.[77] The attitude corresponds to awareness of the obligation and simultaneous neg-

---

77 See the SC order of 12 October 1988, V KRN 212/88, OSNPG 1989/3/44, p. 13; SC order of 06 June 1972, V KRN 122/72, OSNKW 1972/11/177, p. 46-48; SC order of 23 February 1974, IV KRN 17/74, OSNKW 1974/5/95, p. 41; SC order of 17 April 1996, II KRN 204/96, GS 1997/3, p. 7; order of the Court of Appeal in Kraków of 27 October 2005, II AKzw 641/05, KZS 2005/11/34, p. 22; SC order of 07 October 2010, V KK 301/10, Lex No. 612941.

ligence of that obligation. The convict's evasion of the duty to compensate has to be ascertained at the moment that the deadline assigned by the court expires. Nevertheless, the court also must take into account the conduct of the offender during probation, since durng that whole time the convict remains under criminal law evaluation. Assessing the convict's conduct may be more difficult if the wronged party has commenced compulsory execution as soon as the claim became chargeable;[78] still, it is also possible in such situations to assess the good will of the convict with respect to remedying the damage. As in other cases, in the event of ordering the execution of the penalty, the wronged party becomes marginalised in the proceedings, although this time he or she at least has a chance to apply for an enforceability clause and seek satisfaction by way of coercive execution. Also the convict's will with respect to repairing the damage may abate, since the convict is not threatened by any criminal law consequences of the failure to repair damage, and the anticipated duration of isolation in prison will probably incline him or her to financially secure his or her family instead of redressing the wronged party.

The above considerations cast doubt on the proper implementation of the idea of restorative justice in the course of the execution of probative measures. This is the case because these procedures are oriented towards the convict rather than toward the wronged party. The offender is given time to repair the damage, which deprives the wronged party of the time to seek compensation by use of coercive execution. Redress of damage does not trigger any automatic criminal law consequences, as it would be necessary to determine in advance if the convict has purposefully strived to repair the damage. In consequence, both the wronged party and the conflict emeging as a consequence of the crime are put on the margin of the executive proceedings. It might be advisable to create institutions which place convicts in a privileged position in the event of the repair of damage, e.g. by shortening the period of probation, so as to give them additional motivation. One might also consider the exclusion of admissibility to append enforceability clauses to rulings which impose the duty to repair damage as a

---

78 Such a possibility was criticized in literature as it made impossible for a court to assess the rehabilitative influence of the obligation imposed on the person under probation - see Z. Gostyński, Obowiązek naprawienia szkody w nowym ustawodawstwie karnym, p. 248; A. Gadomska-Radel, K. Malinowska-Krutul, 'Problematyka wykonania obowiązku naprawienia szkody' in Z. Ćwiąkalski, G. Artymiak (eds.), Karnomaterialne i procesowe aspekty naprawienia szkody (Warsaw, 2010), p. 618. It is difficult, however, to assume that the wronged party should wait to have his or her claim satisfied for the entire probation period.

probation requisite so as to provide inducement for convicts to make redress to the wronged party also in situations of previous awards of compensation in civil proceedings.

If the convict has not repaired the damage on his or her own accord, the wronged party may apply to append the court verdict with an enforceability clause between the expiration of the term appointed by court to the convict and the end of probation, and file a motion for commencement of the coercive execution. This does not entirely preclude the idea of restorative justice. This situation does not have to result from the unwillingness of the convict to compensate the damage but rather can result from an objective impossibility to do so, which does not preclude the possibility to carry on coercive execution even after the civil law character of these types of resolutions is accepted. In addition, perhaps this is the only way in which the wronged party may find satisfaction, and it may also lead to the dissolution of the conflict caused by crime. Compensation for damage constitutes one of the conditions of realisation of the idea of restorative justice, since without redressing the damage one could not speak of the implementation of its functions. How long may the wronged party enforce his or her claim? Certainly, this opportunity is not geared to periods of limitation of the punitive measure obliging the convict to compensate[79] in the absence of any provision allowing the application of these periods to probation requisites. Since probation duties are legally annulled upon expiry of the probation period, it is inadmissible to apply civil law provisions concerning the statute of limitation.[80] The absence of a separate regulation in that matter follows from the fact of deactivation of probation requisites upon expiration of the probation period. If this should happen, and the wronged party has previously obtained an enforceability clause and filed for coercive execution, the convict may only bring an anti-execution suit in pursuance of art. 840(1) item 2 CCP because the asserted obligation has become extinguished. This, however, has little in common with realisation of the idea of restorative justice, both with regard to unsatisfied claims of the wronged party and the persistence of conflict caused by the criminal offence.

---

79 Differing opinion can be found in: A. Muszyńska, *Naprawienie szkody wyrządzonej przestępstwem*, p. 399.

80 It has been raised in literature that the clause exempting civil law duties concerning the statute of limitations has not been provided in regard to award of probative requisites because of the link between the latter and admissibility of criminal proceedings being carried on against the offender - see A. Muszyńska, *Naprawienie szkody wyrządzonej przestępstwem*, p. 401.

Summary

The discussion presented leads to the clear conclusion that *de lege lata* the model of executive criminal law does not favour the fulfilment of the idea of restorative justice. Several factors are relevant in this respect. First, executive procedures are oriented towards evaluating the convict's attitude; it is he or she that has been placed as the focal point, and not the wronged party. Moreover, the latter is not even a party to the proceedings, which deprives him or her of basic rights, such as the possibility to submit motions or challenge court decisions. This leads in practice to the marginalisation of the wronged party's role at the executive stage. Secondly, the conceivable consequences of the failure to redress damage threatening the convict are dependent on the type of the penalty imposed and the legal basis of the resolution on compensation of loss, resulting in their heterogeneous character and sometimes also the lack of any negative consequences threatening the convict in the event of non-compliance with the court ruling in the analysed matter. This kind of resolution does not lead to the fulfilment of the idea of restorative justice, since the convict is often left without any real incentives to redress the damage in form of pending criminal law consequences, which does not seem logical as this very motivation was the driving force behind the introduction into the criminal law of the institution allowing the award of compensation. Moreover, even if legal norms prescribe consequences for the absence of compensation, these are not uniform but rather dependent on the type of the imposed penalty and legal basis of the resolution on reparation of damage. The differences between the consequences rely on principles which are difficult to explain. Third, it is not uncommon that in the relatively short period since the time when the criminal judgement became final and binding, situations may develop in which the resolution on the repair of damage becomes devoid of its legal existence (for instance, in the case of erasure of entry in the register of penalties), which is unfavourable from the point of view of restorative justice since the wronged party still remains unsatisfied and the conflict emerging from the crime still persists, but the offender may conclude that, because of the absence of any criminal law consequences of the failure to redress damage, fulfilling this obligation is pointless. Fourth, doubts arise even in the context of realising the compensatory function in the course of executive proceedings, which constitutes a *sine qua non* of restorative justice, since in the absence of unsolicited repair of damage by the convict it is left to the wronged party to seek coercive satisfaction of the claim. The wronged party is also made to pay advances towards future bailiff expenses, and in the civil law execution proceedings he or she enjoys in principle no priority over other creditors. This section of legislation does not even favour the realisation of the compensatory function, not to mention the idea of restitution. The arguments deployed above lead to a corollary assertion: the binding model of executive proceedings is focused on the offender and fails to fulfil the postulations of restorative justice.

Leszek Wilk

The Concept of Restorative Justice in Fiscal Penal Law

Introduction

The concept of restorative justice is normally discussed in the context of general criminal law, and especially for crimes with an individual wronged party.

When one considers the background and origin of the concept of restorative justice, each component thereof, and its functions and procedures, they do not appear to suit fiscal penal law, which constitutes a separate area of criminal law. On the other hand, however, it must be noted that the very nature of interests protected by regulations of fiscal penal law are conducive to compensation, since interests protected by fiscal penal law are economic and recoverable.

Therefore, if the objective of this study is a comprehensive and multidimensional analysis of the question of to what extent restorative justice might be spoken of *de lege lata* within the framework of Polish penal law in its widest context, the analysis shall also include careful thinking on the possible transfer of the basic assumptions, components, functions and procedures of restorative justice from general to fiscal penal law.

As restorative justice stems from victimology and requires systematic solutions to bolster the role of the wronged party, the victim of a prohibited act, and to acknowledge the multifacetedness of economic and non-economic losses inflicted on the wronged party, an analysis of the concept of restorative justice in the context of fiscal penal law should start with definitions of the key terms of "damage" and "wronged party" in the context of fiscal penal law.

Damage in fiscal penal law

The fiscal penal law counterpart of the notion of "damage" is the concept of "reduction of public receivables."

What is understood by "public receivables" in the field of the Fiscal Criminal Code in force (hereinafter referred to as the FCC)[1] are state or local receivables

---

1 Act of 10 September 1999 (Dziennik Ustaw 2007 No. 111 item 765, as amended).
   Art. 53(26) In the understanding of the Code, a public receivable shall be any charge owed to the state or self-government that is subject to fiscal offences or contraventions;

that are subject to fiscal offences or contraventions. State receivables include taxes that comprise the revenue for the state budget, receivables from the clearing of granted subsidies or subventions, and customs duties, while local receivables are made up of taxes comprising local government budgets as well as receivables from the clearing of granted subventions or subsidies. In the understanding of the FCC, public receivables, including taxes, also include the receivables which make up the revenue of the European Union general budget or budgets managed by or on behalf of the European Union that are subject to fiscal offences or fiscal contraventions in accordance with those EU regulations which are binding for the Republic of Poland.[2]

The reduction of public receivables that is, as mentioned above, the fiscal penal law counterpart of the notion of damage has its own legal definition in the FCC. According to art. 53(27) of the FCC,[3] a public receivable reduced by a prohibited act is an amount of money expressed in numbers whose payment or declaration of payment in whole or in part has been evaded by the obligor, as a result of which evasion an actual financial detriment has occured. Furthermore, according to the subsequent paragraph (28) of the cited article, exposure to reduction is the induction of a concrete danger of such a reduction, which means that the occurrence of financial detriment is very likely, yet not inevitable.

The concept of "reduction" of public receivables was intended by the lawmaker to be distinguished from the notion of "exposure to reduction," as the two are to serve different functions in the FCC. The former ("reduction") serves as a prerequisite for the application of some institutions which modify the liability of the offender and influence the level of punishment,[4] whereas the latter ("ex-

---

state receivables are fiscal levies which comprise revenue for the state budget, dues on account of the clearance of a subsidy or subvention or customs duty, whereas self-governmental receivables are levies that make revenue of a unit of self-government or clearance on account of a subsidy or subvention.

2   Art. 53(26a) In the understanding of the Code, public receivables, including taxes, are also dues that constitute revenue to the general budget of the European Union or to a budget managed by the European Union or on its behalf that are subject to fiscal offences or contraventions in the light of the European Union law provisions binding for the Republic of Poland.

3   Art. 53(27) A public receivable reduced by a prohibited act is an amount of money expressed in numbers whose payment or declaration has been evaded in whole or in part by an obligor, causing financial damage.

4   Some authors are more precise and present three functions of the notion of reduction of public receivables under the FCC: 1) it is a consequence-related element in the definitions of the set of components of prohibited acts, 2) it is a modal element (referring

posure to reduction") functions mainly as an element determining the degree of penalization in particular provisions of the specific part of the Code. Yet, both these elements affect an assessment of the social noxiousness of the act.[5]

Additionally, the terms are closely related to each other. The risk of financial detriment that is the crux of "exposure to reduction" is characterized by significant dynamism of development resulting from the passage of time alone, as lapse of time causes the due date for the payment of public receivables to expire. As soon as the due date of payment expires, there emerges the situation of the obligor's evasion of payment, which, in turn, implies the reduction of public receivables.[6] For example, if the offender declares false information in a tax declaration or return, the due date for the tax payment usually expires before this false declaration is discovered, and thus "exposure to reduction," an element of the definition of the act referred to in art. 56(1-3) FCC,[7] becomes "reduction."

What usually appears in statutory constructions of the FCC is "exposure to reduction" rather than "reduction" itself. The types of "exposure to reduction" do not have counterparts in the types of "reduction," unlike in general penal law where there is basically symmetry between various types of exposure of legal interests to danger and the actual infringement of those legal interests; for example,

---

to circumstances) on which modified liability is dependent 3) alternatively, it is also a result that conditions the application of some institutions included in the FCC. See G. Łabuda, T. Razowski, "Glosa do postanowienia SN z dnia 27 marca 2003 r., sygn. T KZP 2/03," *Prokuratura i Prawo* 2003, No.11, p. 126.

5 Z. Siwik, "Projekt Kodeksu karnego skarbowego – o kierunkach zmian w materialnoprawnych przepisach części ogólnej," *Czasopismo Prawa Karnego i Nauk Penalnych* 1998, No. 1-2, p. 59-60.

6 See L. Wilk, *Szczególne cechy odpowiedzialności za przestępstwa i wykroczenia podatkowe*, Katowice 2006, p. 64.

7 *Art. 56(1) A taxpayer who, by filing a tax declaration to a tax authority, or another competent authority or tax remitter, declares false data, conceals the truth, or does not fulfil an obligation to provide information about the change of data relevant thereto that may result in tax reduction, shall be subject to the penalty of a fine up to 720 daily rates or to the penalty of imprisonment, or to both penalties jointly.*

(2) If the amount of tax exposed to reduction is of small value, the perpetrator of the prohibited act stipulated in paragraph (1) shall be subject to a penalty of a fine of up to 720 daily rates.

(3) If the amount of tax exposed to reduction does not exceed a statutory threshold, the offender of the prohibited act stipulated in paragraph (1) shall be subject to the penalty of a fine for a fiscal contravention.

there is exposure of a human being to the imminent danger of loss of life or severe health impairment[8] and there are also several variations of intentional or unintentional deprivation of life and of infliction of severe health impairment.[9]

---

8   *Art. 160 of the Criminal Code § 1. Whoever exposes a human being to the immediate danger of death or severe health impairment shall be subject to the penalty of imprisonment for up to 3 years.*

(2) If the offender has the duty to care for the person exposed to danger, he shall be subject to the penalty of imprisonment for a term of between 3 months and 5 years.

(3) If the offender of the act specified in paragraph (1) or (2) acts unintentionally, he shall be subject to the penalty of a fine, restriction of liberty or imprisonment for up to 1 year.

(4) An offender who has voluntarily averted the impeding danger shall not be subject to the penalty for the offence specified in paragraphs (1-3).

(5) Prosecution of the offence specified in paragraphs (1 – 3) shall be pursued at the request of the wronged party.

9   The Criminal Code:

Art. 148(1) Whoever kills a human being shall be subject to the penalty of imprisonment for a minimum term of 8 years, or to the penalty of imprisonment for 25 years, or to life imprisonment.

(2) Whoever kills a human being:

    1) with extreme cruelty,

    2) in connection with the taking of a hostage, rape or robbery,

    3) for motives deserving particular reprobation,

    4) with the use of explosives,

shall be subject to the penalty of imprisonment for a minimum term of 12 years, to the penalty of imprisonment for 25 years, or life imprisonment

(3) Whoever kills more than one person in a single act or has earlier been validly and finally convicted for homicide, and whoever kills a public official on duty or in relation to his duties of protecting people's safety or protecting the safety or public order, shall be subject to the penalty specified in paragraph (2).

(4) Whoever kills a human being with intense emotion that is justified by the circumstances shall be subject to the penalty of imprisonment for a term of between 1 and 10 years.

Art. 155. Whoever unintentionally causes the death of a human being shall be subject to the penalty of imprisonment for a term of between 3 months and 5 years.

Art. 156(1) Whoever causes severe impairment of health in a form which:

    1) deprives a human being of sight, hearing, speech or the ability to procreate,

    2) inflicts on a human being a heavy disability, a chronic or prolonged disease, a disease actually dangerous to life, a permanent mental disorder, a permanent total or substantial incapacity to work in one's occupation, or a permanent severe bodily disfigurement or deformation shall be subject to the penalty of imprisonment for a term of between 1 and 10 years.

In this respect, the Fiscal Criminal Code is different: the lawmaker does not differentiate between types of exposure to reduction and reduction itself, as the introduction of the types of reduction corresponding to exposure to reduction into the FCC would inflate this Code without any practical result.

The reduction of public receivables as a specific type of penal fiscal law damage occurs only in fiscal offences, fiscal contraventions (including also clearances on account of a subsidy and subvention), and customs fraud. This term does not appear in the FCC chapters on foreign currency and gambling. In case of violation of regulations pertaining to foreign currency trading or activities in the gambling industry, the lack of tangible and measurable damage makes the concept of restorative justice pointless. In the context of the reduction of public receivables, however, attention should be paid to the notion of wronged party, which is closely related to damage.

The wronged party in fiscal penal law

There is a stereotype according to which fiscal offences (and contraventions) are categorised as so-called offences without a victim. It would be an overstatement to say, however, that there is no wronged party in fiscal penal law. Art. 113(2) FCC[10] might in fact exclude the application of the rules of the Code of Criminal Procedure that pertain to the wronged party and to mediation in proceedings relating to fiscal offences and contraventions, but it should not be treated as grounds for such a far-reaching conclusion. This regulation does not mean that there is no wronged party or damage. The exclusion of the application of the CCP regulations pertaining to the wronged party and to mediation stems from a different source, namely the lack of discrepancy, or even identity, between the interests of the wronged party and the prosecutor. This convergence is most evident in the preparatory proceedings in which the wronged party and the law enforcement authority are in fact the same entity. The actual wronged party is the State Treasury, units of local government (as far as local taxes are concerned),

---

(2) *If the offender acts unintentionally, he shall be subject to the penalty of imprisonment for up to 3 years.*

(3) *If the consequence of the prohibited act specified in paragraph (1) is the death of a human being, the offender shall be subject to the penalty of imprisonment for a term of between 2 and 12 years.*

10 *Art.113(2) The provisions of:*

  1) the Code of Criminal Procedure pertaining to the wronged party and to mediation,

  2) art. 325f of the Code of Criminal Procedure shall not apply.

and other units of the public finances sector (in cases of clearance of a subsidy and subvention) and, as of May 1, 2004, the European Union.

These institutions are the wronged parties with regard to the right to claim payment of public receivables reduced by the prohibited act. However, considering the final recipient of such receivables, it can be said that society at large as well as local communities are wronged parties as well.

Because of the content of the cited art. 113(2) of the FCC, one should remember that the notion of the wronged party in fiscal penal law may be discussed in terms of substantive but not procedural law. This means that there is no one in penal and fiscal proceedings to take on the status of a wronged party. In actuality, the wronged party here is the fiscal creditor. Financial detriment to its property is the fundamental component of the statutory definition of reduction to public receivables.

The process of redressing damage in fiscal penal law

The preference under the current Fiscal Criminal Code is to execute the public receivables reduced by the prohibited acts.[11] The Code is based on the principle of prioritizing the execution of public receivables over punishment. This fundamental principle of the "philosophy of punishment" of the FCC means that the penal fiscal law response is aimed at execution of public receivables rather than at punishment. This principle is expressed by a number of fiscal penal law regulations that establish a system whose keynote is to induce the perpetrators of fiscal offences and contraventions that result in the reduction of public receivables to act as soon as possible to cover the financial detriment suffered by the fiscal creditor, instead of any far reaching mitigation that takes the form of penal fiscal law punishment. Within this mitigation, it is even possible for a punishment not to be imposed at all, depending on how soon the financial detriment is redressed; it also depends on the amount of time and effort a judicial body has to spend on discovering the financial offence or contravention and conducting the proceedings. This executive objective of fiscal criminal proceedings, i.e. to redress the financial detriment caused by the prohibited act to the State Treasury, a local government entity, or any other authorized agent, has been articulated *expressis verbis* in art. 114 FCC,[12] which also imposes on law enforcement authorities the

---

11 Z. Siwik, "Kodeks karny skarbowy. Ogólne zasady odpowiedzialności i karania," *Przegląd Podatkowy* 1999, No. 12, p. 31.

12 *Art. 114(1) Furthermore, the provisions of the Code are aimed at framing procedures concerning financial offences and financial contravention so as to achieve the objectives*

obligation to instruct the offender about his or her rights with regard to the remedy of the financial detriment caused. These rights are the right to initiate any of the institutions of so-called regress of punishment that are extensively accounted for in the FCC; as one of their elements, they provide for the duty or requirement to pay the public receivable in a reduced amount.

Within the extensive amendment of the FCC of 2005,[13] the principle of prioritizing the executive objective over punishment, as discussed in this study, was essentially rationalized and adjusted to the actual needs involved in protecting public finances.[14] This principle is expressed by the following solutions from the amendment of the FCC mentioned above.

Currently, the relevant provisions of the FCC imposing an obligation or requirement to pay public receivables clearly apply only to receivables which are chargeable (mature) and are actually reduced by the prohibited act; this obligation or requirement is omitted if there was only the exposure of a public receivable to reduction or if the receivable has not become chargeable (with the exception of art. 16a FCC,[15] which is obviously different from other regulations prioritizing the executive objective over punishment, an omission which simply appears to be the doing of the lawmaker). Therefore, the expiry of a tax obligation on account of reduced tax resulting from cancellation of tax arrears, as decided by the fiscal creditor (the wronged party), does not deprive the offender of the opportunity to take advantage of institutions that mitigate fiscal criminal liability related to the obligation or requisite to pay the due public receivable (as in this case receivables are not chargeable).

---

of such procedures with respect to compensating the financial detriment inflicted by a prohibited act to the State Treasury, a local government or other authorized agent.

(2) The authority conducting proceedings is also obliged to instruct the offender about his rights in cases of redress of the financial detriment to the State Treasury, unit of local government or other authorized agent.

13 The act of 28 July 2005 Amending the Act, the Fiscal Criminal Code and Some Other Acts (Dziennik Ustaw No. 178, item 1479).

14 For more, see L. Wilk, "Założenia nowelizacji Kodeksu karnego skarbowego z 28.7.2005," *Monitor Prawniczy* 2006, no 1, p. 7-16.

15 *Art. 16a. Whoever has filed a correction to a tax return that is legally effective according to the provisions of the Tax Ordinance Act or the Financial Control Act of 28 September 1991 (Dziennik Ustaw 2011, No. 41 item 214, as amended) and has explained the reasons for such a correction, and whoever has paid in whole the public receivable reduced or exposed to reduction within a time frame established by the authorized agent, shall not be subject to penalty for either a financial offence or financial contravention.*

The FCC regulations that refer to obligations or requisites to pay a chargeable public receivable reduced by a prohibited act do not require that they be paid directly to the offender. Rather, they prescribe such obligations or requisites impersonally; at the same time, they do not require, as was the case prior to the FCC reform, such an obligation or requisite to be fulfilled by the offender him- or herself. This comes as a result of the consideration of a wide range of possible scenarios in which the offender acts on behalf of someone else, as well as the situations defined in art. 9(3) FCC.[16] The payment of chargeable public receivables reduced by a prohibited act by someone on whose behalf the offender acted is considered to be fulfilment of the statutory obligation or requisite as though the sum was paid by the offender him- or herself.

The execution of reduced public receivables and the concept of restorative justice

Having discussed the notions of "wronged party" and "damage" as used in the FCC, and having briefly outlined how the principle of prioritizing the execution of a reduced public receivable over punishment functions in penal fiscal law, an attempt might be made to answer the question of whether and to what extent the model of penal fiscal response that prioritizes the execution of a reduced public receivable over punishment might be considered a specific counterpart to the model of restorative justice as it appears in general criminal law. In order to answer this question, the definition of "restorative justice" should be first taken up, and the components of the restorative justice model should be confronted with the state of affairs in the field of penal fiscal law that has been described above.

One definition of restorative justice reads that it is a "process in which the offender and the wronged party make a conscious effort to compensate and forgive, and supported by the other parties involved, they look together for opportunities to solve the problems that have arisen from the offender's criminal conduct."[17] This definition, as can be quickly noticed, does not fit well into a fiscal penal law framework. Because of the nature of the protected interest, that is

---

16 *Art. 9(3) Whoever is involved, based on a provision of law, the decision of a proper authority, a contract or actual conduct in business matters, particularly related to finances of a natural or juridical person, or entity without legal personality, yet with legal capacity under special provisions of law, shall be liable for financial offences and contraventions to the same extent as the offender.*

17 D. Jaworska, M. Niełaczna, W. Klaus, "Sprawiedliwość naprawcza a mediacja – konkurentki czy sojuszniczki," *Mediator* 2004, No. 4, p. 23.

the revenue of the State Treasury and other fiscal creditors on account of public levies, and because of the absence of ethical and moral roots for this legal interest and in fact because of the somewhat opposite, even pejorative overtones of the word "tax" in social perception, it is simply impossible to talk about forgiveness or compensation as it is understood in the restorative justice model. Furthermore, from the formal standpoint, neither forgiveness nor compensation is to be considered as there is no one who would hold the status of a wronged party in fiscal criminal proceedings. While it is true that there is an entity injured by a given fiscal act, i.e. the fiscal creditor (the State Treasury or any other respective authority), they do not become involved in a relationship with the offender in fiscal criminal proceedings.

Restorative justice, as discussed in the context of general penal law, covers the process of resolving conflicts, not just the outcome of that process, and it presupposes cooperation between the parties in line with the horizontal model of penal proceedings, which likewise requires the maximum involvement of the wronged party.[18] There is no such an element in fiscal criminal law. Reduction of a public receivable is not a conflict but rather an outcome of social conflict that has arisen out of a fiscal offence or fiscal contravention. The FCC is exclusively aimed at redressing the financial detriment to the fiscal creditor, that is at liquidating the financial consequences of the conflict. The "horizontal model" of fiscal criminal process is not possible as there is no wronged party involved. Another element missing in the process is the presence of the local community, which is an important aspect of restorative justice at the level of general penal law.

Due to the aforementioned legislative reform of 2005, which cancelled the requirement for the offender to directly pay the reduced public receivable and prescribed this requirement in an impersonal way instead (the offender and the obligor under a tax or customs duty are in practice frequently not the same; the consequences of this fact are provided for in art. 9(3) FCC), it is statistically common that the one who redresses the detriment caused by the relevant fiscal act by paying a reduced chargeable public receivable is not the offender him- or herself but somebody else, namely a person replaced by the offender, as described in the art. 9(3) FCC. In many cases this type of redress of financial detriment to the creditor occurs without any initiative or involvement of the perpetrator of the fiscal offence or fiscal contravention.

---

18 See J. Wróblewska, "Rozważania na temat kulturowo-społecznych ograniczeń dla wprowadzania idei mediacji w Polsce," *Mediator* 2003, No. 3, p. 45-47; P. Szczepaniak, "Mediacja po wyroku – w stronę sprawiedliwości naprawczej," *Mediator* 2003, No. 1, p. 57.

Unlike in classic examples of active repentance in general penal law, the relevant regulations of the FCC that ordain the payment of a reduced chargeable public receivable do not make use of certain institutions of regression of punishment in a way that is dependent on the voluntariness of payment. The requirement of "voluntariness" would not make any sense whatsoever as long as the damage that is reduction of a public receivable can be, and actually is, redressed by somebody else than the offender.

The system of institutions governing the regress of punishment in the FCC, prioritizing the execution of reduced public receivables, is not aimed, unlike in restorative justice, at educating society about the norms and values related to the duty to pay public levies, but at making people realize that fiscal offences and fiscal contraventions against State revenue and local revenues from public levies are not profitable. This penal and fiscal system, based as it is on a simple and clear *carrot and stick* approach, actually works as if in the place of fiscal executive authorities. It is aimed at avoiding the necessity to conduct executive administrative proceedings of little practical effectiveness. Instead, the point is to execute public receivables by resorting to fiscal criminal law instruments. The motivation for the offender to redress the damage is the threat of a punishment which would be a greater distress. This is not what restorative justice looks like in the area of general penal law. It employs totally different procedures than those used in fiscal penal law. It should be emphasized that the "negotiations" appearing in the FCC regulations in reference to one of the institutions of regress of punishment, namely voluntary submission to liability, actually do not concern the question of reduced public receivable, as this requirement has been categorically prescribed by the fiscally oriented lawmaker without any room for flexibility. Furthermore, the authority capable of making decisions about liabilities under tax and customs obligations does not take part in these "negotiations" (not to mention the fact that the term "negotiations" is inadequate in this context, as in fact it is a process in which the offender meets the conditions set by the statute and a law enforcing authority), as they are run only by the financial authority that conducts the preparatory proceedings (investigation).

The payment of chargeable public receivables reduced by the prohibited act obviously bars the commencement of execution proceedings in administration, as it makes such procedures redundant. It might be doubted, however, whether this translates into the avoidance of further escalation of the conflict between the obligor and fiscal creditor. The conflict is entrenched in the eternal, multifaceted desire of taxed persons to reduce their tax obligations, a desire that has always been observable and seems impossible to eradicate. Any illegal and punishable reduction of public receivables is a mere consequence of this conflict.

Finally, the classic concept of restorative justice was born in penal law and it was a grassroots movement, while its activists (N. Christie) were supported by science that provided the new paradigm of "horizontal" justice in opposition to the traditional model of "vertical" justice.[19]

There is nothing like this in fiscal penal law: as the lawmaker realised how ineffective economic punishment and, in addition, the administrative execution of public levies are, the lawmaker became inclined to construct a system of solutions based on the principle of prioritising the execution of reduced public receivables over punishment.

Conclusion

To sum up, it should be stated that, at a basic level, the regulations of the FCC analysed do not put the model of restorative justice into practice, whether in view of its background, essence, components or procedures. It should also be highlighted that fiscal criminal law will never be able to deploy this model in practice. The parties to the social conflict resulting from the commission of a fiscal offence or a fiscal contravention are not, and never will be, equal to one another and will not constitute equal partners as the detriment is redressed. What constitutes grounds for conflict is a tax law relationship in which the fiscal creditor authoritatively determines liabilities in the form of administrative decisions. As a result, this is not a suitable field in which to implement the idea of restorative justice in the sense in which this term is commonly used.

---

19 N. Christie, *Dogodna ilość przestępstw* (Warszawa 2004), p. 82 et seq.

Jakub Hanc

The Idea of Restorative Justice: An Attempt at a Comparative Analysis

For some time, it has been apparent that the idea of restorative justice is becoming important to European states. Its postulations, transformed into concrete legal enactments, constitute unique elements of legal systems, and are often considerably diversified (especially considering the degree to which Roman law has been adopted). Unfortunately, it should be noted at the same time that implementations of this idea are often fragmented and cover only certain areas that are separate from the broader context of the model of criminal restorative law. In addition, they do not always properly match their legal environment. This points to the absence of any comprehensive approach.

Because of the limited scope of this publication, it is not the author's intention to thoroughly and meticulously describe the mechanisms leading to the implementation of the idea of restorative justice in a variety of jurisdictions, but only to point to particular instances of its implementation. Moreover, the object of the present study is to identify a typical model of restorative justice in criminal law, situating cases of departure from that model outside the scope of its interest.

Bearing in mind the prospect of further investigations,[1] it is necessary at the outset to make one crucial explanation. The idea of restorative justice is realised in areas influenced by German legal culture. It is based on the assumptions of the concept of the so-called third way (known as either *Dritte Spur* or *Dreispurigkeit*), whose basic postulates have been expressed in a study edited by a working group of German, Swiss and Austrian scholars in the field of criminal law, entitled *Alternativ - Entwurf Wiedergutmachung*.[2] This alternative project concentrates on the German concept *Wiedergutmachung*, which refers to the compensation (restitution, repair) of the consequences (effects) of the criminal

---

1 Especially the fact that the present analysis covers selected regulations in two German-speaking countries, i.e. the Swiss Confederacy and the Republic of Austria.

2 J. Baumann (*et al.*) *Alternativ - Entwurf Wiedergutmachung* (München: C. H. Beck Verlag, 1992); see also C. Roxin, *Zur Wiedergutmachung als einer «dritten Spur» im Sanktionensystem* in G. Arzt, G. Fezer, U. Weber, E. Schlüchter, D. Rössner (eds.), *Festschrift für Jürgen Baumann zum 70. Geburtstag am 22. Juni 1992* (Bielefeld: Verlag Ernst und Werner Gieseking, 1992), p. 243-254.

actions of the offender taken against the victim or society (understood as a whole, the community).[3] According to the authors of this publication, if one is to recognise as an aim of criminal law the preservation of the condition of peace and order, i.e. reaction to any possible disturbances of this condition, then the discussed institution can constitute a separate and independent measure allowing for its achievement.[4] With this in mind, these authors recommend that, in addition to the existing criminal law reactions (amounting to penalties or other measures), *Wiedergutmachung* be introduced as a so-called third type of response, a third independent path within the available instruments of criminal law.[5] Obviously, this notion is not undisputed. It has many adversaries. In the first place, they are against including the institution of *Wiedergutmachung* in the scope of criminal law regulations, and emphasise that its instruments cannot be used to pursue the assumptions of restorative justice. These critics speak in favour of the need to create a separate legal track which would cover the relationship between the offender and the wronged party, both from the purely compensatory perspective and the restorative one (aimed at successful diffusion of conflict).[6] Finally, however, they see the possibility of anchoring the construction of *Wiedergutmachung* as one of the duties to be imposed by court along with conditional suspension of execution of penalty (*Bewährungsauflagen*).[7]

The basic concerns of German academics are, however, caused by two issues. The first is the potential influence of *Wiedergutmachung* on the traditional system of criminal sanctions and their aims.[8] Sceptics of the third way doubt that

---

3   J. Baumann (*et al.*) *Alternativ - Entwurf Wiedergutmachung*, p. 39 *et seq.* A similar interpretation of the term is proposed by Ö. Sevdiren, *Alternatives to Imprisonment in England and Wales, Germany and Turkey. A Comparative Study* (Berlin - Heidelberg - Dordrecht - London - New York: Springer - Verlag 2011), p. 165.

4   J. Baumann (*et al.*) *Alternativ - Entwurf Wiedergutmachung*, p. 23 *et seq.*

5   The main proponent of this understanding of the third way is C. Roxin; see C. Roxin, *Die Wiedergutmachung im System der Strafzwecke*, in H. Schöch (eds.), *Wiedergutmachung und Strafrecht* (München: Wilhelm Fink Verlag, 1987), p. 37-55.

6   See e.g. H. J. Hirsch, *Wiedergutmachung des Schadens im Rahmen des materiellen Strafrecht*, Zeitschrift für die gesamte Strafrechtswissenschaft, vol. 102 (1990), p. 534-562.

7   As in H. J. Hirsch, *Ibid.* For the dispute between H. J. Hirsch and C. Roxin on the essence of *Wiedergutmachung*, see H. Schöch, *Wege und Irrwege der Wiedergutmachung im Strafrecht* in B. Schünemann (ed.), *Festschrift für Claus Roxin zum 70. Geburtstag am 15. Mai 2001* (Berlin - New York: Verlag de Gruyter, 2001), p. 1050 *et seq.*

8   See e.g. J. Kaspar, *Wiedergutmachung und Mediation im Strafrecht. Rechtliche Grundlagen und Ergebnisse eines Modellprojekts zur anwaltlichen Schlichtung* (Münster: Lit

reconciliation between the offender and the victim could realise in any way the goals traditionally attributed to criminal law responses to undesired actions.[9]

The second concern refers to the question of the character of *Wiedergutmachung*, to whether it is a civil law or criminal law institution.[10]

As can be seen, the realisation of the idea of restorative justice in German speaking countries has been preceded by common and thorough preparatory efforts spurred by the urge to find a solution that allows a quick and effective redress of the results of an offender's criminal conduct to be ensured to the wronged party. The analysis here presented will be focused on attempts to find an answer to the question of the implementation of the proposals of restorative justice in the legal systems of two European states.

Swiss Confederation

In analysing provisions of the Swiss Criminal Code (*Schweizerisches Strafgesetzbuch*[11]), one can easily find several traces indicating the presence of the idea of restorative justice in the legal system. At the same time, it must be pointed out, without over-generalising, that these traces are mostly related to the question of compensation.

Verlag, 2004), p. 28 *et seq.*; T. Trenczek, *Within or outside the system? Restorative justice attempts and the penal system* in E. G. M. Weitekamp and H. J. Kerner (eds.), *Restorative Justice in Context: International Practice and Directions* (Devon – Portland: Willan Publishing, 2003), p. 280 *et seq.*

9   One might be under the impression that they perceive the third path as a component that decomposes the specificity of criminal law; it is foreign to its standard functions. Simultaneously, they do not deny that the application of measures resulting from the concept of restorative justice might have positive and eventful consequences, reaching further than restitution and the aims of penalty themselves. They do not exclude the need to create an autonomic and active platform for legal rules to facilitate the resolution of conflict; see T. Trenczek, *Ibid.*

10   There is obviously a big difference of opinions. H. Schöch states that the construction of *Wiedergutmachung* is on the border between penal and civil law; C. Roxin presents evidence that it would be difficult to accept its exclusively civil law character, yet H. J. Hirsch points out that it is not an independent institution, and in this sense it depends on civil law; see J. Kaspar, *Wiedergutmachung und Mediation*, p. 36. It is also worth noticing that the notion of *Wiedergutmachung* is foreign to the civil codes of Austria, Germany and Switzerland; instead they use the terms *Schadenersatz* (damage) and *Genugtuung* (compensation).

11   Schweizerisches Strafgesetzbuch vom 21. Dezember 1937 (Stand am 1. Juli 2013); hereinafter referred to as sStGB.

Special regard should be paid to the provisions of art. 42 sStGB[12] relating to so-called conditional penalties (*Bedingte Strafen*). Clearly the most interesting part of this enactment is paragraph (3), which prescribes that the offender may be obligated to serve a sentence in a conditional system whereby he or she has a chance to repair the damage[13] caused by his or her criminal conduct but omits (fails) to do so. In accordance with paragraph (1), the court suspends execution of fine, community service or imprisonment to the extent of at least six months, but for no longer than 2 years, in situations in which the imposition of an unconditional sentence is not necessary to prevent the offender from perpetrating further felonies or misdemeanours. One negative prerequisite of the benevolence specified in paragraph (1) is the possibility for the offender to redress the damage, which is determined *ad casum*. Undoubtedly, this puts a very difficult task before the court. Although it requires considerable effort, it is not impossible.

Many more serious hardships are posed by the prerequisite of damage (*Schaden*). The Code does not specify how to understand this term. In addition, the statute does not offer any specific reference to its Civil Code, or even indirectly to the doctrine of civil law to which the concept of damage is closely linked. Bearing these observations in mind, it ought to be noted that both arguments which speak in favour of an autonomous understanding of the notion of "damage" under sStGB and those which support the need to resort to the findings of civil law science are equally important.

In the absence of a legal definition of damage in the Swiss Criminal Code, there is no other option but to seek an answer by means of systematic interpretation. The Swiss lawmaker uses the notion of damage in other provisions of the Code (quite many of them). In the general part of the Code, attention ought to

---

12 Art. 42 sStGB: "(1) Das Gericht schiebt den Vollzug einer Geldstrafe, von gemeinnütziger Arbeit oder einer Freiheitsstrafe von mindestens sechs Monaten und höchstens zwei Jahren in der Regel auf, wenn eine unbedingte Strafe nicht notwendig erscheint, um den Täter von der Begehung weiterer Verbrechen oder Vergehen abzuhalten. (2) Wurde der Täter innerhalb der letzten fünf Jahre vor der Tat zu einer bedingten oder unbedingten Freiheitsstrafe von mindestens sechs Monaten oder zu einer Geldstrafe von mindestens 180 Tagessätzen verurteilt, so ist der Aufschub nur zulässig, wenn besonders günstige Umstände vorliegen. (3) Die Gewährung des bedingten Strafvollzuges kann auch verweigert werden, wenn der Täter eine zumutbare Schadenbehebung unterlassen hat. (4) Eine bedingte Strafe kann mit einer unbedingten Geldstrafe oder mit einer Busse nach Artikel 106 verbunden werden."

13 The lawmaker requires that the repair of the damage be "reasonable," "acceptable," and "suited to the capacities" of the offender—rendered by the German adjective "zumutbare."

be paid to the fact that one of the alternative grounds for mitigation of penalty (*Strafmilderung – Gründe*) is the condition in which the offender shows genuine repentance by repairing the damage inflicted by the offence in the manner expected of him or her.[14]

Basic difficulties follow from art. 53 sStGB,[15] which regulates the consequences derived from the institution of *Wiedergutmachung*. Where the offender has redressed the economic loss or made all efforts to compensate the non-economic loss inflicted by his or her actions, the respective authority refrains from criminal prosecution, initiating judicial proceedings or imposing punishment if the prerequisites of conditional sentence (of art. 42 sStGB) are fulfilled and the public interest as well as the interest of the wronged party in criminal prosecution are minor (low).

Doubts emerge already at the stage of interpreting the first part of this regulation. The question arises of how the conjunction *oder*[16] should be understood in this specific provision. Does the obligation of the offender encompass only compensation of economic loss, or also efforts to redress non-economic loss? Moreover, even if it is assumed that the fulfilment of a single premise is sufficient, it remains unclear who has the choice and which prerequisite ought to be met. Unfortunately, this and many other questions cannot be answered on the basis of a literal interpretation of the provision. It also does not seem that other methods of interpretation (i.e. systematic and purposive) could clear up these ambiguities.

Other objections are raised by the requirement of the joint subsistence, on the part of the wronged party and the public interest, of a minor degree of interest in the prosecution of the offender. It would not be difficult to imagine a situation in which the stance of the wronged party and the broadly conceived interest of the

---

14 Art. 48 sStGB: "Das Gericht mildert die Strafe, wenn: (d) der Täter aufrichtige Reue betätigt, namentlich den Schaden, soweit es ihm zuzumuten war, ersetzt hat."

15 Art. 53 sStGB: "Hat der Täter den Schaden gedeckt oder alle zumutbaren Anstrengungen unternommen, um das von ihm bewirkte Unrecht auszugleichen, so sieht die zuständige Behörde von einer Strafverfolgung, einer Überweisung an das Gericht oder einer Bestrafung ab, wenn: (a) die Voraussetzungen für die bedingte Strafe (Art. 42) erfüllt sind; und (b) das Interesse der Öffentlichkeit und des Geschädigten an der Strafverfolgung gering sind."

16 Does this word really mean the same as "or"? In this case it would be a simple alternative (i.e., it would be sufficient to meet one out of the alternative requisites or meet both of them simultaneously); or is it a mutually exclusive "or" (one circumstance is sufficient to create an obligation).

system of justice (i.e., the need to punish originating in criminal policy) should differ significantly.

When it comes to definitions of crime in the specified section, it should be noted that the absence of any approximation of the content of the notion of "loss" negatively translates into interpretation of these rules. The Swiss legislator uses the term "loss" rather inconsequently, as a result of which one may doubt whether it means the same with respect to each type of crime, which in turn undoubtedly impeaches the directive of parallel interpretation of the same expression.

It seems conspicuous, first, that one can encounter definitions of crime in which the notion of damage is independent. Such is the case with most definitions located in the chapter on crimes against property (*Strafbare Handlungen gegen das Vermögen*).[17] Second, one can also find definitions in which the element of "damage" is qualified by an adjective. This situation is the case, for example, with qualified damage to property (*Sachbeschädigung*),[18] where the qualifying factor is the infliction of "serious (great) damage" (*grossen Schaden*), and with regard to the qualified type of crime of corrupting data (*Datenbeschädigung*).[19] Another example is the statutory expression "minor (minimal, inconsiderable) damage"

---

17 The element of damage is present, e.g. in the definition of fraudulent misuse of a data-processing device (*Betrügerischer Missbrauch einer Datenverarbeitungsanlage*), art. 147 sStGB: „(1) Wer in der Absicht, sich oder einen andern unrechtmässig zu bereichern, durch unrichtige, unvollständige oder unbefugte Verwendung von Daten oder in vergleichbarer Weise auf einen elektronischen oder vergleichbaren Datenverarbeitungs- oder Datenübermittlungsvorgang einwirkt und dadurch eine Vermögensverschiebung zum Schaden eines andern herbeiführt oder eine Vermögensverschiebung unmittelbar darnach verdeckt, wird mit Freiheitsstrafe bis zu fünf Jahren oder Geldstrafe bestraft.", or crime against bankruptcy and execution or executory procedure; fraudulent bankruptcy and fraudulent attachment of claims (*Konkurs- und Betreibungs Verbrechen oder Betreibungsvorgehen. Betrügerischer Konkurs und Pfändungsbetrug*) – art. 163 sStGB: „(1) Der Schuldner, der zum Schaden der Gläubiger sein Vermögen zum Scheine vermindert, namentlich Vermögenswerte beiseiteschafft oder verheimlicht, Schulden vortäuscht, vorgetäuschte Forderungen anerkennt oder deren Geltendmachung veranlasst, wird, wenn über ihn der Konkurs eröffnet oder gegen ihn ein Verlustschein ausgestellt worden ist, mit Freiheitsstrafe bis zu fünf Jahren oder Geldstrafe bestraft."

18 Art. 144 sStGB: "(3) Hat der Täter einen grossen Schaden verursacht, so kann auf Freiheitsstrafe von einem Jahr bis zu fünf Jahren erkannt werden. Die Tat wird von Amtes wegen verfolgt."

19 Art. 144 *bis* sStGB: "(1) Wer unbefugt elektronisch oder in vergleichbarer Weise gespeicherte oder übermittelte Daten verändert, löscht oder unbrauchbar macht, wird, auf Antrag, mit Freiheitsstrafe bis zu drei Jahren oder Geldstrafe bestraft. Hat der

(*geringer Schaden*), used in the definition of minor crimes against property (*Geringfügige Vermögensdelikte*),[20] arson (*Brandstiftung*),[21] causing an explosion (*Verursachung einer Explosion*),[22] causing flood or collapse (*Verursachen einer Überschwemmung oder eines Einsturzes*),[23] and damage to electrical or hydraulic installations and protective devices (*Beschädigung von elektrischen Anlagen, Wasserbauten und Schutzvorrichtungen*).[24]

It ought to be stressed that the Swiss Criminal Code contains norms that are unlikely to be classified as conforming to the model of restorative justice. One example of such an enactment may be art. 73 sStGB,[25] which is appended with

---

Täter einen grossen Schaden verursacht, so kann auf Freiheitsstrafe von einem Jahr bis zu fünf Jahren erkannt werden. Die Tat wird von Amtes wegen verfolgt."

20 Art. 172 ter sStGB: "(1) Richtet sich die Tat nur auf einen geringen Vermögenswert oder auf einen geringen Schaden, so wird der Täter, auf Antrag, mit Busse bestraft. (2) Diese Vorschrift gilt nicht bei qualifiziertem Diebstahl (Art. 139 Ziff. 2 und 3), bei Raub und Erpressung."

21 Art. 221 sStGB: "(1) Wer vorsätzlich zum Schaden eines andern oder unter Herbeiführung einer Gemeingefahr eine Feuersbrunst verursacht, wird mit Freiheitsstrafe nicht unter einem Jahr bestraft. (2) Bringt der Täter wissentlich Leib und Leben von Menschen in Gefahr, so ist die Strafe Freiheitsstrafe nicht unter drei Jahren. (3) Ist nur ein geringer Schaden entstanden, so kann auf Freiheitsstrafe bis zu drei Jahren oder Geldstrafe erkannt werden."

22 Art. 233 sStGB: "(1) Wer vorsätzlich eine Explosion von Gas, Benzin, Petroleum oder ähnlichen Stoffen verursacht und dadurch wissentlich Leib und Leben von Menschen oder fremdes Eigentum in Gefahr bringt, wird mit Freiheitsstrafe nicht unter einem Jahr bestraft. Ist nur ein geringer Schaden entstanden, so kann auf Freiheitsstrafe bis zu drei Jahren oder Geldstrafe erkannt werden."

23 Art. 227 sStGB: "(1) Wer vorsätzlich eine Überschwemmung oder den Einsturz eines Bauwerks oder den Absturz von Erd- und Felsmassen verursacht und dadurch wissentlich Leib und Leben von Menschen oder fremdes Eigentum in Gefahr bringt, wird mit Freiheitsstrafe nicht unter einem Jahr bestraft. Ist nur ein geringer Schaden entstanden, so kann auf Freiheitsstrafe bis zu drei Jahren oder Geldstrafe erkannt werden."

24 Art. 228 sStGB: "(1) Wer vorsätzlich elektrische Anlagen, Wasserbauten, namentlich Dämme, Wehre, Deiche, Schleusen, Schutzvorrichtungen gegen Naturereignisse, so gegen Bergsturz oder Lawinen, beschädigt oder zerstört und dadurch wissentlich Leib und Leben von Menschen oder fremdes Eigentum in Gefahr bringt, wird mit Freiheitsstrafe nicht unter einem Jahr bestraft. Ist nur ein geringer Schaden entstanden, so kann auf Freiheitsstrafe bis zu drei Jahren oder Geldstrafe erkannt werden."

25 Art. 73 sStGB: "(1) Erleidet jemand durch ein Verbrechen oder ein Vergehen einen Schaden, der nicht durch eine Versicherung gedeckt ist, und ist anzunehmen, dass der Täter den Schaden nicht ersetzen oder eine Genugtuung nicht leisten wird,

the caption "attachment to the benefit of the wronged party" (*Verwendung zu Gunsten des Geschädigten*). In paragraph (1), the discussed provision prescribes that where the committed felony or misdemeanour caused damage which cannot be covered by insurance, and where it may be surmised that the offender will not redress economic loss or provide compensation for non-economic loss, the court, at the request of the wronged party, awards to the later (up to the value of compensation for economic or non-economic loss ascertained by court or in a settlement) either a fine or vindictive damages payable by the convict,[26] the sequestrated items or assets or the equivalent obtained from their sale, decreased by costs of the executive proceedings, substitute receivable debt (*Ersatzforderung*[27]), or a so-called peace guarantee amount (*den Betrag der Friedensbürgschaft*[28]).

---

so spricht das Gericht dem Geschädigten auf dessen Verlangen bis zur Höhe des Schadenersatzes beziehungsweise der Genugtuung, die gerichtlich oder durch Vergleich festgesetzt worden sind, zu: (a) die vom Verurteilten bezahlte Geldstrafe oder Busse; (b) eingezogene Gegenstände und Vermögenswerte oder deren Verwertungserlös unter Abzug der Verwertungskosten; (c) Ersatzforderungen; (d) den Betrag der Friedensbürgschaft."

26 When awarding vindictive damages (*die Busse*), the court takes into account in particular the gravity of the act, the degree of organisation deficiency, the damage caused and the economic efficiency of the enterprise; see art. 102 sStGB: "(3) Das Gericht bemisst die Busse insbesondere nach der Schwere der Tat und der Schwere des Organisationsmangels und des angerichteten Schadens sowie nach der wirtschaftlichen Leistungsfähigkeit des Unternehmens."

27 This issue is developed in art. 71 sStGB: "(1) Sind die der Einziehung unterliegenden Vermögenswerte nicht mehr vorhanden, so erkennt das Gericht auf eine Ersatzforderung des Staates in gleicher Höhe, gegenüber einem Dritten jedoch nur, soweit dies nicht nach Artikel 70 Absatz 2 ausgeschlossen ist. (2) Das Gericht kann von einer Ersatzforderung ganz oder teilweise absehen, wenn diese voraussichtlich uneinbringlich wäre oder die Wiedereingliederung des Betroffenen ernstlich behindern würde. (3) Die Untersuchungsbehörde kann im Hinblick auf die Durchsetzung der Ersatzforderung Vermögenswerte des Betroffenen mit Beschlag belegen. Die Beschlagnahme begründet bei der Zwangsvollstreckung der Ersatzforderung kein Vorzugsrecht zu Gunsten des Staates.". See notes made by F. Bommer, *Vorlesung Strafrecht I/II. Allgemeiner Teil des StGB. Stichworte*, p. 21 *et seq.*, http://www.unilu.ch/files/12_strafrechtliche-sanktionen.pdf [last accessed Dec. 22, 2013; 15:58].

28 The Swiss Criminal Code distinguishes between penalties (*Strafen*) and measures (*Massnahmen*), which are divided into "preventive" measures ("*sichernden*" *Massnahmen*) defined in arts. 56 to 65 and "other" measures (*Andere Massnahmen*) referred to in arts. 66 to 73. The so-called peace guarantee has been defined in art. 66 sStGB: "(1) Besteht die Gefahr, dass jemand ein Verbrechen oder Vergehen ausführen wird, mit dem er gedroht hat, oder legt jemand, der wegen eines Verbrechens oder eines

Without covering too much detail as regards the construction of particular securities, it should be noted that it is highly doubtful whether this type of criminal law regulation may lead to the effective diffusion of the conflict between the offender and the wronged party. In the literature of the field, one may encounter voices that are sceptical of the effectiveness and actual compensatory capacity of certain securities.[29] In consequence, one should not exclude *a limine* a situation in which the wronged party obtains no satisfaction (i.e. compensation for economic and non-economic loss) through these instruments of criminal law.

Additionally, it does not seem that vindictive damages (*Busse*) suit the overall framework of restorative justice well. They constitute a financial sanction amounting (unless statutory provisions should provide otherwise) maximally to 10000 Swiss francs.[30] Judicial duties stipulate the inclusion of a warning in the judgment that in the event of non-payment of the vindictive damages, they will be substituted for a replacement penalty of imprisonment (*Ersatzfreiheitsstrafe*) in the amount of from 1 to 6 months.[31] When determining the amount of vindictive damages, the court should take into consideration all the circumstances of the case so as to adjust the penalty to the level of

---

Vergehens verurteilt wird, die bestimmte Absicht an den Tag, die Tat zu wiederholen, so kann ihm das Gericht auf Antrag des Bedrohten das Versprechen abnehmen, die Tat nicht auszuführen, und ihn anhalten, angemessene Sicherheit dafür zu leisten. (2) Verweigert er das Versprechen oder leistet er böswillig die Sicherheit nicht innerhalb der bestimmten Frist, so kann ihn das Gericht durch Sicherheitshaft zum Versprechen oder zur Leistung von Sicherheit anhalten. Die Sicherheitshaft darf nicht länger als zwei Monate dauern. Sie wird wie eine kurze Freiheitsstrafe vollzogen (Art. 79). (3) Begeht er das Verbrechen oder das Vergehen innerhalb von zwei Jahren, nachdem er die Sicherheit geleistet hat, so verfällt die Sicherheit dem Staate. Andernfalls wird sie zurückgegeben. " See F. Bommer, *Vorlesung Strafrecht I/II. Allgemeiner Teil des StGB. Stichworte*, p. 2, 14 and 18.

29 F. Bommer draws attention, *inter alia*, to the "minor practical significance" of the peace guarantee; *Ibid.*

30 Vindictive damages have been envisaged in art. 106 sStGB: "(1) Bestimmt es das Gesetz nicht anders, so ist der Höchstbetrag der Busse 10 000 Franken. (2) Der Richter spricht im Urteil für den Fall, dass die Busse schuldhaft nicht bezahlt wird, eine Ersatzfreiheitsstrafe von mindestens einem Tag und höchstens drei Monaten aus. (3) Das Gericht bemisst Busse und Ersatzfreiheitsstrafe je nach den Verhältnissen des Täters so, dass dieser die Strafe erleidet, die seinem Verschulden angemessen ist. (4) Die Ersatzfreiheitsstrafe entfällt, soweit die Busse nachträglich bezahlt wird. (5) Auf den Vollzug und die Umwandlung sind die Artikel 35 und 36 Absätze 2–5 sinngemäss anwendbar."

31 See art. 106(2) sStGB, *Ibid.*

the offender's guilt.[32] Vindictive damages constitute an element that separates crimes, i.e. felonies (*Verbrechen*), and misdemeanours (*Vergehen*) from contraventions (*Übertretungen*), as art. 103 sStGB[33] stipulates that contravention is an act for which there is the threat of the penalty of vindictive damages. In the light of further provisions of the Swiss Criminal Code, this means that in the case of misdemeanours,[34] the adjudication of vindictive damages is always unconditional (*immer unbedingt*), while with regard to crimes one may speak of the conditional (*bedingt*) character of the measure.[35]

At first glance, it would seem that the layer on which the postulates of restorative justice could be realised is mediation. Unfortunately, as regards criminal law, one may encounter the view that the task of ensuring the proper legal framework for mediation and effectively utilising this instrument in order to evaporate the conflict between the victim and the offender is still "in its infancy."[36] The problems of mediation in criminal matters have been addressed in art. 317 of the draft of the new Code of Criminal Procedure,[37] which, however, has not entered

---

32 See art. 106(3) sStGB, *Ibid.*

33 Art. 103 sStGB: "Übertretungen sind Taten, die mit Busse bedroht sind."

34 Regulated within sStGB in arts. from 103 to 109.

35 See F. Bommer, *Vorlesung Strafrecht I/II. Allgemeiner Teil des StGB. Stichworte*, p. 4 *et seq.*

36 I. Meier, *Mediation und Schlichtung in der Schweiz. Unter besonderer Berücksichtigung der gesetzlichen Rahmenbedingungen für Mediation*, p. 7, http://www.175jahre.uzh. ch/fakultaeten/recht/fachbereiche/zprschkg/ Dokumente/report_mediation_deu_ EZPO.pdf [last accessed: Dec 24, 2013, 08:01].

37 Art. 317 EStPO: "(1) Die Staatsanwaltschaft kann jederzeit eine Mediatorin oder einen Mediator mit einer Mediation betrauen. Sie holt dazu das Einverständnis der beschuldigten und der geschädigten Person ein und orientiert sie über die Tragweite einer Mediation. Sie stellt der Mediatorin oder dem Mediator eine Kopie der Akten zu. (2) Die Verantwortung für die Strafverfolgung bleibt bei der Staatsanwaltschaft. Diese kann sich jederzeit über den Stand der Mediation unterrichten lassen. (3) Die Mediatorin oder der Mediator soll auf eine zwischen den beteiligten Personen frei verhandelte Lösung hinarbeiten. Um dieses Ziel zu erreichen, agiert die Mediatorin oder der Mediator in völliger Unabhängigkeit von der Staatsanwaltschaft, unparteilich und ohne auf die beteiligten Personen Druck auszuüben. (4) Die Mediatorin oder der Mediator lädt die beschuldigte und die geschädigte Person unter Hinweis auf die Freiwilligkeit ihrer Beteiligung zu einem Gespräch ein. Erachtet die Mediatorin oder der Mediator die Aufgabe als erfüllt, so teilt sie oder er der Staatsanwaltschaft das Ergebnis der Mediation mit. Die Mitteilung enthält: (a) den Wortlaut der getroffenen Vereinbarung und den Nachweis, dass sie umgesetzt worden ist; oder (b) die blosse Feststellung des Scheiterns. (5) Die Strafbehörden tragen dem Ergebnis einer

into force. As regards the more essential provisions of this article, it should be stressed that the prosecutor was given the option to refer a case to mediation at any stage of the preparatory proceedings (investigation).[38] Most obviously, this type of mediation would require consent on the part of the offender and the wronged party.[39] Certain regulations refer to the legal position of mediator; the authors of the draft prescribe that a mediator is to carry out his or her duties entirely independently of the prosecutor, in a manner unbiased and without the pressure of persons directly engaged in the conflict.[40] The draft envisaged the main task of the mediator to be to invite the offender and the wronged party to voluntarily take up conversation. Upon completion of his or her task, the mediator would inform the persecutor about the results of the mediation, including in the notice the following: the content of the settlement reached and a declaration that its provisions had been executed, or information that a settlement had not been concluded.[41]

In the Swiss system the instrument of mediation does not exist, which indicates the factual impossibility of implementing of the idea of restorative justice even to the most modest extent.

Elements of restorative justice can be found in the Code of Criminal Procedure for Juveniles (*Jugendstrafprozessrechts*[42]). In the first place, attention should

---

erfolgreichen Mediation angemessen Rechnung. (6) Keine der beteiligten Personen kann sich im späteren Verlauf des Strafverfahrens auf Äusserungen berufen, die vor der Mediatorin oder dem Mediator gemacht worden sind, wie auch immer die Mediation ausgegangen ist. (7) Die Mediatorinnen und Mediatoren sind zur Verschwiegenheit verpflichtet. Sie können unter keinem Titel über Tatsachen, die ihnen in Ausübung ihrer Funktion zur Kenntnis gekommen sind, oder über Handlungen, die sie vorgenommen oder an denen sie teilgenommen haben, befragt werden; ihr Dossier kann nicht beschlagnahmt werden. (8) Bund und Kantone bestimmen die Modalitäten für den Einsatz von Mediatorinnen und Mediatoren im Strafverfahren. Sie legen namentlich die fachlichen und persönlichen Voraussetzungen für die Ausübung der Mediationstätigkeit fest und erlassen Bestimmungen über die Berufsregeln, die Registereintragung und die Aufsicht," *www.admin.ch/ch/d/ff/2006/1389.pdf* [last accessed December 23, 2013; 09:47]; I. Meier, *Mediation und Schlichtung in der Schweiz. Unter besonderer Berücksichtigung der gesetzlichen Rahmenbedingungen für Mediation*, p. 8.

38 See Art. 317(1) EStPO, *Ibid.*
39 *Ibid.*
40 See Art. 317(3) EStPO, *Ibid.*
41 See Art. 317(4) EStPO, *Ibid.*
42 Schweizerische Jugendstrafprozessordnung vom 20. März 2009 (Stand am 1. Januar 2011); hereinafter referred to as sJStPO.

be payed to the norm on settlement and restitution (*Vergleich und Wiedergutma-chung*) found in art. 16 sJStPO.[43] This provision gives the authorities in charge of investigation and the courts competent to hear juvenile cases the opportunity to attempt to induce the wronged party and the incriminated juvenile to a settlement (as long as the proceedings refer to crimes prosecuted at the wronged party's request) or obtain compensation on the condition of the fulfilment of premises of art. 21(1) letter (c) of the Juveniles Criminal Act (*Jugendstrafrecht*[44]). Art. 21 sJStG[45] contains a catalogue of premises entitling the authority with jurisdiction to refrain from imposing a penalty (*Strafbefreiung*), and in letter (c) one can find provisions to the effect that resignation on imposition of penalty is possible where the juvenile has repaired the economic damage caused by his or her act through his or her provision (as far as it has been possible) or has taken special effort in order to compensate for non-economic loss. It is possible to refrain from punishment solely in a situation when at the same time the only penalty that could be adjudged is a reprimand (*Verweis*) specified in art. 22 sJStG or if the public and private (i.e. the wronged party's) interests in criminal prosecution are minor.[46]

---

43 Art. 16 sJStPO: "Die Untersuchungsbehörde und das Jugendgericht können versuchen: (a) zwischen der geschädigten Person und der oder dem beschuldigten Jugendlichen einen Vergleich zu erreichen, soweit Antragsdelikte Gegenstand des Verfahrens sind; oder (b) eine Wiedergutmachung zu erzielen, sofern eine Strafbefreiung nach Artikel 21 Absatz 1 Buchstabe c JStG in Frage kommt."

44 Bundesgesetz über das Jugendstrafrecht vom 20. Juni 2003 (Stand am 1. Januar 2013); hereinafter referred to as sJStG.

45 Art. 21 sJStG: "(1) Die urteilende Behörde sieht von einer Bestrafung ab, wenn: (a) die Bestrafung das Ziel einer früher angeordneten oder im laufenden Verfahren anzuordnenden Schutzmassnahme gefährden würde; (b) die Schuld des Jugendlichen und die Tatfolgen gering sind; (c) der Jugendliche den Schaden so weit als möglich durch eigene Leistung wieder gutgemacht oder eine besondere Anstrengung unternommen hat, um das von ihm begangene Unrecht auszugleichen, als Strafe nur ein Verweis nach Artikel 22 in Betracht kommt und die Strafverfolgung für die Öffentlichkeit und den Geschädigten nur von geringem Interesse ist; (d) der Jugendliche durch die unmittelbaren Folgen seiner Tat so schwer betroffen ist, dass eine Strafe unangemessen wäre; (e) der Jugendliche wegen seiner Tat von den Eltern, andern erziehungsberechtigten Personen oder Dritten schon genug bestraft worden ist; oder (f) seit der Tat verhältnismässig lange Zeit verstrichen ist, der Jugendliche sich wohlverhalten hat und das Interesse der Öffentlichkeit und des Geschädigten an der Strafverfolgung gering sind."

46 See Art. 21(1) letter (c) sJStG, *Ibid.*

In turn, art. 17 sJStPO[47] prescribes that authorities conducting investigation or courts may, at any stage, stay the proceedings and appoint (in the area of mediation) a proper organisation or individual to mediate if the application of preventive (protective) measures is not necessary, or the civil law authority has awarded proper measures, and as long as the prerequisites specified in art. 21(1) sJStG are not met. If mediation proves successful, the criminal law procedure initiated by the juvenile will be discontinued.[48] The provision of art. 17 sJStPO is directly correlated to art. 5 sJStPO,[49] which refers to the situation of abandonment of criminal law prosecution (*Verzicht auf Strafverfolgung*), where one of the conditions enabling application of the construction is the conclusion of a settlement or a positive outcome to mediation.[50]

This synthetic and fragmented attempt at presenting the degree of implementation of the idea of restorative justice in Swiss legislation affirms beyond all doubt the general thesis put forward in the introduction with respect to the incomplete and not entirely successful adaptation of its postulations. Despite the good will (as it might seem) shown by the Swiss legislator, the quoted criminal law enactments aimed at the promotion of restorative justice are superficial provisions which do not always guarantee real satisfaction to the wronged party, which would be manifest for instance in the effective and quick redress of the damage inflicted. Obviously, individual diffusion of the conflict between the offender and the wronged party is always possible; yet, it is not easy to resist the

---

47 Art. 17 sJStPO: "(1) Die Untersuchungsbehörde und die Gerichte können das Verfahren jederzeit sistieren und eine auf dem Gebiet der Mediation geeignete Organisation oder Person mit der Durchführung eines Mediationsverfahrens beauftragen, wenn: (a) Schutzmassnahmen nicht notwendig sind oder die Behörde des Zivilrechts bereits geeignete Massnahmen angeordnet hat; (b) die Voraussetzungen von Artikel 21 Absatz 1 JStG1 nicht erfüllt sind. (2) Gelingt die Mediation, so wird das Verfahren eingestellt."

48 See art. 17 ust. 2 sJStPO, *Ibid.*

49 Art. 5 sJStPO: "(1) Die Untersuchungsbehörde, die Jugendstaatsanwaltschaft und das Gericht sehen von der Strafverfolgung ab, wenn: (a) die Voraussetzungen für eine Strafbefreiung nach Artikel 21 JStG1 gegeben und Schutzmassnahmen entweder nicht notwendig sind oder die Behörde des Zivilrechts bereits geeignete Massnahmen angeordnet hat; oder (b) ein Vergleich oder eine Mediation erfolgreich abgeschlossen werden konnte."

50 See art. 5 ust. 2 sJStPO, *Ibid.* and C. Domenig, *Behördeninterne Mediation im strafrechtlichen Kontext*, http://www.baselland.ch/fileadmin/baselland/files/docs/jpd/juga/projekt/behoerdeninterne-mediation-strafrecht.pdf [last accessed December 27, 2013; 08:03].

impression that the shape of the present Swiss legislation does not favour the achievement of that end.

Republic of Austria

The Austrian Criminal Code,[51] as compared to its Swiss equivalent, is much ampler. However, this does not imply, *ipso facto,* fuller implementation of postulates associated with the idea of restorative justice.

Just as in the case of the Swiss Criminal Code, the Austrian lawmaker uses the term damage without any closer explanation of what is understood by such a formulation. That is why it is necessary also in the case of this piece of legislation to refer to the context in which the term appears. Within the general part of the Code, the concept of "damage" appears, among other places, in the catalogue of special mitigating circumstances (*Besondere Milderungsgründe*). §34 aStGB provides that one such mitigating circumstance is the situation in which the offender has virtually taken every effort to compensate for the damage inflicted as a result of his or her acts or to prevent further detrimental effects.[52] The same applies where the offender on his or her own accord has refrained from causing greater damage while he or she had the occasion to do so, or where the offender or a third party acting in their place has repaired the damage.[53] Moreover, another mitigating circumstance is the condition in which the offender, in spite of having completed the act, has not caused any damage, or in which his or her conduct did not reach beyond the phase of attempt.[54][55] One may notice that these premises bear a certain resemblance to the Polish construction of active repentance.

---

51 Bundesgesetz vom 23. Jänner 1974 über die mit gerichtlicher Strafe bedrohten Handlungen (Strafgesetzbuch - StGB) Stand am 18. Januar 2014, hereinafter referred to as aStGB.

52 §34(1) item 15 aStGB: "Ein Milderungsgrund ist es insbesondere, wenn der Täter sich ernstlich bemüht hat, den verursachten Schaden gutzumachen oder weitere nachteilige Folgen zu verhindern."

53 §34(1) item 14 aStGB: "Ein Milderungsgrund ist es insbesondere, wenn der Täter sich der Zufügung eines größeren Schadens, obwohl ihm dazu die Gelegenheit offenstand, freiwillig enthalten hat oder wenn der Schaden vom Täter oder von einem Dritten für ihn gutgemacht worden ist."

54 §34(1) item 13 aStGB: "Ein Milderungsgrund ist es insbesondere, wenn trotz Vollendung der Tat keinen Schaden herbeigeführt hat oder es beim Versuch geblieben ist."

55 See J. H. Ebner in F. Höpfel, E. Ratz (eds.), *Wiener Kommentar zum Strafgesetzbuch*, §§ 32 – 36 (Wien: Manzsche Verlags- und Universitätsbuchhandlung, 2003), p. 70 – 72.

As regards the special part of the Code, the term "damage" is present as an independent element of definitions of crime, for exemple, in the case of the offence of misrepresentation (*Täuschung*),[56] one of a couple of types of serious damage to property (*schwere Sachbeschädigung*),[57] as well as in qualified types of breach of trust (*Untreue*)[58] or thwarting execution (*Vollstreckungsvereitelung*).[59] However, one may maintain basic doubts about whether the concept of "damage," despite its ubiquity in the Austrian Criminal Code, is of universal character and whether it signifies exactly the same thing in each occasion.

Sometimes it may happen that the term "damage" is qualified by various adjectives. For instance, we may encounter crime definitions involving "serious damage" (*schweren Schadens*). This element is one of the circumstances that justifies the exemption of the punishability of abortion (*Schwangerschaftsabbruch*[60]). The provision of §97(1) item 2 aStGB[61] envisages that an act of abortion (in the form set out in §96 aStGB) shall not be liable to penalty if the abortion

---

56 §108(1) aStGB: "Wer einem anderen in seinen Rechten dadurch absichtlich einen Schaden zufügt, daß er ihn oder einen Dritten durch Täuschung über Tatsachen zu einer Handlung, Duldung oder Unterlassung verleitet, die den Schaden herbeiführt, ist mit Freiheitsstrafe bis zu einem Jahr zu bestrafen."

57 §126 (1) item 7 aStGB: "Mit Freiheitsstrafe bis zu zwei Jahren oder mit Geldstrafe bis zu 360 Tagessätzen ist zu bestrafen, wer eine Sachbeschädigung begeht durch die der Täter an der Sache einen 3 000 Euro übersteigenden Schaden herbeiführt."

58 §153(2) aStGB: "Wer durch die Tat einen 3 000 Euro übersteigenden Schaden herbeiführt, ist mit Freiheitsstrafe bis zu drei Jahren, wer einen 50 000 Euro übersteigenden Schaden herbeiführt, mit Freiheitsstrafe von einem bis zu zehn Jahren zu bestrafen."

59 §162(2) aStGB: "Wer durch die Tat einen 3 000 Euro übersteigenden Schaden herbeiführt, ist mit Freiheitsstrafe bis zu drei Jahren zu bestrafen."

60 §96 aStGB: "(1) Wer mit Einwilligung der Schwangeren deren Schwangerschaft abbricht, ist mit Freiheitsstrafe bis zu einem Jahr, begeht er die Tat gewerbsmäßig, mit Freiheitsstrafe bis zu drei Jahren zu bestrafen. (2) Ist der unmittelbare Täter kein Arzt, so ist er mit Freiheitsstrafe bis zu drei Jahren, begeht er die Tat gewerbsmäßig oder hat sie den Tod der Schwangeren zur Folge, mit Freiheitsstrafe von sechs Monaten bis zu fünf Jahren zu bestrafen. (3) Eine Frau, die den Abbruch ihrer Schwangerschaft selbst vornimmt oder durch einen anderen zuläßt, ist mit Freiheitsstrafe bis zu einem Jahr zu bestrafen."

61 §97(1) item 2 aStGB: "Die Tat ist nach § 96 nicht strafbar, wenn der Schwangerschaftsabbruch zur Abwendung einer nicht anders abwendbaren ernsten Gefahr für das Leben oder eines schweren Schadens für die körperliche oder seelische Gesundheit der Schwangeren erforderlich ist oder eine ernste Gefahr besteht, daß das Kind geistig oder körperlich schwer geschädigt sein werde, oder die Schwangere zur Zeit der

takes place in a situation in which there are no other ways to avert serious threat to life or serious damage to the physical or mental health of the pregnant woman, or in which it is highly probable that the child will be seriously harmed, mentally or physically, or in which the pregnant woman was a minor during conception (in all the above situations abortion is performed by a physician). This situation is considered by most representatives of the doctrine as a statutory exonerating factor (*Rechtfertigungsgründe*).[62]

At another point, the Austrian legislator uses the phrase "serious damages" (*ernstlichen Schaden*). It occurs in §102 aStGB,[63] in which the Code defines the crime of kidnapping with a view to extorting a specific behaviour (*Erpresserische Entführung*). §102(4) aStGB introduces a privileged form of that crime (*Privilegierung*), which allows for the possibility of imposing a less severe criminal sanction (within the bracket of between 6 months and 5 years) if the offender's conduct amounts to voluntary resignation on extortion of a specific result, as long as the abducted (*entführen*) or forcefully intercepted (*bemächtigen*) individual has not suffered serious damages and may return to his or her living environment. In the literature, the understanding of "serious damages regarding life" in the cited crime definition is quite specific. It is emphasised that it covers

---

Schwängerung unmündig gewesen ist und in allen diesen Fällen der Abbruch von einem Arzt vorgenommen wird."

62 See M. Eder – Reider in F. Höpfel, E. Ratz (eds.), *Wiener Kommentar zum Strafgesetzbuch*, §§ *96 – 98* (Wien: Manzsche Verlags- und Universitätsbuchhandlung, 2001), p. 25 *et seq.*

63 §102 aStGB: "(1) Wer einen anderen ohne dessen Einwilligung mit Gewalt oder nachdem er die Einwilligung durch gefährliche Drohung oder List erlangt hat, entführt oder sich seiner sonst bemächtigt, um einen Dritten zu einer Handlung, Duldung oder Unterlassung zu nötigen, ist mit Freiheitsstrafe von zehn bis zu zwanzig Jahren zu bestrafen.

(2) Ebenso ist zu bestrafen, wer 1. in der im Abs. 1 genannten Absicht eine unmündige, geisteskranke oder wegen ihres Zustands zum Widerstand unfähige Person entführt oder sich ihrer sonst bemächtigt oder 2. unter Ausnützung einer ohne Nötigungsabsicht vorgenommenen Entführung oder sonstigen Bemächtigung einer Person einen Dritten zu einer Handlung, Duldung oder Unterlassung nötigt. (3) Hat die Tat den Tod der Person zur Folge, die entführt worden ist oder deren sich der Täter sonst bemächtigt hat, so ist der Täter mit Freiheitsstrafe von zehn bis zu zwanzig Jahren oder mit lebenslanger Freiheitsstrafe zu bestrafen. (4) Läßt der Täter freiwillig unter Verzicht auf die begehrte Leistung die Person, die entführt worden ist oder deren sich der Täter sonst bemächtigt hat, ohne ernstlichen Schaden in ihren Lebenskreis zurückgelangen, so ist er mit Freiheitsstrafe von sechs Monaten bis zu fünf Jahren zu bestrafen."

only serious bodily injury or health detriment (*schweren Körperverletzung oder Gesundheitsschädigung*) in the understanding of §84(1) aStGB.[64] Minor bodily injury (*leichte Körperverletzung*) §83(1) aStGB,[65] on the other hand, falls outside the scope of the above formulation. The same refers to damage of a merely economic type (*bloße Vermögensschäden*).[66]

Some terminological confusion is linked to the term "detriment" (Nachtail), recurrent throughout the Code. To add to this confusion, it is frequently supplemented by numerous adjectives, such as heavy (*schwer*), particularly serious (*besonders schweren*), considerable (*beträchtlich*), inconsiderable (*gering*), legal (*rechtlich*), significant (*bedeutend*), or economically significant (*bedeutenden vermögensrechtlichen*). It would be difficult to find a convincing reason that the Austrian legislator opted for such diversification. On many occasions, one may have the impression that the terms "damage" and "detriment" in fact refer to the same thing. Unfortunately, this reading of the cited passages is precluded by the prohibition of synonymous interpretation, which means that within a given legislative act, the same meaning should not be attributed to differing expressions.

The institution of redressing damage caused by a punishable act is also vital from the point of view of the idea of restorative justice, yet, it has not been comprehensively regulated in the Austrian Code. It appears only incidentally, along with rules on active repentance (*tätige Reue*) shown after commission of the prohibited act in §167 aStGB.[67] The prerequisites of active repentance

---

64 §84(1) aStGB: "Hat die Tat eine länger als vierundzwanzig Tage dauernde Gesundheitsschädigung oder Berufsunfähigkeit zur Folge oder ist die Verletzung oder Gesundheitsschädigung an sich schwer, so ist der Täter mit Freiheitsstrafe bis zu drei Jahren zu bestrafen."; Cf. K. Schwaighofer in F. Höpfel, E. Ratz (eds.), *Wiener Kommentar zum Strafgesetzbuch*, §§ 99 – 104a (Wien: Manzsche Verlags- und Universitätsbuchhandlung, 2010), p. 36.

65 §83(1) aStGB: "Wer einen anderen am Körper verletzt oder an der Gesundheit schädigt, ist mit Freiheitsstrafe bis zu einem Jahr oder mit Geldstrafe bis zu 360 Tagessätzen zu bestrafen."

66 As in K. Schwaighofer in F. Höpfel, E. Ratz (eds.), *Wiener Kommentar zum*, p. 37.

67 §167 aStGB: "(1) Die Strafbarkeit wegen Sachbeschädigung, Datenbeschädigung, Störung der Funktionsfähigkeit eines Computersystems, Diebstahls, Entziehung von Energie, Veruntreuung, Unterschlagung, dauernder Sachentziehung, Eingriffs in fremdes Jagd- oder Fischereirecht, Entwendung, Betrugs, betrügerischen Datenverarbeitungsmißbrauchs, Erschleichung einer Leistung, Notbetrugs, Untreue, Geschenkannahme durch Machthaber, Förderungsmißbrauchs, betrügerischen Vorenthaltens von Sozialversicherungsbeiträgen und Zuschlägen nach dem

quoted in this provision (bearing in mind the absence of its definition in the general part of the Code) refer only to crimes listed in §167(1) aStGB, among which one can enumerate, for example, damage to property (*Sachbeschädigung*), energy theft (*Entziehung von Energie*), and gross negligence resulting in detriment to creditors' interests (*grob fahrlässiger Beeinträchtigung von Gläubigerinteressen*).

Active repentance is taken into account to the benefit of the offender as long as the offender has, before the competent authority learns about the culpable conduct, and under the influence of the wronged party but not under duress, (1) repaired all damage resulting from his or her conduct or (2) contractually undertaken to remedy the damage to the wronged party before a specific deadline; the punishability of the crime "revives" (*aufleben*) if the offender does not carry out his or her obligation (to repair the damage caused by his or her act).[68]

Moreover, the offender will not be liable to a penalty if he or she, along with revealing and denouncing his or her offence (*Selbstanzeige*), compensates the entire damage following from his or her act by depositing with the law enforcing authority an appropriate amount of money.[69]

Paragraph 167(4) aStGB prescribes moreover that the offender who has earnestly tried to redress the damage inflicted by his or her acts shall not be liable

---

Bauarbeiter-Urlaubs- und Abfertigungsgesetz, Wuchers, betrügerischer Krida, Schädigung fremder Gläubiger, Begünstigung eines Gläubigers, grob fahrlässiger Beeinträchtigung von Gläubigerinteressen, Vollstreckungsvereitelung und Hehlerei wird durch tätige Reue aufgehoben. (2) Dem Täter kommt tätige Reue zustatten, wenn er, bevor die Behörde (§ 151 Abs. 3) von seinem Verschulden erfahren hat, wenngleich auf Andringen des Verletzten, so doch ohne hiezu gezwungen zu sein, 1. den ganzen aus seiner Tat entstandenen Schaden gutmacht oder 2. sich vertraglich verpflichtet, dem Verletzten binnen einer bestimmten Zeit solche Schadensgutmachung zu leisten. In letzterem Fall lebt die Strafbarkeit wieder auf, wenn der Täter seine Verpflichtung nicht einhält. (3) Der Täter ist auch nicht zu bestrafen, wenn er den ganzen aus seiner Tat entstandenen Schaden im Zug einer Selbstanzeige, die der Behörde (§ 151 Abs. 3) sein Verschulden offenbart, durch Erlag bei dieser Behörde gutmacht. (4) Der Täter, der sich um die Schadensgutmachung ernstlich bemüht hat, ist auch dann nicht zu bestrafen, wenn ein Dritter in seinem Namen oder wenn ein anderer an der Tat Mitwirkender den ganzen aus der Tat entstandenen Schaden unter den im Abs. 2 genannten Voraussetzungen gutmacht." See also K. Kirchbacher, W. Presslauer in F. Höpfel, E. Ratz (eds.), *Wiener Kommentar zum Strafgesetzbuch*, §§ 166 – 168e (Wien: Manzsche Verlags- und Universitätsbuchhandlung, 2009), p. 14 *et seq*.

68 See §167(2), *Ibid.*
69 See §167(3) aStGB, *Ibid.*

to a penalty if a third party acting on his or her behalf or another participant in the prohibited act remedies all damages inflicted by that act (according to the principles set forth in §167(2) aStGB).[70] Undoubtedly, the possibility that a joint participant, or even a person unrelated to the conlict between the offender and the wronged party, could repair the damage points to the stronger accentuation of compensatory elements at the cost of elements of a restorative nature.

Certain elements of the idea of restorative justice can be found in the Austrian Code of Criminal Procedure.[71] This statute makes use of several constructions that allow for refraining from criminal prosecution (*Rücktritt von der Verfolgung*). The first of them is the payment of a specific sum of money (*Zahlung eines Geldbetrages*), regulated in §200 aStPO.[72] Acting in pursuance of this enactment, a prosecutor may refrain from entering indictment where the offender voluntarily (1) pays within 14 days of the service of notice towards the state a specific sum of money (which may not, however, be higher than the equivalent of 180

---

70 See §167(4) aStGB, *Ihid*

71 Strafprozeßordnung (StPO), Stand am 18. Januar 2014, hereinafter referred to as aStPO.

72 §200 aStPO: "(1) Unter den Voraussetzungen des § 198 kann die Staatsanwaltschaft von der Verfolgung einer Straftat zurücktreten, wenn der Beschuldigte einen Geldbetrag zu Gunsten des Bundes entrichtet. (2) Der Geldbetrag darf den Betrag nicht übersteigen, der einer Geldstrafe von 180 Tagessätzen zuzüglich der im Fall einer Verurteilung zu ersetzenden Kosten des Strafverfahrens (§§ 389 Abs. 2 und 3, 391 Abs. 1) entspricht. Er ist innerhalb von 14 Tagen nach Zustellung der Mitteilung nach Abs. 4 zu bezahlen. Sofern dies den Beschuldigten unbillig hart träfe, kann ihm jedoch ein Zahlungsaufschub für längstens sechs Monate gewährt oder die Zahlung von Teilbeträgen innerhalb dieses Zeitraums gestattet werden. (3) Soweit nicht aus besonderen Gründen darauf verzichtet werden kann, ist der Rücktritt von der Verfolgung nach Zahlung eines Geldbetrages überdies davon abhängig zu machen, dass der Beschuldigte binnen einer zu bestimmenden Frist von höchstens sechs Monaten den aus der Tat entstandenen Schaden gutmacht und dies unverzüglich nachweist. (4) Die Staatsanwaltschaft hat dem Beschuldigten mitzuteilen, dass Anklage gegen ihn wegen einer bestimmten Straftat beabsichtigt sei, aber unterbleiben werde, wenn er einen festgesetzten Geldbetrag und gegebenenfalls Schadensgutmachung in bestimmter Höhe leiste. Des weiteren hat die Staatsanwaltschaft den Beschuldigten im Sinne des § 207 sowie über die Möglichkeit eines Zahlungsaufschubs (Abs. 2) zu informieren, soweit sie ihm einen solchen nicht von Amts wegen in Aussicht stellt. (5) Nach Leistung des Geldbetrages und allfälliger Schadensgutmachung hat die Staatsanwaltschaft von der Verfolgung zurückzutreten, sofern das Verfahren nicht gemäß § 205 nachträglich fortzusetzen ist."

daily fine rates plus costs of the proceedings[73]), or (2) proves to have repaired the inflicted damage (unless there are specific reasons allowing for the cancellation of this duty).[74]

Another institution is the so-called social provision (*Gemeinnützige Leistungen*) of §201 and 202 aStPO.[75] According to the directives prescribed in §201, the

---

73 See §200(2) aStPO - *Ibid.*

74 See §200(4) and (5) aStPO – *Ibid*; O. Maleczky, *Strafrecht Allgemeiner Teil II. Lehre von den Verbrechensfolgen* (Wien: Fakultas.wuv, 2011), p. 20; M. Neumair, *Strafrecht Allgemeiner Teil II* (Wien: LexisNexis Verlag, 2010), p. 57.

75 §201 aStPO: "(1) Unter den Voraussetzungen des § 198 kann die Staatsanwaltschaft von der Verfolgung einer Straftat vorläufig zurücktreten, wenn sich der Beschuldigte ausdrücklich bereit erklärt hat, innerhalb einer zu bestimmenden Frist von höchstens sechs Monaten unentgeltlich gemeinnützige Leistungen zu erbringen. (2) Gemeinnützige Leistungen sollen die Bereitschaft des Beschuldigten zum Ausdruck bringen, für die Tat einzustehen. Sie sind in der Freizeit bei einer geeigneten Einrichtung zu erbringen, mit der das Einvernehmen herzustellen ist. (3) Soweit nicht aus besonderen Gründen darauf verzichtet werden kann, ist der Rücktritt von der Verfolgung nach gemeinnützigen Leistungen überdies davon abhängig zu machen, dass der Beschuldigte binnen einer zu bestimmenden Frist von höchstens sechs Monaten den aus der Tat entstandenen Schaden gutmacht oder sonst zum Ausgleich der Folgen der Tat beiträgt und dies unverzüglich nachweist. (4) Die Staatsanwaltschaft hat dem Beschuldigten mitzuteilen, dass Anklage gegen ihn wegen einer bestimmten Straftat beabsichtigt sei, aber vorläufig unterbleiben werde, wenn er sich bereit erklärt, binnen bestimmter Frist gemeinnützige Leistungen in nach Art und Ausmaß bestimmter Weise zu erbringen und gegebenenfalls Tatfolgenausgleich zu leisten. Die Staatsanwaltschaft hat den Beschuldigten dabei im Sinne des § 207 zu informieren; sie kann auch eine in der Sozialarbeit erfahrene Person um die Erteilung dieser Informationen sowie darum ersuchen, die gemeinnützigen Leistungen zu vermitteln (§ 29b des Bewährungshilfegesetzes). Die Einrichtung (Abs. 2) hat dem Beschuldigten oder dem Sozialarbeiter eine Bestätigung über die erbrachten Leistungen auszustellen, die unverzüglich vorzulegen ist. (5) Nach Erbringung der gemeinnützigen Leistungen und allfälligem Tatfolgenausgleich hat die Staatsanwaltschaft von der Verfolgung endgültig zurückzutreten, sofern das Verfahren nicht gemäß § 205 nachträglich fortzusetzen ist."

§202 aStPO: "(1) Gemeinnützige Leistungen dürfen täglich nicht mehr als acht Stunden, wöchentlich nicht mehr als 40 Stunden und insgesamt nicht mehr als 240 Stunden in Anspruch nehmen; auf eine gleichzeitige Aus- und Fortbildung oder eine Berufstätigkeit des Beschuldigten ist Bedacht zu nehmen. Gemeinnützige Leistungen, die einen unzumutbaren Eingriff in die Persönlichkeitsrechte oder in die Lebensführung des Beschuldigten darstellen würden, sind unzulässig. (2) Die Leiter der Staatsanwaltschaften haben jeweils eine Liste von Einrichtungen,

offender is informed that he is in a position within 6 months as of the service of proper notice to (1) take on voluntary unpaid labour in his or her spare time (2) prove to have repaired the damage caused or compensated for consequences of the prohibited act, (3) pay the lump sum of the proceeding costs.[76] More or less "in exchange" for the fulfilment of these requisites, the prosecutor may temporarily refrain from criminal prosecution. In the case of compliance with the requisites provided by statutory provisions, the case is not continued, which means that the prosecutor refrains from further actions and from entering indictment before the court. In the opposite situation, preparatory proceedings are resumed.

The most interesting content, however, can be found in §204 aStPO,[77] which contains rules on compensation for the act committed by the offender

---

die für die Erbringung gemeinnütziger Leistungen geeignet sind, zu führen und erforderlichenfalls zu ergänzen. In diese Liste ist auf Verlangen jedermann Einsicht zu gewähren. (3) Fügt der Beschuldigte bei der Erbringung gemeinnütziger Leistungen der Einrichtung oder deren Träger einen Schaden zu, so ist auf seine Ersatzpflicht das Dienstnehmerhaftpflichtgesetz, BGBl. Nr. 80/1965, sinngemäß anzuwenden. Fügt der Beschuldigte einem Dritten einen Schaden zu, so haftet dafür neben ihm auch der Bund nach den Bestimmungen des bürgerlichen Rechts. Die Einrichtung oder deren Träger haftet in diesem Fall dem Geschädigten nicht. (4) Der Bund hat den Schaden nur in Geld zu ersetzen. Von der Einrichtung, bei der die gemeinnützigen Leistungen erbracht wurden, oder deren Träger kann er Rückersatz begehren, insoweit diesen oder ihren Organen Vorsatz oder grobe Fahrlässigkeit, insbesondere durch Vernachlässigung der Aufsicht oder Anleitung, zur Last fällt. Auf das Verhältnis zwischen dem Bund und dem Beschuldigten ist das Dienstnehmerhaftpflichtgesetz, BGBl. Nr. 80/1965, sinngemäß anzuwenden. (5) Erleidet der Beschuldigte bei Erbringung gemeinnütziger Leistungen einen Unfall oder eine Krankheit, so gelten die Bestimmungen der §§ 76 bis 84 des Strafvollzugsgesetzes dem Sinne nach."

76 See §200(1), (4) and (5) aStPO, *Ibid*; O. Maleczky, *Strafrecht Allgemeiner Teil*, p. 21; M. Neumair, *Strafrecht Allgemeiner Teil*, p. 58.

77 §204 aStPO: "(1) Unter den Voraussetzungen des §198 kann die Staatsanwaltschaft von der Verfolgung einer Straftat zurücktreten, wenn durch die Tat Rechtsgüter einer Person unmittelbar beeinträchtigt sein könnten und der Beschuldigte bereit ist, für die Tat einzustehen und sich mit deren Ursachen auseinander zu setzen, wenn er allfällige Folgen der Tat auf eine den Umständen nach geeignete Weise ausgleicht, insbesondere dadurch, dass er aus der Tat entstandenen Schaden gutmacht oder sonst zum Ausgleich der Folgen der Tat beiträgt, und wenn er erforderlichenfalls Verpflichtungen eingeht, die seine Bereitschaft bekunden, Verhaltensweisen, die zur Tat geführt haben, künftig zu unterlassen. (2) Das Opfer ist in Bemühungen um einen Tatausgleich einzubeziehen, soweit es dazu bereit ist. Das Zustandekommen

(*Tatausgleich*). Under subparagraph (1), the prosecutor may refrain from prosecution if the offender's act directly infringed on the legal interests of another person, and the perpetrator is able to pledge that he or she will compensate for the results of his or her conduct.[78] The offender should be especially prepared to redress the damage or compensate for the consequences of his or her act.[79] If it turns out to be necessary, the offender has to declare readiness to take steps that will prevent the future commission of acts producing effects that are relevant from the viewpoint of criminal law.[80] As examples of such conduct, scholars speak of treatment against alcohol addiction, anti-aggression training, and other types of therapy.[81] As a rule, the victim must agree to compensation.[82] The prosecutor's office may use the assistance of a conflict manager (*Konfliktregler*).[83] This person's main tasks include (1) managing the efforts of the victim and the accused in order to elicit the negotiation of an agreement that determines the manner of compensation and (2) providing assistance to both these parties.[84]

---

eines Ausgleichs ist von seiner Zustimmung abhängig, es sei denn, dass es diese aus Gründen nicht erteilt, die im Strafverfahren nicht berücksichtigungswürdig sind. Seine berechtigten Interessen sind jedenfalls zu berücksichtigen (§ 206). (3) Die Staatsanwaltschaft kann einen Konfliktregler ersuchen, das Opfer und den Beschuldigten über die Möglichkeit eines Tatausgleichs sowie im Sinne der §§ 206 und 207 zu informieren und bei ihren Bemühungen um einen solchen Ausgleich anzuleiten und zu unterstützen (§ 29a des Bewährungshilfegesetzes). (4) Der Konfliktregler hat der Staatsanwaltschaft über Ausgleichsvereinbarungen zu berichten und deren Erfüllung zu überprüfen. Einen abschließenden Bericht hat er zu erstatten, wenn der Beschuldigte seinen Verpflichtungen zumindest soweit nachgekommen ist, dass unter Berücksichtigung seines übrigen Verhaltens angenommen werden kann, er werde die Vereinbarungen weiter einhalten, oder wenn nicht mehr zu erwarten ist, dass ein Ausgleich zustande kommt."

78 See §204(1) aStPO – *Ibid.*
79 See §204(1) aStPO; O. Maleczky, *Strafrecht Allgemeiner Teil*, p. 22; M. Neumair, *Strafrecht Allgemeiner Teil*, p. 59 *et seq.* The statute does not resolve at the same time what results are at play. It is, thus, unclear, if all types of results come into question which make a consequence of the offender's conduct, which covers even remote results?
80 *Ibid.*
81 O. Maleczky, *Strafrecht Allgemeiner Teil*, p. 22.
82 See §204(2) aStPO.
83 That is court-appointed probation officer (*Bewährungshelfer*) or professional social welfare officer (*Sozialarbeit erfahrene Person*) – see reference to §29a Bundesgesetz vom 27. März 1969 über die Bewährungshilfe (Bewährungshilfegesetz).
84 See §204(3) aStPO.

The *Konfliktregler* is obligated, among other things, to present to the prosecutor accords concerning the compensation (reached between the victim and the offender) and to control their implementation.[85] Moreover, he or she is to submit a final report on whether the offender has complied with the freely incurred duties, and whether, after having monitored the offender's conduct hitherto, he or she may be expected to continue to observe the agreement, or may no longer be expected to complete the compensation.[86] The *Konfliktregler* is under the duty to maintain the secrecy of all he or she has learned in the course of providing assistance to the parties to the conflict. On an exceptional basis, the conflict manager may be examined by court as a witness, but only with regard to contents of agreement on compensation.[87]

Taking into consideration the shape of the institution *Tatausgleich,* it has been noted that it makes a relatively good allowance for the more flexible handling of conflicts that exist in the closest social environments, such that of the family, the neighbourhood, or the workplace, as well as of many conflicts conditioned by certain circumstances (for example, acts caused by an outbreak of aggression in a pub).[88]

As regards the comparison of criminal law institutions for redressing damage (*Schadensgutmachung*) and compensation for consequences caused by the offender's act (*Tatfolgenausgleich*), it is stressed that they are to support the interests of the victim to the prohibited act.[89] Strangely enough, it is highlighted at the same time that the concept of *Wiedergutmachung* regulated by means of the above criminal law institutions may not be automatically identified with civil law compensation (*zivilrechtlich Schadenersatz*).[90] The determination of compensation on the basis of criminal procedure is expected to fulfil specific functions, such as inducement of the parties (victim and offender) to interact with one another, alleviation of the emerged criminal conflict, and complete dissolution of conflict.[91] Accepting these assumptions suggests that compensation can take the form of non-economic values, such as, for example, an apology to the victim or reconciling with or providing assistance to him or her. It is not ruled out that

---

85 See §204(4) aStPO.

86 *Ibid.*

87 O. Maleczky, *Strafrecht Allgemeiner Teil*, p. 23.

88 *Ibid.*

89 O. Maleczky, *Strafrecht Allgemeiner Teil*, p. 23 *et seq.*

90 Such view is adhered to by O. Maleczky, *Ibid.*

91 *Ibid.*

damage might be repaired only symbolically (if such is the will of the parties expressed in their agreement).[92]

In attempting to summarise this part of the present study, it must be stated that broadly conceived, Austrian law provides for certain mechanisms that serve the purpose of implementing restorative justice postulations. Unfortunately, the scattering of the regulation throughout various pieces of legislation and the absence of terminological consistency makes it seemingly very difficult to reconstruct the intentions of the lawmaker with regard to particular provisions. It cannot be granted that solutions proposed by the Austrian lawmaker are of a comprehensive character; however, originality is a feature that cannot be denied them. First of all, the scope of rights and obligations of *Konfliktregler* ought to be emphasised, as they fit well into the concept of restorative justice. Moreover, from this point of view it seems particularly crucial that Austrians move away from the forms of compensation that are defined in accordance with civil law norms. Secondly, the solutions discussed gear the questions of redressing damage toward procedural rather than substantive provisions. It remains open for evaluation whether this type of entrenchment in criminal procedure can be deemed successful and sufficient. It is worth pointing out that the provisions quoted above do not use the term "duty" to repair damage but only tie voluntary reparation of damage by the offender to specific benevolences prescribed by law. This solution seems perfectly correct, since the ramifications of the concept of "duty" could effectively thwart the assumptions of restorative justice. In criminal legislation, one could not find direct references to questions connected with mediation, which validates the thesis that the Austrian legislator perceives the resolution of dispute that may be tracked to the punishable act as one issue, and the evaporation of conflict set in a criminal law environment as another.[93]

Thus far, certain considerations have been presented with respect to the binding model of criminal law in connection with the factual relationship between the offender and the victim. With regard to this, it ought to be pointed out that, bearing in mind certain shortcomings of the statutory regime, it may turn out to be difficult to extinguish the actual conflict.

To sum up very briefly the arguments made above concerning Swiss and Austrian law, as compared with the Polish model, one could conclude that the three

---

92 *Ibid.*

93 Problems of mediation in civil cases are regulated by a separate Act, Bundesgesetz über Mediation in Zivilrechtssachen (Zivilrechts-Mediations-Gesetz - ZivMediatG).

legal systems only partially allow for the pursuit of the idea of restorative criminal law. This is the case because they concentrate more on compensation itself than on the mechanisms of diffusing the conflict between the offender and the wronged party, and because the degree of empowerment of these two parties appears to be limited.

Final Conclusions

The concept of restorative justice is rooted in the resolution of conflict between an offender and a wronged party. Dissolution of conflict is reached through the empowerment of both parties, in most cases with the participation of an impartial mediator, and, possibly, the involvement of the local community. There will be no possibility of putting such a model into practice unless certain mechanisms are created to meet these requirements. Therefore, the papers presented in this volume have focused on provisions related to the relationship between the offender and the wronged party and rules pertaining to the compensatory function. It would not be possible to speak of a resolution of the social conflict related to the commission of a crime without taking into account the position of its parties and without redressing the damage caused by the offender (at least without partial redress, although obviously it would be an overstatement to say that this condition is absolutely necessary in this model).

The Criminal Code does not define the basic concepts that serve the compensatory function (it only specifies the amounts of considerable economic damage and of economic damage of great dimensions). Nearly all authors who make a statement on this matter hold the view that the implementation of criminal law instruments serving compensation must, under such circumstances, be based on provisions of civil law, and this leads to the thesis that in order to understand the damage and to define the mechanisms of redressing it, provisions of the Civil Code should be examined, as well as statements by civil law scholars and rulings by civil courts. This solution, however, has run up against obstacles of fundamental significance; on one hand, these obstacles stem from properties of civil law norms, accomplishments of the doctrine of civil law and rulings by civil courts; on the other hand, they are posed by certain fundamental principles of the Criminal Code in force.

In a nutshell, but not without a simplification that seems justified in concluding points, it can be argued that there are no legal definitions which grasp without doubts the essence of economic and non-economic loss in the framework of the Civil Code to which the Criminal Code would refer *a contrario*; furthermore, there is no uniform position within the doctrine and case law. As a consequence, there is no clarity about whether:

– damage as a fact should be consequently distinguished from the duty to redress the damage (as is important in relation to the wronged party's consent, and so-called natural detriment or wear and tear),
– non-economic loss should be perceived as a form of damage,
– non-economic loss might be equated with infringement of personal interests,
– infringement of personal interests is not only non-economic loss, but might also lead to the so-called bodily injury that is a special case of economic damage,
– compensation for non-economic loss occurs only under delictual claims.

Another question that is essential for criminal liability concerns the difficulties civil law scholars are faced with when determining *lucrum cessans*, as well as the difference between direct and indirect (consequential) damage.

Despite this state of affairs, the necessity of adapting civil law solutions to penal law has been widely accepted in statements hitherto among representatives of the doctrine of penal law (only B. Janiszewski has raised some doubts). It was also expressed that the compensatory function becomes dominant in the event of redressing damage, and therefore damage becomes the primary determinant of criminal law response. The only objection that has been raised was in regard to the adjudication of the duty to redress damage jointly and severally (and the Supreme Court has allowed such possibility). As a result, while imposing the duty to redress the damage, criminal courts follow civil law regulations to a significant extent.

The opinion that criminal courts should follow civil law regulations, and make use of the findings of both the doctrine and case law established in pursuance of civil law provisions while imposing the duty to redress the damage, has been examined in the present study with respect to fundamental principles of the Criminal Code, that is the principle of specificity and the principle of guilt. The directives on the level of penalty have also been taken into account. Consequently, it turns out that compensation based on the rules of the Criminal Code should be subject to far reaching restrictions.

As the principle of specificity is in force, the grounds for the duty to redress might only include offences with actual consequences, and the scope of this duty is confined by the form of such consequences as described in statutory law. In other words, the obligation is limited by the detriment inflicted to the legally protected interest (both primary and secondary interests, and by a consideration of the consequences of the legal classification of the prohibited act). Therefore, the concept of damage in civil law, though not fully specified, must be understood in reference to the legal interest affected by the prohibited act.

The principle of *nulla poena sine lege* requires a statutory provision to define the essence of criminal law response. This requirement is not met with regard to the duty to redress the damage, as the Criminal Code only envisages such a duty, and the Executive Penal Code does not allow for this gap to be filled. At this point, reference is made to civil law regulations, in particular by pointing to such provisions as are not applicable. The lawmaker used a so-called total blanket clause that redirects the reader to an area of law with different functions. What is more, the reference has been made in a particular way. This condition of the legislation should be considered almost without any doubt to be contradictory to the principle of specificity.

The significant restriction of the scope of the duty to redress damage stems from the function of guilt in penal law, as there is no doubt that penalty must not overstep the level of guilt, and the attribution of guilt is conditioned by the presence of the necessary elements of *mens rea* in the prohibited act.

The violation of fundamental principles of criminal law, as pointed out above, justifies this critical assessment of the existing legislation. However, the bottom line is that even if there were no weak points like the ones described above, the necessity to observe the principles of specificity and guilt would (as it actually does) limit the opportunity to satisfy the wronged party in a way that is true to the concept of restorative justice, merely because restorative justice is limited to result crimes, and because there are more crime definitions in penal law which would recognize only intentional commission of a prohibited act. It is also of significant importance that civil law provides *de facto* for only a single way to compensate, i.e. monetary compensation (in case of crimes, restitution is of minor importance), whereas the resolution of a conflict that has arisen from the commission of a crime is more frequently better served by the offender's conduct of another kind.

The prospects of satisfying the wronged party diminish also as a result of indicatives of the level of penalty found in the Criminal Code, which are applicable as appropriate to other penal measures including the duty to redress the damage.

Without any doubt, punishment should correspond to the extent of social noxiousness of the prohibited act, and determinants of social noxiousness are normatively specified. There is no reason to assign any special importance to damage, which has been listed as one of the determinants. The limiting function of guilt is of equal significance.

Another factor of certain relevance is the set of solutions offered by the Polish lawmaker to prevent excessive accumulation of economic distress. They do not refer to the duty to redress the damage, so there is a risk that such accumulation might happen in the event of awarding this obligation. In such cases compensation might become a fiction.

In the model of restorative criminal law, mediation between the offender and the wronged party essentially contributes to the reduction of conflict between the parties, an assertion that holds especially true to settlement as an outcome of mediation. Polish criminal law, however, does not compel the court to take the outcomes of mediation into account by ordering them to be "transposed" in the area of penal measures, because, above all, such a transposition would be impossible in many cases due to regulatory provisions pertaining to the selection of a penal measure and its level, which result from a particular axiology underlying penal codification. Therefore, the existing statutory regime does not provide a suitable environment for the ideas professed by adherents of restorative justice or the implementation of its components in criminal law. Although the general part of the Criminal Code is replete with compensatory components, and even with components directly pertaining to mediation, the performance of obligations awarded to the benefit of the wronged party is hardly ever supported by provisions of penal law (what is more, penal law does not back up the obligations of the wronged party in relation to the offender, even if they are likely to be included in a settlement).

Attempts to render the offender's commitments as penal measures produce limited effects, especially if their functioning at the executive stage is likewise taken into account. Functions associated with penal measures are not contradictory to the concept of restorative justice, yet ending the conflict in a way that satisfies both parties perfectly complements such functions. However, the standard extent of penalty in a criminal case, understood as distress inflicted on the offender by the court on behalf of the state, appears not to depend exclusively on the offender's arrangements with the wronged party or with the local community. The interference in the personal rights (of the offender) that results from criminal sanctions does not allow for resignation on the guarantees afforded by criminal substantive law, such as the principle of *nullum crimen sine lege, nulla poena sine lege*. What might turn out to be a good solution is a new regulation, indicated above, provided in article 59a CrimC, in light of which the renouncement of punishment does not deprive state authorities of control over the accomplishment of the objectives of punishment. Such an amendment should not be, however, expected to actually put restorative penal law into practice, because the assessments of provisions pertaining to active repentance after commission of a crime cited below are still valid for this legislative measure. Furthermore, such a solution does not provide mechanisms against mutual blackmail between the parties of the conflict (which would be possible if the requirement were introduced to establish the terms of compensation exclusively through mediation).

What is strongly highlighted in doctrinal statements is the problem of how significant active repentance is from the perspective of putting the restorative justice model into practice. However, if active repentance is subjected to a closer analysis from such a viewpoint, different conclusions are reached, and it is necessary to take into account two forms of active repentance: before perpetration of a crime and following perpetration of a crime.

The objective of pre-perpetration active repentance is nothing other than the additional (that is, in addition to the "regular" or repressive criminal law) protection of the wronged party's legal interests. Demonstration of active repentance by the offender not only benefits him or her (as he or she gains impunity) and the wronged party but also the society and the system of justice. This form of active repentance, however, neither guarantees nor actually even offers anything to the wronged party except prevention of the damage in a narrow understanding of the term and, possibly, redress of the damage *sensu largo*. The wronged party has no chance to express his or her feelings related to victimization and to find out why he or she has become the victim of a crime. Additionally, he or she is deprived of the opportunity to forgive the offender. This kind of active repentance is neither guaranteed to make the offender show remorse nor to become conducive to taking responsibility for the wrong he or she has committed. Motivation of this nature might be present, but it is not required by the institution as such. On the other hand, even this type of positive attitude in the offender does not facilitate obtaining the forgiveness of the wronged party. The "only" benevolence for the offender is impunity; what is missing is emotional experience that might influence his or her future life. Furthermore, the unconditional nature of non-liability to a penalty in the event of active repentance prior to commission of a prohibited act excludes the process of repairing the relationship between the offender and the wronged party. In other words, while penal legal consequences of active repentance lead (only) to a conclusion of the legal dispute, they *de facto* make both further lawsuit and resolution of any conceivable conflict impossible.

What then is active repentance in such a form from the viewpoint of restorative justice? It is automatic forgiveness expressed by the state without making sure whether the wronged party is satisfied and the conflict resolved. This means that although the institution of active repentance bears paramount significance to the wronged party, it cannot be perceived *de lege lata* as a component of restorative justice. Therefore, the institution of active repentance demonstrated prior to the commission of a crime, in its current form, appears to complement the retributive model of penal law, in which it plays an important role.

Active repentance demonstrated after commission of a crime, but prior to infringement of material interest, is functionally identical to pre-perpetration active repentance and, thus, it also entails "automatic" forgiveness expressed by the state without making sure whether the wronged party is satisfied, and the conflict resolved. This means that although the institution of active repentance bears much importance to the wronged party, *de lege lata,* it cannot be perceived as a component of restorative justice. Since constituent components of restorative justice are missing in this form of active repentance, active repentance cannot be included among the mechanisms of restorative justice.

Without any doubt, active repentance after perpetration of a crime and after causing the damage is *de lege lata* easier to fit into the framework of restorative justice. Restorative justice is not debarred from this form of active repentance, which makes the latter more effective from the viewpoint of restorative justice; still, it merely opens the way for resolving the conflict.

In briefly formulating postulates *de lege ferenda,* it should be stressed that, according to the conception of restorative justice, the model of active repentance demonstrated after causing the damage would have to be based on a morally positive attitude of the offender, and constitute resolution of the conflict by recourse to the position of the wronged party. The achievement of such an effect requires abolishment of time restrictions.

Yet another thing that ought to be stressed is that this form of active repentance is of much stronger compensatory impact than the duty to redress the damage imposed on the offender. These solutions might constitute a component of both a retributive model of penal law and a model intended to fully implement the concept of restorative justice.

Provisions of executive penal law, as described in the present study, are not conducive to implementing the concept of restorative justice, for several reasons. First, such proceedings are intended to assess the convict's attitude; these proceedings are focused on the offender, and not the wronged party. Furthermore, the latter is not even a party in these proceedings, which deprives him or her of such fundamental rights as the opportunity to file motions or challenge judicial decisions. This leads to the marginalization of the wronged party in the executive stage. Second, the consequences of not redressing the damage that a convict might be faced with are dependent on the type of punishment imposed and the legal basis for the resolution concerning redress of the damage. This leads to heterogeneity or sometimes even the absence of any negative consequences for the convict in the event of his or her non-compliance with the court ruling in this respect. This solution is not conducive to the implementation of the concept of restorative justice because penal consequences threatening the convict do not stimulate him or her to redress the damage, an illogical situation since it was nothing other than this very opportunity that was the reason for which instruments allowing rulings concerning compensation were introduced to criminal law. Third, a situation might occur, sometimes within a relatively short period following the validation of the penal judgment, in which the decision to redress the damage loses its legal subsistence (for example in the event of erasure of entry in the register of penalties). From the viewpoint of restorative justice, such situations are disadvantageous, as the wronged party remains unsatisfied, the conflict that was caused by the crime remains unresolved, and the offender might have the impression that it is pointless to redress the damage as there will be no penal law consequences if he or she fails to compensate. Fourth, within executive proceedings, even performance of the compensatory function raises some doubts, and redress of damage is the focal point of restorative justice, since if the offender does not voluntarily compensate, the wronged party will be obligated compulsorily to seek coercive execution of compensation, which involves a necessary down-payment for bailiff fees, and in executive proceedings he or she has no priority over other creditors waiting for their dues. Such a legislative framework does not serve the compensatory function, not to mention restorative justice. The points presented above lead to a conclusion that the currently binding model of executive proceedings is focused on the offender and does not serve the postulates of restorative justice.

Penal fiscal law is aimed at producing the effect of enforcing liabilities owed to the State Treasury or to units of self-government; therefore, it is driven by the compensatory objective. However, the "inequality of arms" resulting from the joinder of the roles of the wronged party and the prosecutor closes off an opportunity to achieve objectives inherent to penal restorative justice.

Final conclusion

The classical model of penal law may be formed in a way that corresponds to the concept of restorative justice only to a degree; it is limited because of the principle of specificity and the principle of guilt, whereas putting such a model into practice requires the selection of crime categories that allow recourse to mediation so as to properly frame the legal and penal response, proper statutory grounds for a correct understanding of the term of damage, and specification of the means of redressing the damage; it also requires an ascertainment of the relation between directives of the level of penalty and settlement between the offender and the wronged party. Both procedural and executive provisions would have to be modified to fit such a model of substantive penal law.

Lex et Res Publica
Polish Legal and Political Studies

Edited by
Anna Jarón

Vol. 1   Anna Jarón: Socio-Economic Constitutional Rights in Democratisation Processes. An Account of the Constitutional Dialogue Theory. 2012.

Vol. 2   Stanisław Filipowicz: Democracy – The Power of Illusion. 2013.

Vol. 3   Teresa Dukiet-Nagórska (ed.): The Postulates of Restorative Justice and the Continental Model of Criminal Law. As Illustrated by Polish Criminal Law. 2014.

www.peterlang.de